Theo Harris

BLESSED *and* HIGHLY FAVORED

Memoirs of a Multiple Felon

TATE PUBLISHING
AND ENTERPRISES, LLC

Published by Tate Publishing & Enterprises, LLC
127 E. Trade Center Terrace | Mustang, Oklahoma 73064 USA
1.888.361.9473 | www.tatepublishing.com

Tate Publishing is committed to excellence in the publishing industry. The company reflects the philosophy established by the founders, based on Psalm 68:11,
"The Lord gave the word and great was the company of those who published it."

Book design copyright © 2012 by Tate Publishing, LLC. All rights reserved.
Cover design by Allen Jomoc
Interior design by Jake Muelle

Published in the United States of America

ISBN: 978-1-62147-186-8
1. Biography & Autobiography / Personal Memoirs
2. Biography & Autobiography / General
12.09.17

Me, my sister Retie, and Mom. (1954)

My 3rd grade school photo.
(1957)

My 6th grade school photo.
(1960)

DEDICATION

This book is dedicated to my wife, Phyllis. It is her love and support that have given me the motivation to keep writing, even through the pain.

It is also dedicated to my Lord and Savior Jesus Christ, without whose love and blessings I would not be alive today. Thank you, Lord.

FOREWORD

Scripture is full of stories about prisoners—Joseph, Daniel, Paul, John, and many others. Some are imprisoned for their faithful witness; others are imprisoned for breaking the law. But in every case, to be shut away and deprived of abundant life is against the dream that God has for any man or woman. Through the good news of the gospel, Jesus makes it clear that we are called to set the oppressed free, to visit the prisoner, to break down the dividing walls of hostility.

With depth and honesty, Theo Harris tells the story of imprisonment—and freedom. A seven-time felon, Theo Harris takes us on a journey. Drawn into the joys and sorrows of an unfolding life, we come to see and understand how crime and drug addiction can creep into the narrative of an all-American story. We feel Theo's guilt, we see and taste the cruelty of the criminal justice system, we experience the trauma of incarceration, we marvel at the forgiveness of family, and we celebrate the ultimate power of God's grace to heal and liberate.

Post imprisonment, Theo Harris is now an author, a storyteller, a playwright, a song stylist, a poet, a motivational speaker, and a mentor to formerly incarcerated men. He also serves as the prison ministry associate for the Presbytery of Hudson River, where he shares his testimony and calls people to become advocates for criminal justice reform throughout the Hudson Valley. Theo shares a joy and enthusiasm for the gospel that is contagious, and he reminds all of us that freedom, in body and soul, is the birthright of every human being.

As you read this intriguing story, be prepared to be changed. All to the Glory of God!

—Susan R. Andrews
General Presbyter, Hudson River Presbytery
Moderator of the 215th General Assembly
Presbyterian Church, USA

PROLOGUE

Sirens split the air as I raced across the parking lot of the Ramada Inn. Police cars converged behind me, screeching to a halt. Guns had drawn, angry shouts, heavy footsteps. The Binghamton, New York, Police were in hot pursuit. As I ran into the darkness, away from their yells, I wanted to escape from everything—the pounding of my feet, my heaving lungs, the spasms of my heart—as I tried to outrun the expected bullet. Then, out of nowhere, a German shepherd police dog fastened its teeth into my upper arm. Born down by its weight, my flesh tore in its clamped teeth as I fought to shake off the snarling beast. A swarm of cops brought me to the ground as the dog continued to chew on my arm. One of the cops kicked me hard in the ribs as another clamped handcuffs tightly around my wrists. Only after the handcuffs were secured, cutting off my circulation, did they call the dog off.

Bloody and disheveled, I was yanked to my feet and searched. My shirt was ripped to shreds in the area where the dog had latched on to me, and blood dripped from the exposed flesh of my arm, the same dark-red blood that now stained the pavement as it reflected the revolving reds and blues of the police cruisers.

My breathing was slowing down, and the pain in my arm was just a hot throb. Although mere minutes old, the robbery of the frightened Ramada Inn hotel clerk seemed a lifetime away.

The fact that I had only pretended to have a gun didn't matter in the least. To all concerned, this was an armed robbery. To make matters even worse, the money from the robbery was in my pocket in a crumbled knot, along with my identification, letting the police know immediately who I was. The hotel security guard, who had witnessed the entire robbery, stood off to one side staring smugly at me. It was his 911 cell phone call that led to the scene before him. I turned my eyes away and lowered my head. I was caught.

Suddenly, an ambulance rolled into the parking lot, adding the glare of its lights to the excitement. Squawk boxes and walkie-talkies crackled with activity. I was strapped to a gurney and rolled toward the waiting ambulance. All I could think about was that I had finally gone and done it. In a crack-cocaine-induced moment of madness, I had thrown myself into the bottomless pit of a life sentence. Amazingly, after seven years clean and seven years out of prison, this current robbery would make my seventh felony. The date was April 14, 2002, and I had just turned fifty-three years old. *Some birthday present*, I thought to myself as the medics loaded me inside the ambulance.

At the hospital I was greeted with more shouting as rough hands rushed me to a treatment room. The glare of the hospital lights gave the hustle and bustle of the doctors and nurses an almost dreamlike sequence. My immediate thoughts focused on trying to escape. My emotional wounds were more profound than my physical ones, bordering on the unbearable. I was at the point where I didn't care whether I lived or died. In my anguished state of mind, escape or death appealed more to me than any other options. My intent was to utilize the element of surprise, hoping that it would work in my favor. The plan was to wait until my handcuffs were removed, then rush to the open window and jump out. *Death* or *escape*, either or, whichever came first; I truly didn't care.

As if reading my mind, the cop in the treatment room with me removed just one of the cuffs from my wrist, attaching the free cuff to the bed railing. Now that escape was virtually impossible, I was left with only the tortured thoughts of my wife, my marriage, my family, my grandchildren, and how I had just thrown my whole life away.

After treatment, I was taken directly from the hospital to the police station in downtown Binghamton. I immediately became the center of attention, suffering through the hostile stares and snide remarks of the cops and detectives. When they learned that it actually was my birthday, that's when I really became the object of ridicule and tasteless jokes. As I was being booked, fingerprinted, and photographed, I was told that, since it was my birthday, I could have my pick of available cells. The station erupted in laughter. I was in no state of mind to feed their taunts and endured them in silent anger. The instinctive rage that welled up in me was intensified by displaced anger against my own guilt and me.

After being strip searched, I was placed inside a bare holding cell. The only furnishings were a metal slab extending from the wall, a filthy toilet bowl, and a crust-infested sink. I had no blanket, no pillow, and no mattress. And, because it was the weekend, that cell was where I would spend the next two days, as the courts were closed until Monday morning.

Also, there was no avoiding the inevitable: I had to call my wife. Even though she knew about my criminal history, it didn't make telling her where I was any easier. I slowly dialed the phone, certain that she was going to leave me. Tears welled up in my eyes as I listened to the phone ringing on the other end. I was determined to make this call as brief as possible—short and to the point. Finally, my wife answered the phone with a sleepy hello, followed by a long silence. I closed my eyes and blurted out a hello of my own. She clearly knew that it was I on the line but remained silent, waiting for me to speak first.

"Guess where I'm calling from," I whispered.

"Either a drug program or jail," Phyllis replied.

"I'm in jail, baby," I said, my voice cracking.

"For what?" she asked calmly.

"Robbery."

"Did you do it?"

"Yes."

An even longer silence followed. As I waited for her to respond to my last answer, I wanted to lie down and die. As the silence lingered, I began to prepare myself for the worst. It was all over for us as husband and wife. She was going to leave me.

"Do you love me?" she asked, finally.

"What?" I croaked, puzzled.

"I said do you love me?"

"Yes, Phyllis. I love you more than anything."

"That's all I want to know," she said softly.

I held my breath, still trying to fight back the tears.

"I'll be there for you," she continued. "We'll get through this together.

I was too stunned to respond, but the love I felt for my wife at that moment seared through me like an electric current, but it only served to intensify my anguish. I couldn't stay on the line in my present state of mind. I had to hang up.

"I'm so sorry, Phyllis," I cried.

"Are you okay?" she asked.

"No," I said, honestly.

"When will you be in court?"

"Monday morning."

"I'll be there," she whispered.

"I love you," I cried and hung up the phone.

I was formally arraigned that Monday morning on a charge of first-degree robbery. Pending assignment of counsel, I pled not guilty and was quickly hustled out of the courtroom. The judge remanded me to the Broome County Jail without bail and did not permit me to speak with my wife or other family members present at the arraignment. I was in no condition—emotionally—to speak with them anyway, so that was fine with me.

In a matter of weeks, I was indicted by a Broome County grand jury on the first-degree robbery charge. I was surprised at the speed of the indictment until it became apparent that the district attorney prosecuting my case was determined to paint me in the worst possible light. My extensive criminal history was going to make that very easy for him to do.

In the weeks leading up to my indictment, I was required to stand in a lineup to see if the Ramada Inn hotel clerk, the security guard, and other witnesses to the robbery could positively identify me. Just before standing in that lineup, I learned from my lawyer that there would be victims of other robberies present at the lineup as well. The police and district attorney probably figured that if they could pin those unsolved robberies on me, so much the better. I wasn't surprised. I knew it was standard operating procedure, but that didn't stop me from worrying. The last thing I needed were additional robbery charges against me.

My brother Danny agreed to stand in my lineup with me, and for that I was extremely grateful. We closely resemble one another, so his presence in the lineup was a major plus for me. Five Broome County Jail inmates were paid ten dollars each—as was my brother—for their participation in the lineup as well.

I was positively identified in the Ramada Inn robbery, but to my great relief, I was not identified by any of the other robbery victims. I learned this from my court-appointed attorney in the three minutes of time he gave me. I told him that I wanted to speak with him concerning the charge against me, but he said he was in a hurry and would speak with me at length at a later date.

Three days later I was brought back to court to be arraigned. I spied my lawyer as soon as I entered the courtroom. He was wearing a rumpled suit and scuffed shoes, with glasses perched on the bridge of his nose like a college professor. With his snow-white hair and permanent smirk, he reminded me a little of

Albert Einstein or the stereotype of the absent-minded professor, from whom I would probably have received better legal counsel. My present lawyer's skills and interest in a possible defense on my behalf left everything to be desired. He spoke with me for about thirty seconds, and then the judge entered the courtroom. All talking ceased at that point as the bailiff called the court to order, and I was directed to stand next to my lawyer directly in front of the judge.

The judge immediately asked to see my rap sheet, which is nothing more than a record of my criminal history. It seemed like it took him forever just to *skim* through the papers in front of him. My criminal history dated clear back to 1965, and I could see that it was shocking to the judge. He kept glancing down at me and then back at my rap sheet, piercing me each time with an icy glare. Finally, after what seemed like hours, the judge looked at the district attorney and asked him if there was an offer on the table. Usually a plea bargain will be offered to a criminal defendant to avoid a costly trial. In my case, however, the district attorney knew that my criminal history would make it easy for him to win a conviction.

All that is required for persistent offender status is *three* felony convictions, and this would be my seventh. If it were determined that I was a persistent-felony offender, I would be looking at a maximum sentence of twenty-five-years to life. My own past would be more than enough to assure that I would spend the rest of my life behind bars. I could only pray that the district attorney was not considering prosecuting me under the persistent felony statute.

After careful review of my rap sheet, the judge looked at the district attorney and said, "This case appears to be a possible persistent-felony offender prosecution." The courtroom seemed to darken, and I became extremely nervous and agitated.

I was ordered held on a fifty-thousand-dollar property or twenty-five-thousand-dollar cash bail, neither of which I could post. In the unlikely event that I was able to come up with the bail money, however, the judge further stipulated that he would have to make the final approval before I could be released. At that point the arraignment was over, and I was hustled out of the courtroom to a waiting Broome County Jail van.

On the ride back to the county jail, it was all that I could do to maintain my composure. I wanted to cry! I wanted to die! The situation I had placed myself in did not make sense. I dug deep for answers that just would not surface. I had a thousand questions for myself. Was my addiction that powerful? Was it controlling to the point that it would literally cause me to throw my whole life away? Apparently it was, and the scary thing was that I didn't see any of it coming until it was too late.

It is amazing how heightened one's beliefs become when faced with a crisis. Locked inside of that prison van, facing what would more than likely be the rest of my life behind bars, I felt more connected to God than at any other time in my life, believing with all my heart that the miracle I needed to save me from a life sentence would somehow be provided. For some inexplicable reason, I just felt that this was not the way God intended for my life to end, pining away in a prison cell and waiting to die.

I shuddered at the thought. I simply could not resign myself to that fate. I had to find the answers. What led me to this point in my life? Was this how my life was destined to end? It was clear to me that the answers to these questions—among others—could only be found by going over every event that had led up to my current situation. I had to start at the beginning.

CHAPTER ONE

Although sketchy, some of my fondest memories as a child are of growing up in the small town of Bloomsburg, Pennsylvania. Born out of wedlock, when my mother was about seventeen or eighteen years old, I never knew my biological father. I lived in a faded white corner house at 920 Catherine Street, surrounded by a host of aunts, uncles, and cousins. Gram, however, was the beloved matriarch of the family.

I remember Gram telling me that my great-grandparents were full-blooded Blackfoot Indians. With her jet-black, silky hair; high cheekbones; and regal posture, my grandmother's Indian heritage could not be denied. There was a lot of love in that small house, and Gram was at the center of it all.

I was also the center of attention as a child, and it seemed that every time I turned around, I was being picked up, hugged, cuddled, and kissed. My mother always made sure that I was clean and well groomed. As far as she was concerned, there was nothing too good for her "Teddy Bear." I had loads of baby items, toys, and clothes, and my mom would sometimes change my outfits two or even three times a day. I loved my mother dearly and always looked forward to her coming home from her job as a presser in the nearby town of Milton, Pennsylvania. She almost always had a gift for me, and of course I looked forward to that.

When I was about four years old, my mother suddenly left Bloomsburg for New York City, leaving me in Gram's care. I didn't know it at the time, but my mom married a man named Daniel Harris, a Korean War veteran from Lewisburg, whom she had been dating. At the time of her departure, she was pregnant with the first of five children they would have together. My stepdad was working in New York City, and of course he wanted my mother with him. It was during that period, in 1954, when my mother gave birth to my oldest sister, Nereida, or "Retie," as she would come to be called by family and friends.

Back in Bloomsburg, however, life went on as usual for me, so much so that I didn't have time to miss my mom. Gram had stepped in to take her place, and by all accounts I was a happy, well-adjusted, and much-loved child.

One of my most vivid memories as a child is when Gram took me to the annual Bloomsburg Fair. It was my first fair. I was fascinated by the rides, the games of chance, and the enticing smell of popcorn, candy apples, and cotton candy. Along with us were a few of my cousins and two of my uncles, Sonny and Sam. A booth in the middle of the fairway with an abundant display of baked goods caught my attention. I was enticed by a huge coconut cake that was sitting in the middle of the display. I quickly took my uncles by the hand and pulled them over to the booth, pointing excitedly at the coconut cake. On the counter in front of the baked goods were painted squares with numbers in the center of each square. Next to the baked goods was a large wheel displaying the same numbers as those in the squares on the counter. I was told that, for a nickel, I could try and win the pastry of my choice. All I had to do was correctly pick the number that the spinning wheel would stop on. I was so excited. I pleaded with my uncles to put a nickel on a number for me. I wanted to win that coconut cake more than anything in the world.

My Uncle Sam reached into his pocket and handed me a nickel. He then picked me up so that I could place it on the number of my choosing. As I leaned over to put the nickel down, my uncle whispered something to the booth operator. I didn't think anything of it at the time because I was too intent on watching the spinning wheel as the operator gave it a hefty turn. As it began to slow down, my eyes were glued to the wheel edging closer and closer to my number. I was so caught up in trying to *will* the wheel to stop on my number that I didn't see the exchange of money between the booth operator and my Uncle Sam. I also failed to notice the operator's hand softly brushing the underside of the wheel, causing it to stop directly on my number. I screamed my delight as the operator asked me what I wanted from the baked goods display. It was all I could do to control myself as I pointed a trembling finger at the beautiful coconut cake. When it was handed to me, I floated away from the game booth, not paying attention to anything but my cake, not even the exchange of winks that surely occurred between the booth operator and my Uncle Sam. I'll never forget that experience at the Bloomsburg Fair because it was one of my happiest memories.

I do not want to give too much weight to this childhood event, but it is a possible clue to a pattern I blindly followed from childhood, to adolescence, to adulthood. The pattern that I have gambled much more than a nickel; indeed I have gambled my life, my freedom, and the welfare of those I loved more times than I care to remember.

About a year after my mother had been in New York City, a strange black lady showed up at the house. I remember coming into the house from playing when I immediately sensed that something was wrong. It was just too quiet. The somber look on the faces of my family members also alerted me to the fact that something was not right. Gram introduced the stranger to me, telling me that she was my *other* grandmother. The lady grabbed me and hugged me close, telling me to call her "Nana." I gave her a weak hug in response, all the time looking up at Gram. I didn't want another grandmother, and as far as this *other grandmother* stuff was concerned, I wasn't trying to hear it. Gram was my grandmother, and that was that.

So when Gram told me that "Nana" lady was there to take me back to New York City with her, I went berserk! I didn't want to go...nobody could *make* me go...I wasn't going, but my clothes were already packed, and there was nothing I could do to keep from going. My world was coming to an end, and there was nothing that anyone could do about it. No amount of protest on my part could prevent it.

After an endless number of hugs, kisses, and tears, Nana took me firmly by the hand and led me away from the paradise that was Bloomsburg, Pennsylvania. My heart was breaking as I looked back through tear-filled eyes at my family and my beloved Gram. In a strange way, this scene has reechoed numerous times in my life when I have been taken away from people I loved and sent to jail, just as more than once I have gambled with my freedom, as well as my life, expecting the wheel of fate to stop on my number.

If I were asked to pinpoint a moment in time where my life took a turn for the worst, it would have to be this event, when I was taken from 920 Catherine Street—because if Pennsylvania's Bloomsburg was *Eden*, surely New York's Harlem was the *Apple*.

CHAPTER TWO

I was immediately caught up in the allure of Harlem's *Sugar Hill*. Not only was the pace faster than what I was used to back in Bloomsburg, but I had never seen so many black people together in one place in my life. Harlem was a canvas of personalities of various colors and shades, and to my five-year-old eyes, it was as if I was on another planet. The kids my age and older were rough, tough, and extremely street smart. It would be through them, along with the pimps, players, prostitutes, and neighborhood gangsters, that I would learn the tough lessons of the street.

My mom grabbed me in a bear hug as soon as I walked through the door of the small fifth-floor apartment at 1642 Amsterdam Avenue on the corner of 141st Street. We both cried tears of joy as we held on tightly to one another, and it was only at that moment that I realized just how much I had missed her. Still holding tightly to her, I heard the sound of a baby crying in the next room. She smiled, took me by the hand, and led me in to the adjoining bedroom.

"Who's that?" I asked in puzzlement.

"That's your baby sister, Nereida," Mom said, bending down to pick her up from the small crib.

"*Nereida?*" I said, making a face at the weird-sounding name.

"Yes"—my mother laughed—"but we call her Retie."

"Well, I'm gonna call her that too," I said firmly, making my mom laugh. It was clear that I would no longer be the baby of the family, but I wanted to fit in, and maybe having a little sister wouldn't be so bad.

"I would've come to get you, Teddy," my mother said as she fixed me something to eat, "but I couldn't travel with the baby."

I nodded my head in understanding as my mother continued to explain that since my stepdad had to work, his mother— "Nana"—had volunteered to bring me to New York City from Bloomsburg.

"So how do you like the big City so far?

"I miss Bloomsburg, Mom," I responded sadly.

"You'll be fine," my mom said, hugging me tightly. "You'll get use to the City, especially once you start making new friends."

Although not very confident about getting used to my new environment, I did begin to seek companionship, recognition, and stimulation outside of the family, as my mother encouraged me to do. But despite her hopeful prediction, I was anything but fine.

I started playing hooky from school as early as the third grade. The New York City subway system fascinated me, and I would ride for hours on end to various boroughs of the city. It didn't take long to familiarize myself with the five boroughs and the many different neighborhoods in each one. Usually I would do all of my traveling alone, but then I met my soon-to-be new "hangout" buddy, Little Johnny Hart.

Little John lived just around the corner from me and was well known in the neighborhood as a troublemaker. He was a few years older than I was and much more street-smart. I had seen him around the neighborhood from time to time, and we would exchange stares, not really knowing what to make of each other. However, each time our paths would cross, there was something about Little John that attracted my interest. We would acknowledge each other cautiously with a brief nod and then go our separate ways. Somehow I knew, though, that we would become close friends. And eventually we did—even though one of his first acts toward me was one of betrayal and deceit.

My brother Danny, named after my stepdad, was the newest addition to the Harris family. As a result, we moved into a bigger apartment across the street at 1634 Amsterdam Avenue. Early one summer evening, I made my way out of the building to find a large crowd gathered around a truck that was burning out of control. I saw Nana in the crowd talking with some of her friends as they stared at the raging inferno directly in front of our apartment building. To my surprise, I also saw Little John in the crowd, pointing in my direction.

"That's him!" he yelled as all eyes turned to look at me.

I stood there in shock, confusion, and disbelief as I tried to make sense out of Little John's accusation.

"It was him!" he yelled again. "He set that truck on fire! I seen him do it!"

I looked at Little John with pure hatred as anger boiled up inside of me. He knew what he was saying was a lie, and it was all I could do to convince Nana that I had nothing to do with the fire. At that, Little John laughed and bolted around the corner, out of sight. I followed closely on his heels. I had been lied on, and it hurt terribly.

It didn't take me long to locate him, just one block over from Amsterdam Avenue in Hamilton Park. He was sitting on one of the park benches, smiling as he watched me approach.

"Why'd you lie on me?" I shouted, approaching Little John with clenched fists.

Laughing, he said, "Man, I was just playin' with you. I wanted to see if you could talk your way out of it—that's all!"

Personally, I failed to see the humor in what he had done, but I decided to let it go. Even at that young age, the gift of gab fascinated me, and if anyone had that, it was Little John. He was quick-witted and a sharp dresser. For some reason, I felt honored that this older kid was interested enough in me to test my reaction to what he knew to be a blatant *lie*. I guess I passed his test because we became inseparable after that. When you saw one, you saw the other, even sleeping over from time to time at each other's house.

Little John introduced me to marijuana and wine, neither of which I enjoyed very much. To cement our friendship, I tried them. Then as a means of funding our many *escapades*, he showed me how to shoplift and snatch purses. The problem with that, however, was that Little John didn't teach by example—he simply told me how to do it—so I was the one doing the actual stealing. Somehow he always managed to stay *far* in the background.

I didn't mind. I simply chalked it up to my having more nerve than he did. I was becoming addicted to risk, as well as being hungry for recognition. As would prove to be my nature, I didn't think things through enough to realize I had allied myself with a little Judas who knew how to exploit these tendencies in me to the hilt.

CHAPTER THREE

When I was in the fifth grade, I got caught stealing money from my teacher's pocketbook. At first I just took a few dollars every now and then, but ultimately it was my greed that got me caught.

It was payday for the teachers, and my class was doing a penmanship assignment. My teacher, Mrs. Webber, was outside of the classroom in the hallway, talking with another teacher. After first making sure that none of the kids were paying any attention to me, I took my assignment paper up to the desk at the front of the classroom. Again, making sure that I was not being watched, I ducked behind the desk where I knew her pocketbook was kept. I quickly unsnapped her bag, reached inside, and removed a large wad of bills—more than I had ever taken before. I didn't realize it at the time, but I had just taken Mrs. Webber's entire paycheck. Stuffing the money in my pocket, I walked slowly back to my desk, careful not to draw attention to myself. My heart was thumping, my palms were sweating, and my pocket was swollen, but I was certain that I had gotten away with it.

When Mrs. Webber returned to the classroom, to my horror and disbelief, she headed directly for her pocketbook. After looking through it briefly, she turned to the class with a piercing glare and ordered us all into the hallway. She told us to form a double line, and that's when I knew that we were going to be searched. In desperation, I looked for the right opportunity to get rid of the wad of bills in my pocket. Mrs. Webber walked up and down the line of students, and as she passed by the middle of the line where I was standing, I eased the bills out of my pocket and flung them hard behind me.

To my dismay, the money simply fluttered to the ground around my feet. Then, adding to my problems, a girl standing directly behind me pointed to the money, and shouted, "Look at all that money!"

"Where?" I asked, trying to act as surprised as everyone else.

"Right there"—the girl pointed—"at your feet!"

Mrs. Webber came running over and told me to pick the money up. She then sent the rest of the class back inside the classroom, and I was taken immediately to the principal's office. I denied taking the money of course, but they called my mother anyway. When she arrived at the school, she was angry but not surprised. She told the principal and Mrs. Webber that she had suspicions from recent purchases that I had made that I was stealing money, but when she questioned me about the money, I told her that it was a prize for winning spelling and penmanship competitions at school. After being made to apologize to Mrs. Webber, I was taken home, where an even *worse* fate waited: being reprimanded by my stepdad.

Whenever my stepdad punished or disciplined me, it was always taken to the extreme. In this day and age, almost all of what he subjected me to in terms of punishment would be viewed as child abuse; of that I have no doubt. I considered it a treat if he simply used a belt on me. The majority of the time, he would punch me with his fists. He would knock me down and sit on my chest, pinning me to the floor as he repeatedly punched me in the face. My mother would cry and scream for him to stop, but most of the time it didn't do much good. If my stepdad were working late, I would hurry and go to bed in an attempt to put the beating off until the morning, but even finding me sound asleep would not save me from his wrath. Whenever he got home, no matter how late, my mother would tell him what I had done. Then, in his anger, he would jerk the bedcovers off me and lay his belt across my body so hard that it would shock me awake. The real punishment, however, would come after the offense.

Our apartment had a large walk-in closet just off the living room, and that's where I would have to go when I was home. During school days I would be required to come straight home from school, do whatever homework I may have had, and then take a chair into the closet. I would have to sit in there in solitary confinement with the door closed until dinnertime. After dinner it would be back in the closet until bedtime. On weekends I would have to sit in the closet from the time I got up in the morning straight through until bedtime, only being allowed out for bathroom and meal breaks. Whenever my stepdad left the house, I could usually talk my mom into letting me out to watch television for a couple of hours, but I would keep an ear out for my stepdad's footsteps in the hallway, and then I would rush back into the closet. My behavior never changed as a result of this punishment. If anything, I became more practiced at ignoring the possible negative consequences of my behavior. The amount of time I spent in that closet is perhaps why I have such a vivid and active imagination and enjoy my own company as I do. After all, in the closet, I was all that I had. Ironically, as I write this memoir in prison, I see myself constantly repeating this pattern.

The odd thing about my relationship with my stepdad was that I both feared and loved him. Was one outcome of this that I came to feel out of touch with my stepdad's love if not periodically bringing punishment down on my head? I also notice that I did not feel angry with him. Where did that anger go? Have I acted it out through my criminal history, even though I couldn't feel it? I am not angry to this day. It may be difficult to understand, but I didn't view him as a cruel person. In my eyes, he was just a strict disciplinarian. In all honesty, he made me feel like his real son, worked hard to provide for his family, loved my mother, and gave us a home. Still, he was definitely harder on me than he was on my siblings. I'm inclined to believe that the reason for that was because I was the oldest child in the family and he felt that I should set a better example. Plus, I have to admit I was the only one of the kids getting into trouble outside the home. I did, however, wonder at times why none of my sisters and brothers ever had to go to the closet as punishment for their offenses. Perhaps by the time they were old enough to experience that form of punishment, my stepdad had figured out that it was not only wrong but psychologically abusive as well. Who can say? All I know is that I was the only one to be punished in that manner. Meanwhile, despite the closet, I continued to steal and play hooky from school.

Whenever I decided to skip school, I would take my books to the rooftop of my building and leave them there until school was out for the day. Then, on my way home, I would pick them up and enter the apartment as if I had just returned from a busy day of learning. This system worked pretty well for a while, but as the old saying goes, "All good things must come to an end." The end for me came after an average day of truancy.

On the day in question, I left my books on the rooftop as usual, riding the subway all over the city. When I returned home, I went to the roof to retrieve my books. However, to my horror, my books were gone! I had no choice but to return home without them. I wasn't too worried about this, though, because sometimes I would leave my books at school. So if I were questioned about them, which I doubted, I would just say that we didn't have any homework and I had left them in my locker at school. That would give me enough time to come up with an excuse for their disappearance at a later date.

When I walked into the house, I expected just my mom to be home, but to my surprise, my stepdad was there as well. But it didn't worry me all that much because, as far as my parents knew, I hadn't done anything wrong. I did, however, pick up on the fact that they were both unusually quiet. My stepdad was seated at the kitchen table, drinking coffee, while my mom just busied herself in the kitchen. I poked my head inside the refrigerator, looking for something to eat. The silence was now beginning to bother me a little, but finally my stepdad broke it.

"So," he said, taking a sip of coffee, "how was school?"

"Okay," I said calmly, my head still inside the refrigerator.

"Where are your books?"

"I left them in school," I replied, taking some lunchmeat from the refrigerator. "We didn't have any homework." I had to give it to myself as I walked over to the kitchen table—I was playing it pretty cool.

Then, without another word, my stepdad stood and walked into his bedroom. Because all of the rooms in our apartment were in a straight line, we lived in what is referred to as a "railroad apartment," so I was able to follow him with my eyes from my position at the table. The bedroom was the last room in the apartment, and he was only in there for a few minutes. When he came back toward the kitchen, I could see that he was carrying something in his hand. Now I was beginning to get nervous. I could no longer concentrate on the sandwich that I was making. As he got closer, I was able to make out exactly what it was that he had in his hand: my books. As I stared at them in shock, my appetite completely evaporated.

"What are these?" he shouted, throwing the books on the table.

Tears welled up in my eyes. I knew what was coming, and I was trying desperately to prepare myself for it.

"My books," I whispered.

"Go to your room," he said, "and wait for me."

The beating that I received was as expected, but not even that was as bad as the lecture that followed hours later. Whenever my stepdad got a few drinks in him, he would give marathon speeches, which was torture in and of itself. And so it was, later that evening, that I was summoned from my place inside the closet to receive one of his talks.

"You think I'm stupid, don't you, Ted?" he asked through his whiskey breath.

"No," I mumbled, eyes to the floor.

"Yes, you do," he slurred. "You think I'm stupid."

Knowing what was coming, I began to cry. As always, when trying to make a point that he wanted to drive home, he would take his forefinger and jab my forehead to punctuate his questions.

"Look at me!" he screamed.

I raised my head to look at him, bracing myself for the inevitable.

"When are you going to get it through that *thick*"—he jabbed—"*skull* of yours"—he jabbed again—"that I am not *stupid?*"

On the word *stupid*, he poked my head so hard with his stiff forefinger that he nearly knocked me out of my chair. By then, however, I had learned that his questions were purely rhetorical, so I didn't even attempt to answer. I just sat there, trying my best to endure the rest of his talk. The interrogation went on for hours, and I prayed that he would get as sleepy as I was becoming. I would gladly have taken another beating if it meant that I would be sent to bed afterward.

Finally, after being allowed to use the bathroom for the fourth or fifth time—in as many hours—I returned to find him fast asleep. I immediately went to bed, leaving him at the kitchen table. Before drifting off to sleep, however, I vowed never to hide my books on the roof again. No—I needed to find a better, more secure hiding place. I smiled as I listened to my stepdad snoring in the kitchen.

CHAPTER FOUR

Music and singing have always been a motivating factor in my life. For as long as I can remember, I had dreams of becoming a professional singer. I attribute my interest in singing to my mother. When I was about six or seven, she took me to the world-famous Apollo Theater on 125th Street in the heart of Harlem. I don't remember everyone who was on the show at the time, but I do know that Mickey & Sylvia were the headliners. Their hit record "Love Is Strange," one of my mom's favorite songs, was out at the time. I used to listen to records on the radio and on our record player, but that could in no way compare to seeing the songs performed live on stage by the actual artists. I was mesmerized by that Apollo experience and couldn't get enough of Apollo shows after that. I would play hooky and sneak in to see my favorite singers. Then I would go home and practice the songs, using the top of our kitchen table as a stage. My absolute favorite entertainer at the time was Jackie Wilson—Mr. Excitement himself! Jackie Wilson was an all-around showman, and he had a voice that just blew me away. Whenever he was at the Apollo, I would make it my business to be there.

I also enjoyed the *Motown Review*, with its lineup of up-and-coming stars. My two favorite Motown groups were Smokey & the Miracles and The Temptations. I would watch Smokey Robinson make the girls swoon with his mellow tenor voice. He had a major influence on my style of singing, and the fact that we looked a little bit alike didn't hurt any either. Smokey was light complexioned and wore his hair in what was called a "process." I—like Smokey—am light complexioned with naturally curly hair. So, of course, I used those attributes to my advantage—especially when it came to the opposite sex. Yes, Smokey was smooth, and I imitated him to the hilt.

However, when it came to pure harmony and choreography, there were none better than the "tempting" Temptations. With their fancy footwork and melodic vocals, the audience was always sure to get their money's worth. I would spend my formative years watching groups like them while practicing my own singing every chance I got. And as far as I could tell, people enjoyed my singing. They would never tell me to be quiet or to shut up. As a matter of fact, it was quite the contrary—they would often ask me to sing. And knowing that people actually wanted to hear me sing, I was happy to oblige.

My first opportunity to sing in front of a live audience came when I was in the sixth grade. Our class was preparing to do a production of *Snow White & the Seven Dwarfs*. Our teacher, a young white guy named Mr. Cavicky, was enthusiastic about the play. Everyone in the class was encouraged to try out for a part, and I decided that I wanted to be one of the seven dwarfs. After all, the girl playing Snow White would, of course, be *white*—so I just assumed that the part of Prince Charming would be given to one of the few white guys in my class, but when Mr. Cavicky suggested that I try out for the role of Prince Charming, I was shocked to the core.

Two white guys from the class were reading for the part as well, and we were able to take the script home. Therefore, when we came to the audition, each of us had our lines down pat. There was one minor detail, however, the other two guys didn't factor into the audition: the play was a musical, which, of course, meant that there would be singing. And Prince Charming would be required to sing at least two songs in the play. When Mr. Cavicky heard each of us sing "The Girl That I Marry," one of the required songs, I knew immediately that the part was mine. As I belted out the lyrics, the other guys didn't stand a chance, and they knew it. However, ever the diplomat, Mr. Cavicky told us that we had each done well and that he would make his decision in a couple of days. Exactly two days later, in front of the entire class, he made it official—I would be Prince Charming.

I could hardly contain my excitement as I ran home after school to tell my mother that I had gotten the part. She was so proud of me that instead of simply buying a prince costume for the role, she asked a neighbor friend of hers, a seamstress, to make one for me. We went shopping for the material for the costume, and I picked out a bright-blue velvet material, along with a piece of red silk for a sash. After being measured from head to toe, the end result was nothing short of amazing. The prince costume fit me like a glove. The colors coordinated beautifully, and I was pleased to find that the seamstress had enough of the red silk left over from the sash to make a bright-red cape. I must have posed in the mirror for hours on end in the days leading up to the play. You couldn't tell me anything—I was going to knock them dead. I poured myself into the script, memorizing all of my lines, determined to be the best Prince Charming ever.

The girl playing the part of Snow White was an attractive Jewish girl named Francis. I was a little nervous about that because there had been times, even before the play was proposed as a class project, that I had wondered what it would be like to kiss a white girl. Any thoughts of fulfilling that fantasy, however, were quickly dismissed by Mr. Cavicky. In no uncertain terms, he made it plain that in the scene where Prince Charming awakens Snow White with a kiss, I was to kneel with my back to the audience and simply pretend to kiss Francis. So, not wanting to jeopardize my role in the play, I followed Mr. Cavicky's instructions to the letter, doing everything he told me to do—and *not* to do. As a result, the rehearsals went as smooth as butter. However, opening night was a different story all together.

The night of the play, PS 192's small auditorium was packed with parents, teachers, students, and invited friends. Peering out at the crowd through a crack in the curtain, I was approached by one of the white guys who didn't get the Prince Charming role. He was now one of the seven dwarfs, and I knew he resented his role as well as mine. Therefore, I should have been suspicious when he told me that he overheard Francis telling one of her girlfriends that she wished I would kiss her for real when it came time to awaken her. My ego immediately took charge, swelling my head and causing me to take temporary leave of my senses. I didn't even question the source of the information, just planned my response based on what I had just been told.

As the curtain rose on the first act, a hush came over the audience as they settled in to watch the play. I was nervous—not because I was afraid of messing up my lines, but because I wanted to make a good impression on my parents. I was especially anxious to sing "The Girl That I Marry." I had practiced that song for hours on end and had it down pat, but since I had never before sung in front of a live audience, I didn't really know what to expect. That was the reason for my nervousness, but when it came time to stand out there on stage alone, with the spotlight shining directly on me, I rose to the occasion without hesitation. The moment I opened my mouth to sing, I knew I was in my element. There is something about the theater, about performing in front of a live audience—something magical— and I was caught up in the moment. I felt like that was my calling in life—what I was born to do.

I received a resounding applause at song's end, and Mr. Cavicky gave me a big hug when I came off stage. I stood there in his embrace, relishing the moment, already preparing for the scene where I had to awaken Snow White from her sleep. The decision as to how I was going to handle that had already been made, and I looked forward to it.

As I approached the sleeping figure of Francis, I was more nervous than in any other part of the play. Although I had long since doubted the truth of Francis's actually wanting me to kiss her in the scene, my curiosity had gotten the best of me. So I decided to go for it. After all, I reasoned, she couldn't do anything about it—not without ruining the scene—and I didn't think that she would do that.

I could smell her sweet, warm breath as I leaned over her pretty face. My back was to the audience, so I was able to take full advantage of them not being able to see the actual kiss. Francis lay there, eyes closed, looking luscious and inviting. I pressed my lips to hers. She jerked in response, but her eyes remained closed. Taking that as an invitation to proceed, I stuck my tongue deep inside her mouth. The effect was as if I had touched her with a live wire. Her eyes flew open, and her whole body went rigid. As she rocked her head back and forth, signaling me to stop, I hung in there, kissing her hard and deep.

After being awakened from her "sleep," Francis sat up, staring long and hard at me. Her face was flush with anger, but to the audience it was an amazing performance, and they applauded wildly. The rest of the scene played out to even louder applause, but when the curtain came down, it was curtains for me as well.

When Francis told him what I had done, Mr. Cavicky was furious. It was all that I could do to convince him to keep me in the play for the next performance. We had two more performances that weekend, and I played the scene right from that point on.

After the play, my popularity soared in school and in the community. I was constantly asked to sing by guys and girls alike. Even some of the older guys in the neighborhood—members of singing groups—tried to recruit me to join them. I was in my glory. Here I was, not even twelve yet, and guys sixteen and older wanted me to sing with them.

We would sing whenever and wherever we could—street corners, parks, or hallways. Personally, I enjoyed singing in hallways better because of the acoustics. The echo of the hallway gave the harmonies a richness that couldn't be duplicated outside of a recording studio. I usually sang lead but loved the tight harmony of background singing as well. I would jump into the background every chance I got. Most of the time at these singing sessions, the guys would pass a bottle of wine around, but I didn't indulge at the time. I was only interested in singing and in the girls who were always standing around listening. It wouldn't be long, though, before I found myself right in there drinking with the best of them. After all, I was one of the guys.

From that point on, I was hooked on singing and performing. It was a gift from God that would serve me well in the years to come and would ultimately be my saving grace both inside prison and out. Back then, however, a lifetime of confinement was the furthest thing from my mind. My dream was to be a professional singer, and I was well on my way.

CHAPTER FIVE

I graduated from the sixth grade and spent the summer looking forward to going to junior high school in the fall. Even though this particular summer recess was, for the most part, uneventful, there was one incident that stands out in my mind, even to this day.

My mother had given me two dollars one Sunday morning and asked me to buy her a copy of the Sunday *Daily News*. She told me that I could keep the change, motivating me that much more to run the errand, especially since the Sunday newspaper only cost about fifteen cents at the time.

There was a candy store across the street from our apartment building, about one block down, and that's where I headed to purchase the paper. The flow of traffic, even at that time of morning, was heavy on Amsterdam Avenue, so it took me a few minutes to cross the street.

As I entered the candy store, I noticed this older kid, extremely well built, who must have been around fourteen or fifteen years old. I didn't pay him much attention, but I should have. I pulled both of the dollar bills out of my pocket, using one of them to pay for the paper, and put the other one back in my pocket. When I received my change, I bought a couple pieces of candy and put the rest of the change in my pocket.

I walked out of the store, holding the paper under my arm while unwrapping one of the candies. That's when the kid approached me and demanded the money in my pocket. He was so big that I didn't even think about fighting him, so I did the next best thing: I ran—right into oncoming traffic! In my haste to get away, I tripped and fell directly into the path of a speeding taxi. It was bearing down on me from only about a block away, so there was no way it would be able to stop in time without hitting me. I lay there in the street, frozen in shock, watching the taxi approach at full speed. I turned my head away in anticipation of the impact and closed my eyes. Almost immediately, I heard the screeching of brakes and the honking of the taxi's horn. Then, all of a sudden, there was complete and total silence. It was as if my ears were stuffed with cotton.

I opened my eyes, turned my head slowly in the direction of the taxi, and bumped my nose on the car's tire! Then, as if someone suddenly yanked the cotton from my ears, I heard people screaming and shouting, asking if I was okay. I didn't bother to answer. I just jumped up and ran home, thankful that my mom wasn't looking out the window at the time. Knowing her, she would have had a heart attack.

Friends later told my mother it was only the hand of God that stopped that speeding taxi that day—a miracle pure and simple, they said. As for me, I didn't know what to believe. I was just happy to have gotten home with the change from the paper in my pocket.

At summer's end I transferred to my new school, Junior High School 43. It was located on 127th Street between Amsterdam Avenue and Old Broadway, just fourteen blocks from home. I continued to play hooky, however, so I didn't last long there. It was while playing hooky one day that I got myself into serious trouble with the law.

Little John and I had decided to go to see some girls who lived on the lower eastside of Manhattan. We were in the housing project where one of the girls lived.

"You guys live in this building?" a housing authority security guard asked as Little John and I entered the lobby.

"Naw," Little John replied. "We're looking for the apartment of some friends."

"*Friends*, huh?" the guard sneered, obviously questioning our motives. "You sure you ain't lookin' to *break in* some apartments?"

"No!" I hollered. "We just came to visit some girlfriends, that's all."

"Well, we had some recent burglaries, an' you guys fit the descriptions."

"Man, we don't know nothin' about no burglaries! I told you what we're here for!" Little John yelled.

"Why ain't you guys in school?" the guard asked. "How old are you anyway?"

"Twelve," I said proudly.

"I'm *fourteen!*" Little John yelled, sticking out his chest. "An' we don't have no school today."

"Yeah, it's a *holiday*," I lied.

Because of our ages, however, and the fact that we were not in school at the time, the police were called. As we waited for our parents at the local police station, Little John and I were separated and interrogated. There were two detectives in the interrogation room with me, one of which held a short black club in his hand. As a measure of intimidation, he kept smacking the club against his palm, staring intently at me all the while.

"What you gonna do with *that*?" I asked nervously.

"Oh, that's his *truth stick*," the other detective added.

"*Truth* stick?"

"Yeah," the cop with the club replied. "I'm gonna ask you some questions, an' every time you tell me a *lie*, I'm gonna hit you with this *truth* stick—got it?"

I nodded my head slowly.

My eyes never left the dreaded club. I knew that they wanted me to say that Little John and I had something to do with the project burglaries, so, to keep from getting hit with the club, that's exactly what I told them. I figured that once our parents showed up, the truth would come out. In the meantime, there was no way I was going to get hit with that club.

My confession was quickly committed to paper, and I was required to sign it. Then Little John was brought back into the room, where he was urged to admit his role in the burglaries. When he learned about my confession implicating him as well, he went berserk! He shouted that I was lying and that we never robbed any apartments in the projects. When he asked why I was lying on him, for a brief moment my mind flashed back to the time he had lied on me about setting that truck on fire. *Payback*, I thought, but of course that wasn't the reason I had lied at all. I turned my head without answering and waited for our parents to arrive.

Upon my stepdad's arrival, I told him that I admitted to the burglaries because they threatened to beat me with a club. Of course, the detectives denied it, but I could see that my stepdad had his doubts about that. Either way, it didn't matter, because they had a signed statement from me. Little John, on the other hand, continued to deny everything, so his mother was permitted to take him home. I was taken to the juvenile detention facility on Spofford Avenue in the Bronx, better known as the Youth House.

It was my first time locked up, and I was scared. I was also angry with myself for not having the nerve to stand up to those cops the way Little John had. Now he was home, and I was locked away in the Youth House, possibly on my way to one of the upstate detention facilities, or "training schools," as they were called at the time. I knew the majority of the kids in these places were members of Brooklyn street gangs, and for them it wasn't about acting tough—it was the real deal for them, no acting involved. The stories I heard while in the Youth House about training schools like Warwick and Otisville made me want to avoid them at all costs.

I had my first fight—if it could be called that—during this period of detention. While lining up to go to supper, a boy jumped in front of me in line. I was going to let it go and not say anything, but a couple of guys had already seen what he had done, so they waited to see what I was going to do about it. I took a deep breath and put my hand on the boy's shoulder— big mistake! He turned around, punched me in the eye, and proceeded to beat the crap out of me. He was pulled off me by the same guys who were watching to see what I was going to do in the first place. Later that evening one of them pulled me aside and told me that if I was sent to Warwick, I had better learn how to fight. I knew he was right because if even half of what I had heard about Warwick was true, I was definitely going to need to learn how to defend myself.

While waiting to go back to court, I went to school during the day and sang with a group during evening recreation.

My group and I were singing in the bathroom one evening when I was called into the unit supervisor's office. The unit supervisor, Mr. Super, was a huge black man who looked as if he might have played linebacker for the National Football League. I had only been at the Youth House a few weeks with no disciplinary problems, so I wondered why Mr. Super was calling me into his office. He asked if I was the one singing lead in the bathroom. I didn't know if I had done anything wrong or not, but I admitted that I was the one singing lead. Mr. Super's face lit up with a big grin, and he slapped me on the back. I simply stood there, confused, not saying anything, waiting to see what was coming next. We were singing the new hit song by The Drifters, "Up on the Roof," and, although I didn't know it at the time, it was Mr. Super's favorite song.

"Sing 'Up on the Roof' for me," Mr. Super said with a huge grin.

"Right here—in your office?" I asked cautiously.

"Hell yeah!" he said slapping me on the back. "Right here in *my* office!"

He slapped me on the back once again and then opened the door to his office, calling some of his staff inside.

I sang "Up on the Roof" for them, and everyone was pleased with my performance. Needless to say, during the rest of my stay at the Youth House, I never had to worry about anyone bothering me again. As a matter of fact, Mr. Super gave me the nickname "Up on the Roof," and I was happy to sing it for him whenever he requested it.

Still, I was anxious to go home. So when I finally appeared in juvenile court, I was extremely happy to see my mom and stepdad there. They smiled at me and assured me that everything was going to be fine. The judge, however, didn't agree. She said that because of my persistent truancy and misbehavior at home, I needed a more "structured environment." With that, she directed that I be sent to the Warwick State Training School for Boys, not to exceed a period of eighteen months. I was shocked and dismayed. It seemed that my whole world was falling apart. I wanted to go home so badly. Tears welled up in my eyes as I hugged my parents tightly. They promised to visit regularly, but that didn't make me feel any better. On the ride back to the Youth House, I stared out of the bus window without really seeing anything. My worst fear had just been realized—I was going Upstate! I was thirteen years old and scared to death.

The grounds of Warwick State Training School for Boys had an administration building, a vocational building, and a school building. There were also sixteen housing units—or cottages— grouped into sections of four and prefixed by the letters A, B, C, and D. For example, the A group of cottages was known as A-1, A-2, A-3, and A-4, with the same applying to the B, C, and D groups. Married couples—or "house-parents," as they were called—were assigned to each cottage, and it was their job to oversee the daily activities of the boys in their care.

The cottage to which I was assigned was called C-4. The house-parents were an elderly couple named Mr. and Mrs. Hall, but everyone called them "Mom" and "Pop." The cottage had a dormitory that slept about fifteen boys, and there were also private rooms that could be earned with good behavior. Being a new arrival, however, I was directed to the dormitory section of the cottage. I settled in pretty much without incident, but I was soon to learn that, like most of the cottages at Warwick, the cottage I was housed in held some of the toughest gang members in New York City.

Warwick had a number of rival gangs, with the leaders ruling their respective cottages. The concrete walkways leading to and from academic or vocational programs were virtual "battlefields" for gang rivalries. Everything at Warwick was based on posturing and ritual, from the way we lined up whenever we left the cottage as a group to the way we marched along the walkways to and from our destination.

The line formation of each cottage was based on hierarchy, with the cottage leaders taking their positions three abreast in front of the line. This particular grouping designated the positions known as front-right, front-middle, and front-left. The rest of us in the cottage formed a double-line behind the three in the front, with each position in the line still based on hierarchy or seniority, which meant, of course, that my place in the line was dead last.

The three guys in the front of the line were the toughest guys in the cottage, and it was their responsibility to prevent "traffic" through the middle of the line in either direction. If, for some reason, it were necessary for me to leave my place in line, I would have to step out of the line completely to get to wherever I had to go. Attempting to walk through the middle of the line was called "bugging" the middle, something that I found out the hard way not to do.

We were lined up outside of the cottage in formation, waiting for mail call. I heard my name called and quickly moved toward the front of the line. Instead of stepping completely out of the line to get my mail, I innocently attempted to walk through the middle to get to the front. I was immediately bombarded with fists in the chest, knocking me backward. It felt like everyone in the cottage was punching me, and I quickly realized my mistake. I jumped out of the line, rubbing my chest, and everyone started laughing at me—even Mom and Pop Hall. Needless to say, I never "bugged" the middle again.

When our cottage ventured out onto the walkway, we sang cadence under the direction of a cadence leader. Cadence served as a warning to other cottages that we were on the move and to step aside or suffer the consequences. Cadence, in effect, was saying that our cottage was the toughest and "baddest" on the grounds. Although each cottage had its own form or style of cadence, C-4 cottage's cadence went something like this:

Cadence leader:
Y'all git off the walk, ya know!
The cottage in unison:
High, low!
Cadence leader:
The eenie, meenie, miney, moe
The cottage in unison:
High, low!
Cadence leader:
The birds and the bees and the sycamore trees,
Y'all git off the walk, ya know.
The cottage in unison:
High, low!

Following the cadence leader's rhythmic chant, the entire cottage moved in a choreographed, synchronized movement—arms swinging, hips dipping—as we continued down the walkway:

Cadence leader:
C-4 up, C-4 down, C-4 cottage got the take of the grounds!
Y'all git off the walk, ya know!
The cottage in unison:
High, low!
Cadence leader:
The eenie, meenie, miney, moe!
The cottage in unison:
High, low!
Cadence leader:
The birds and the bees and the sycamore trees,
Y'all git off the walk, ya know!
The cottage in unison:
High, low!

Saying we had the "take of the grounds" meant that our cottage was the toughest on the grounds of Warwick and the rest of the cottages had better recognize who we were. Once I got the hang of the rhythm and melody of the cadence, I started making up new verses to go with the chant. I became so good at it that when our cadence leader went home, I was elevated to his position, something I took great pride in.

I also learned how to fight during my stay at Warwick, pretty much holding my own during our supervised boxing matches. Whenever there was an argument or disagreement between two guys in the cottage, Pop Hall would bring out the boxing gloves and referee the fight, but even if there were no arguments or disagreements to settle, we would fight for the mere fun and competition of it. Pop Hall refereed the matches, and it was always exciting whenever fights were scheduled.

There was a guy from my neighborhood in Harlem that I would box on a regular basis. His name was Ralph Cody, and he was the first to tell me that I had a "knockout punch"—a compliment coming from him, since he was one of the best fighters in Warwick. He would later go on to become one of the "firstborn" of the Five Percent Nation and would change his name to Born Allah. Born and I became lifelong friends and would run into each other from time to time in various upstate prisons.

Upon my release from Warwick, I was pleased to find that having been in the "joint" elevated me in the eyes of my peers, and I enjoyed the attention I received as a result. In terms of street status, my reputation had preceded me. My new school was Robert Wagner Junior High on the east side of Manhattan. I didn't mind that I was no longer going to 43 because it gave me an opportunity to meet new girls, and believe me there were a lot of cute girls at Wagner. Also, being the "new" boy at the school worked to my advantage as well.

I still played hooky from time to time and continued to hang out with my man Little John, who had long since forgiven me for implicating him in our "burglary." I imagine, however, that forgiving me wasn't all that difficult, especially since I was the one who actually did the time. We continued to drink and get into minor trouble every now and then, but nothing that would cause us to have police contact.

In my case, however, I had to report to a probation officer, so it wasn't long before my truancy caught up with me, and I was sent back Upstate. This time, though, I was sent to Otisville State Training School for Boys.

Located in Orange County, near Middletown, New York, Otisville was basically the same as Warwick—I went to school, worked, and sang in a group in my free time. By this time I had the routine down pat, and the time passed relatively fast. I was close to fifteen at the time, so I stayed there until my sixteenth birthday.

Before I knew it, I was back in Harlem, a little older, a little more street-smart, but unfortunately not any *wiser*. I continued my wayward lifestyle—drinking, hanging out, and stealing. So it was only a matter of time before I was back in police custody.

CHAPTER SIX

Two blocks from my house, on the corner of 139th and Amsterdam Avenue, was a restaurant that I had passed many times on my way home from the school park at PS 192. The restaurant was closed for the evening, and I stopped to see if there was anything inside that I could steal. I peered through the large plate-glass window but didn't see anything worth taking.

Before continuing on my way home, however, I looked around the corner and saw a staircase leading to the restaurant's basement storeroom. Checking to make sure I wasn't being observed, I walked to the bottom of the staircase, where a wooden door prevented me from going any further. I tested the door with my shoulder and found that it was pretty flimsy. One good thrust with my shoulder would open it. I peered upward toward the sidewalk, again making sure that no one was watching. I then pressed my shoulder hard to the door, flinging it open with a loud clatter.

Once inside, I looked around quickly to see what—if anything—was worth taking. To my disappointment, the only items of value were empty soda bottles stacked in wooden crates. I decided to take them, stash them, and redeem them the next day. However, before I could bring all of them to the doorway, I heard the crackle of police radios outside. Someone had called the police, and they were right outside the basement door!

In a panic, I quickly looked for a hiding place, but I could only find a cramped closet with a lone apron hanging from a hook on the wall. With angry shouts and police radios still crackling, the police entered the basement, going immediately to the closet.

When they came upon me, I was crouched down under the apron, with my feet sticking out from under it, the outline of my body in plain view. I could hear them snickering over me and realized that I must have looked like an ostrich with its head in the sand.

Wham! The kick came hard and fast to my head, knocking me over. The apron was snatched from my head, and I was yanked roughly to my feet, handcuffed, and hustled outside to a waiting police car. All I could think about as the car sped away from the crime scene was that there was nothing in the basement but empty soda bottles. *It's not going to be so bad*, I thought. *After all, I didn't take anything.* I figured I would get off with probation, or, at the very worst, get thirty days on Riker's Island.

At the station I was charged with unlawful entry, a misdemeanor that carried no more than a year in jail. After being photographed and fingerprinted, I was taken to night court, arraigned on the charge, and then taken to the Brooklyn House of Detention.

The Brooklyn House of Detention is a ten-story monstrosity taking up an entire city block on Atlantic Avenue. With each floor holding dark, foreboding cellblocks, it was a far cry from the Youth House. This was the real deal—the big leagues.

I was quickly processed in and assigned to a cell on the sixth floor. There were two tiers of cells numbered one through forty-two. I was assigned to a cell on the second tier. As I approached my cell, it seemed that all eyes were on me. I tried to walk with a swagger in an attempt to give the impression that this was nothing new for me.

As I walked to the staircase leading to the second tier, I had to pass the recreation room, or "day room," as it was formally called. As I passed, I saw a group of guys in the corner of the room, harmonizing. That made me anxious to put my things in my cell and get back to see if I could join them. After being instructed by one of the guards to put my pillow, sheets, and blankets on the bed, I was told that I could go to the day room.

I headed straight for the singing group and stood off to the side, listening. They were singing "Ooh Baby Baby" by Smokey & the Miracles, and the harmony was pretty good. The guy leading the song was a big muscle-bound kid named Joe Harvel. He sounded pretty good, but he wasn't really all that impressive. After the song was over, the group asked me if I sang, and I told them that I did. Joe invited me to join them, so I thought they wanted to hear me lead a song. I asked them if they knew the new song by The Delfonics, "La-La Means I Love You," and they said they did.

Before I could begin, however, Joe Harvel jumped in: "Many guys have come to you, with a line that wasn't true…," making it obvious that he considered himself the lead singer of the group. So, without protest, I quickly found my note and joined in the background harmony. They were impressed with what they heard and made me an official member of the group.

The group member whose singing impressed me the most was Eddie Zant. Everyone called him by his initials, E-Z—pronounced like the word *easy*. E-Z was locked in the cell right under mine, and he and I quickly became friends. We also served as the cellblock "radio" after the lights went out. Not only did I enjoy singing with him, I also enjoyed his company.

Once everyone was locked in for the night, E-Z and I would take song requests. More often than not, we would harmonize on duets, but if only one of us knew a particular song, we would also take solo requests. No one ever asked Joe Harvel to sing, and I think that's what made him pick a fight with E-Z during one of our singing sessions.

We were in the process of rehearsing for a facility talent show, and Joe wanted to lead a song more suited to E-Z's voice. A fistfight ensued, with E-Z getting the worst of it. When the fight was over, one of his eyes was swollen to the size of a handball. E-Z was transferred to another cellblock, and I never saw him again. It wasn't the same without him, and although I continued to sing with the group, I found myself secretly wishing that Joe Harvel had been transferred instead of E-Z. In later years, I was pleased to learn that E-Z would go on to sing with Ace Spectrum, a popular black recording group in the late sixties.

By the middle of August, I had been back and forth to court a number of times, and my court-appointed lawyer told me that he was trying to work out a deal that would have me home soon. I figured he knew what he was doing, so I spent my time at the Brooklyn House reading; watching TV; and, of course, singing.

Our group was excited about the upcoming talent show we were rehearsing for. We harmonized constantly, with Joe Harvel, of course, leading all the songs. Joe had taken a liking to a new song by The Temptations titled "I Wish It Would Rain" and decided that we would sing it in the show. Since everyone liked the song, there were no objections. Still, there were those in the group who felt that my voice was more suited for the lead. I knew there was no way Joe was going to relinquish the lead, so I continued to work on perfecting my background note. In all honesty, Joe didn't sound bad leading the song, but I knew that—given a chance—I could deliver it better than him, but again, he was the leader, so I didn't say anything.

A couple of days before the actual show, we were in the auditorium rehearsing with the inmate band members. Everyone in the auditorium at the time was performing in the show in some capacity, and I was particularly impressed with a young singer by the name of Victor Sanders. I had heard about Vic through the prison grapevine, and everyone spoke highly of him as a vocalist. This was my first time, however, actually hearing him, and his rendition of the song "My Mother's Eyes" literally blew me away. Vic put so much of himself into the song it was clear that he was singing it with his own mother in mind—even going so far as to actually cry during the song's climax. His rendition was so powerful that I had no doubt he was going to be one of the show's top winners.

As fate would have it, Joe Harvel developed a bad case of laryngitis and was unable to sing the night of the show. That didn't hurt us, though, because there were still four of us left—enough for a lead singer and three-part harmony. I was given the lead, and we did justice to the song, but as almost everyone had predicted, including me, Victor Sanders easily took first place. No way was anyone was going to top "My Mother's Eyes"—not the way Vic sang it.

I returned to court in early September and was told by my lawyer that a deal had been arranged. If I would agree to plead guilty to unlawful entry, I would be given "youthful offender" status and sentenced to three years' probation. My attorney assured me that I would be going home that very same day. All I heard were the words *home* and *same day*. So that was all I focused on as I stood in front of the judge and pled guilty to unlawful entry. I was then given youthful offender papers to sign as my lawyer explained that this conviction could not be used against me if I were later arrested as an adult. I then turned back to the judge for sentencing, and that's when the deal fell apart. I couldn't believe my ears. I turned to my lawyer, but he simply shrugged his shoulders, leaving me standing there in a daze. Fully expecting the judge to live up to the promised three years' probation, I was shocked when he sentenced me to three years in Elmira Reformatory.

CHAPTER SEVEN

A few days after my sentencing, I was taken to the Erie Lackawanna train station along with nineteen other guys. We were on our way to Elmira Reception Center and were shackled together by twos. The guy I was shackled to was about two years older than me, and from the time we were seated together on the train until we pulled into a rest stop in Albany, New York, I cried to him almost nonstop about my three-year sentence. He never said a word. He just sat there in silence, listening to my whining.

As the rest of the train's passengers departed and boarded from separate cars, the guards passed out bag lunches consisting of bologna and cheese sandwiches. I noticed that my traveling companion wasn't eating his sandwiches. He just sat staring out the window, lost in thought.

"You gonna eat that?" I asked, pointing to his bag lunch.

Piercing me with his stare, he shook his head.

"Can I have it then?" I said innocently.

"On *one* condition, my man," he replied.

"What's that?"

"That you stop *crying* to me about that little *three-year* sentence you got!"

Little! I thought. *What was he talking about*—little *sentence?* But I was hungry enough to agree to almost anything, so I accepted the paper bag from him.

After eating, with no further words from my traveling companion, curiosity got the best of me. I was still thinking about him referring to my sentence as little.

"How much time *you* doin', man?" I asked, wiping crumbs from my lap.

Jerking his head toward me, and with a penetrating glare, he nearly spit the words out: "Natural…*life! That's* what I'm doing, my man!" He then turned back toward the window, leaving me sitting there in shock.

I immediately raised my hand, signaling that I needed to use the bathroom. The guard came over, unchained me, and escorted me to the restroom at the rear of the car.

"I don't really have to use the bathroom," I told the guard as we approached the bathroom door.

"What kind of *games* are you playing, son?" the guard asked angrily.

"No games, sir. I just want to change my seat, that's all."

"And why should I let you do that?"

"Because my seat partner has natural *life*, and I've been complaining to him about my *three-year* sentence. He just makes me nervous—if you know what I mean."

"Yeah, I know what you mean" the guard said, "but that should teach you to keep your mouth shut."

I must admit, it did. I returned to my seat and didn't say another word for the rest of the trip.

I didn't know it at the time, but the guy I was complaining to about my sentence was Robert Rice, a member of the infamous Harlem Seven. He and six others had just been sentenced for the double murder of a white Harlem storekeeper and his wife. They had each been given natural life with no possibility of parole. Although he and I later became friends, I learned two valuable lessons that day. One: keep your mouth shut because you never know who you're talking to. And two: no matter how bad you think your situation is, there's always someone who is worse off. Remembering those two lessons served me well in the years of incarceration to follow.

I was told at the reception center in Elmira that I would be there for about two months, just long enough to be tested and evaluated for permanent placement. Coxsackie was the only other reformatory in the state at the time, so I knew I would either be sent there or remain at Elmira's Reformatory next door.

I also learned from a reception center guidance counselor that my stepdad was not my real father. We were going over some background information, and he asked me what my father's name was. I told him Daniel Harris, of course, and he said he meant my *real* father's name. I said Daniel Harris *was* my real father's name. He shook his head in the negative and told me that Daniel Harris was my stepfather. Needless to say, I was devastated. I don't know if I was angrier that I had been told by a stranger or that my parents had been keeping that information from me. I just shrugged it off, acting as if it didn't really matter to me, stuffing the anger deep inside.

I was sent to Coxsackie Reformatory on November 9, 1965. I remember the date because that was the day all of the power up and down the eastern seaboard was knocked out, reaching into Canada and parts of Michigan. The blackout didn't affect operations at Coxsackie, though, nor did it stop me from being processed in as inmate #14946.

Coxsackie was right out of my worst nightmare. There was a total silence rule in effect, with talking only allowed in the recreation yard. No talking was permitted in the corridors or in the mess hall, and anyone caught violating the rule was dealt with severely—usually with thirty or more days in solitary confinement.

Each cellblock held forty-two cells, and we were required to line up in cell order when marching to the mess hall. On one side of the cellblock were cells numbered one through forty-one, and on the other side were cells numbered two through forty-two. When finished eating, each inmate was required to exit the mess hall and stand in the assembly hall in cell order with his hands behind his back, legs apart, eyes straight ahead, in total silence until each man was finished eating.

Coxsackie was segregated at the time, with all the black inmates located on the north wall in what is known as "center yard," the prison's main recreation yard. Sections of the north wall, known as "cribs," designated the geographical area each inmate was from. For example, Manhattan, Bronx, Brooklyn, Queens, and Staten Island cribs represented the five boroughs of New York City. If an inmate came from Manhattan, he would stand in the "Manhattan" crib. Inmates from Upstate New York (Syracuse, Rochester, and Buffalo) had their own cribs as well, as did the white and Puerto Rican inmates. The Puerto Rican crib was known as "Spain," and it could be confusing to the newcomer.

It was also a territorial arrangement, with each crib member required to stand guard when other members were away at school or vocational programs or on a visit. If an "outsider" attempted to enter a crib without being invited in, he would be dealt with severely. Not knowing all of this ahead of time, of course, caused me a serious problem the first time I entered the yard.

I naturally headed toward the north wall and was immediately approached by a huge inmate who was guarding the "Manhattan" crib. With leather-gloved hands balled into fists, he stopped me from passing the imaginary borderline. Thinking that I was Puerto Rican, he told me that I belonged in Spain. Of course I had no idea what he was talking about. I assumed he meant Spain the country, so I immediately wrote him off as a nutcase. Before I could decide how to handle the situation, a guy that I knew from Harlem came to my rescue. He told the guy that I wasn't Spanish and that I was from Manhattan. That apparently was good enough for him. He apologized, stepped to the side, and allowed me access to the north wall. I walked into "Manhattan," where the rules of survival were clearly laid out.

Coxsackie was known as "Gladiator School." The environment was so hostile and dangerous that anyone allowed access to any section of the wall—black, white, or Puerto Rican—was required to fight.

So a few day after my place on the north wall was established, I was approached by Billy Elias, from the Lincoln Projects in Harlem and one of the most feared fighters at Coxsackie.

"You know how to fight?" he asked, his eyes glaring deep into mine.

Knowing there were guys there who lived and breathed physical confrontation, I was cautious with my response. "Yeah, but I'm always open for improvement."

Billy smiled, apparently pleased with my answer. "Show me your fighting stance."

I stood nervously with my back against the wall and put my hands up in a defensive posture.

"All right then. You ready?"

Although not completely comfortable with the question, I apprehensively nodded my head.

WHAM! The jab came from nowhere, and it felt like a mule had kicked me in the chest. My chest bone felt like it was broken, and the wind was knocked completely out of me. I had never been hit that hard in my life and was determined not to let it happen again. I began to block Billy's jabs and punches as he nodded his head in approval, encouraging me to throw punches of my own.

As my boxing skills increased, I knew I was deemed ready when Billy handed me a pair of black leather gloves one day and told me that they were my "guns." I proudly accepted them and was instructed to keep them on me at all times. He then gave me the nickname "Two-Guns"—a "handle" that I made every effort to live up to. I felt like a gunslinger and the center yard was Dodge City.

During my time at Coxsackie, I took typing and music classes and also received my General Equivalency Diploma. My typing instructor was a black man named Mr. Cody, who encouraged me to take typing seriously. He told me it would come in handy one day. So after diligently applying myself, I was typing forty-five words a minute before long. Shortly after acquiring that speed, Mr. Cody made me his clerk, and my proficiency continued to increase.

The music classes were more recreational than anything else. The instructor, Mr. Francis, was also a black man, and he easily weighed five hundred pounds. An accomplished vocalist and musician in his own right, Mr. Francis took a special interest in my vocal development. He gave me weekly voice lessons and encouraged me to sing at Catholic services each Sunday. He also paired me at those services from time to time with an inmate by the name of Philip Luciano.

Philip was from Spanish Harlem and was an extremely gifted vocalist as well. We would sing duets written and arranged by Mr. Francis, and our voices blended nicely. He and I also sang with various groups in the yard and would always draw a crowd whenever we sang together. Unfortunately, however, Philip and I would take different paths upon our release. He would go on to make a name for himself, performing and recording with *The Last Poets* in the late sixties and early seventies, work as a disc jockey for a major Latin radio station in New York City, and finally become a respected television newscaster.

Still angry over the news concerning my stepdad, I had resolved not to say anything to him or my mom. The few times they visited me at Coxsackie served only to fuel my anger. There were times I wanted to bring it up, to let them know just *how* I had found out, but for some reason I couldn't. So I went through the motions with them, acting as if everything was fine. I probably should have discussed it with them. Perhaps if I had, things would have turned out different for me as far as my future was concerned, but as things stood at the time, I did not feel connected as a family member, so my path took a totally different direction. It was all about me, as far as I was concerned. I still had a lot of growing up to do.

CHAPTER EIGHT

In May of 1967, after spending eighteen months at Coxsackie, I was paroled to my parents' house. I returned to my neighborhood to find most of my hangout buddies still hustling and getting high. Only because it was a parole requirement, I started looking for a job the first couple of weeks that I was out. I had my own criteria for accepting or rejecting a job. It was simple: if I couldn't steal anything, I didn't take the job. So when I accepted a job as a janitor at Steinway Pianos in Midtown Manhattan, I questioned that decision as soon as the broom was placed in my hands. After all, what was I going to do, sneak a piano out of the showroom?

I was in one of the rehearsal rooms in the basement, sweeping and mopping. It was my second day on the job, and I had pretty much made up my mind that I would finish out the week, collect my paycheck, and never return. After all, where was the incentive? There was absolutely nothing for me to steal. That's when I saw the cast-iron Indian statue in the corner of the room.

It was an Indian warrior about five-feet high, brandishing a tomahawk and a shield. I immediately put my broom down and attempted to move it—just to get a feel for how heavy it was. I could barely budge it, so I guessed it weighed at least two hundred pounds or better. I quickly located a dolly and managed to maneuver the statue onto it. I then rolled it to a side door that led to an alley just off of the storeroom. I placed the statue in the alley and went back to work. When lunchtime rolled around, I left, and so did the Indian. I headed straight for the uptown subway.

One thing about living in New York City, it takes a lot to turn the head of a New Yorker, no matter the situation. As I rolled the iron Indian through the city streets, passersby gave it a casual glance, but that was the extent of their curiosity. I turned a few heads on the subway, but the passengers quickly lost interest, going back to whatever it was they were doing.

I exited the train station at 145th Street and Broadway and rolled the statue up to 143rd Street and Hamilton Place. I knew it would only be a matter of time before a passing police car stopped me, so I ducked into a hallway and placed the statue behind the staircase. I then went to Johnny & Moe's Bar, located on the corner of 143rd Street and Hamilton Place, and loudly announced that I had a cast-iron Indian statue for sale. The majority of the patrons looked at me as if I had lost my mind. However, there is always one curious enough to see exactly what it is that's being offered. He's the one that I took into the hallway behind the staircase, where the statue had been placed.

"Man, you got to be out your mind!" the guy said. "What am I supposed to do with that?"

I told him that he could put the Indian in his apartment to use as a coat rack, a hat rack, or simply as a conversation piece. He wasn't going for it. And I must admit, the more I looked at the iron Indian, the more it was losing its appeal for me as well. He asked me how much I wanted for it, and I told him two hundred dollars. In his eyes, however, that only served to verify my insanity.

"Man, I'll give you twenty-five dollars," he said. "Take it or leave it."

I told him I would take it. I couldn't see myself continuing to walk the streets with the statue and risk being stopped by the police.

As he counted the money out in my hand, I felt like a complete idiot. And to add insult to injury, he demanded that I roll the Indian to his apartment—two blocks away!

Since he lived on the fifth floor, I was relieved to find that there was an elevator in the building. I left him at the door to his apartment and promised myself I would never again take a job where there was nothing for me to steal.

A few months later, I was in Johnny & Moe's Bar again when a young black guy I had never seen before approached me while I was washing my hands in the men's room. He had just finished relieving himself, and we greeted one another with a nod.

"You wanna make some money?" he asked, pulling out a shiny .38 revolver.

"I'm *always* interested in makin' money," I said. "What you got in mind?"

"Since I'm not from here, I'm open to suggestions."

"Robbing a cab would be the easiest," I said. "They don't usually put up a fight."

"Sounds good," he said. "Let's do it."

I noticed that he didn't put up much of a "fight" either in terms of going along with my suggestions, so we exited the bar as future partners in crime.

Just outside the bar, as we looked for a cab, he told me a little about himself. His name was Ed, and according to him, he was on the run from Chicago. He didn't go into detail, which was fine with me. All I wanted to do was make some quick money. I certainly didn't plan on hanging out with him on a regular basis. As far as I was concerned, he was on his own after the robberies. Only half listening, I saw a gypsy cab coming down the street and waved it over.

I directed the driver to take us to Greenwich Village but changed my mind as we approached 72nd Street and Amsterdam Avenue. I told the driver to pull over, and he glanced at me briefly in the rearview mirror. When the cab came to a stop at the corner, Ed pulled out the gun, and we relieved him of his money without incident. We then headed for the nearest subway station and proceeded to the Village by train.

We split the proceeds from the robbery—which really wasn't worth the risk we had just taken—then hung out in the Village for a while. Then, anxious to get back uptown and let Ed go his own way, we looked for another cab to rob.

We were standing on a corner just outside of a pizza parlor when a cab pulled up in front of us, seemingly from out of nowhere. The driver stuck his head out and asked if we needed a cab. For a fraction of a second, I felt that something wasn't right, but Ed immediately opened the rear door of the cab, and we climbed in. There was something strange about the way the cab just *appeared* without us having to flag it down, a feeling that I just couldn't shake. I should have voiced my reservations to Ed right away, but I didn't. As the cab pulled away from the corner, I directed the driver to take us to 110th Street and Central Park West.

The cab driver engaged us in conversation along the way, but I still felt uncomfortable. As we approached our destination, Ed slowly removed the gun from his waistband. Noticing that the chamber was open, he attempted to close it without the driver hearing it. The clicking sound of the chamber closing, however, gave him away, and I watched as the driver's head jerked in the direction of the gun.

He turned his head quickly back to the road, but I knew he had seen the gun. I motioned to Ed to put the gun away, but he didn't understand what I was trying to tell him. In one swift motion, Ed pointed the gun at the cab driver's head and told him to pull over to the curb. The driver immediately complied, bringing the cab slowly to a stop at the corner. Then, with a move that one would expect to see only in the movies, the driver whipped out a gun of his own and pointed it directly at Ed's head!

I sat there stunned, trying to act like an innocent bystander, watching the drama unfold before me. It was a classical Mexican standoff, and I prayed that nobody started shooting.

While this was going on inside the cab, police cars quickly surrounded us. That's when it dawned on me—the driver was an undercover cop! The cop ordered Ed to give him the gun. I held my breath in anticipation, trying to will him to comply. To my relief, Ed handed the gun over. We were roughly hustled out of the cab and handcuffed. We were then taken in separate cars to the police station and placed in separate interrogation rooms.

I told the cops that I didn't know Ed; I was simply in the Village trying to get home when he offered to let me share a cab with him. I insisted that I didn't know he was going to rob the cab. The story was plausible, and they seemed to buy it. All I needed was for Ed himself to go along with my version of events.

We were booked on a charge of first-degree robbery and then taken to night court, where we entered a not guilty plea. Although it really didn't make a difference, I was given a ransom for a bail. It could just as well have been one dollar. Because of my status as a parole violator, a parole warrant had been lodged against me.

I did, however, get a chance to talk with Ed in the bullpen, just before going into the courtroom. He agreed to tell the district attorney that that he offered me a ride and that I didn't know he was going to rob the cab. He said it didn't make any sense for both of us to go to jail. That really shocked me, because rarely is someone willing to take all of the weight when the bust goes down. Right then and there I had a newfound respect for Ed. He was a real trooper.

From night court I was taken back to the Brooklyn House of Detention. Even though Ed agreed to take full responsibility for the robbery, as a parole violator, I would still have to go back to Coxsackie to finish out my three-year sentence. That didn't matter to me, though, because all I wanted to do was get the current robbery charge dropped. I only owed one year on the parole violation, and I could do another year standing on my head.

The robbery charge was formally dismissed against me in early September of 1967. Ed had earlier pled guilty to the robbery and to the gun possession, so he was in New York Supreme Court for sentencing as well. We had an opportunity to talk in the bullpen before going into the courtroom, and I thanked him for what he had done. I told him he was a "stand-up" guy. He simply smiled and nodded his head.

Inside the courtroom, as we prepared to stand before the judge, Ed and I were seated apart from one another. He was the first to stand before the judge, however, and was promptly sentenced to thirty to sixty years in prison!

Ed didn't so much as flinch, but I sat there in complete shock as he was led from the courtroom in handcuffs. Then it was my turn to stand in front of the judge. After witnessing what had just happened to Ed, I didn't know what to expect. Suppose they reneged on the deal? Suppose they decided not to dismiss the robbery charge against me?

I stood before the judge on shaky legs right next to my court-appointed attorney. A lot of the legal jargon went right over my head, but when the judge said, "Case dismissed," I understood that clearly.

I smiled in relief and walked back to the bullpen in a daze. I was thankful that Ed was not there waiting for me. After all, having just been sentenced to thirty to sixty years, somehow "Thanks again" didn't seem like it would cut it. The ride back to the Brooklyn House was a silent one. I could not stop thinking about Ed.

One week later I was taken to the property room, signed my release papers, given my property, and told that I was free to leave. I couldn't believe it. *Somebody has just made a huge mistake,* I thought. In light of the fact that at the time of my arrest for the robbery I had been out past my curfew, I was certain that I would be held in violation of my parole. I was expecting to be picked up by parole officers and returned to Coxsackie to finish out the remainder of my three-year sentence. I certainly wasn't going to say anything, though. I just wanted to get out of the jail before the mistake was discovered.

The huge steel door in the lobby slammed shut behind me. I stood there a few seconds in disbelief. The door to freedom was mere feet away! I hurried toward the door with a great big "Kool-Aid" grin on my face.

Just as I reached for the door handle, two burly parole officers appeared on each side of me, blocking my exit.

"Theodore Harris?" the one with the folder said. It was more of a statement than a question.

I knew that it wouldn't do any good to deny my identity, so I gave him a reluctant nod. They quickly handcuffed me, took me outside, and placed me inside of an unmarked car.

As we inched our way into rush-hour traffic, heading for the New York state thruway, I shook my head sadly. I had come so close to freedom, but then the thought that I had just dodged a heavy prison sentence put things into perspective.

From that point on, I settled into my seat and actually enjoyed the ride.

CHAPTER NINE

I was released from Coxsackie in June of 1968, two months after the assassination of Dr. Martin Luther King Jr. My parents still resided at 1634 Amsterdam Avenue, and I went to live with them. The neighborhood had not changed much during my time away. There was, however, one exception.

Directly next door to my apartment building was a storefront branch of the slain civil rights leader's "Poor People's Campaign." Over the doorway in big red letters was a large wooden sign that read "Harlem Poor People's Campaign." In smaller letters beneath those words read "Charles Mobley, Campaign Manager." There was a constant stream of people coming and going, and I was pleased to note that there were quite a few attractive young ladies in the office as well. Their style of dress reflected the "Back to Africa" mentality prevalent at the time, with a number of African dashikis and large Afro hairstyles prominently on display. It was the sixties, with "Black Power" the battle cry in almost every ghetto neighborhood.

One day I stopped in the office to ask if I could use one of their typewriters. All eyes were on me as I prepared to type a résumé that I had drafted earlier by hand. When I started typing, my fingers flew across the keyboard. As I was typing, someone went in the back of the office and told the director, Charles Mobley, to come and check me out. Charles came out and stood directly behind me as I continued to type.

"You're pretty fast, my man," Charles said, as I finished typing. "Can you type that fast if someone's dictating?"

"Yeah, that's no problem," I replied without looking at him.

"Stick a fresh sheet in there and let's see what you got," he challenged.

I did as Charles directed, and began to type as he dictated a "test" letter. I was typing as fast as he talked, with no mistakes and proper letter structure. Charles perused the finished product.

"Where'd you learn to type like that?" he asked, obviously impressed.

"In Coxsackie," I said as if everyone knew exactly what that meant. "It's a Reformatory Upstate," I clarified. "I did three years there."

Charles pondered that for a moment, and then asked if I would be interested in working for him at the office. I told him I would think about it and let him know later.

I decided to work for Charles because I was very much impressed with him. Almost immediately I noted that he was a "ladies man." However, I was most impressed with the way he verbally expressed himself. Charles reminded me of an older version of myself or the "image" of me that I aspired to be. With his light complexion and curly hair, we even looked a lot alike. Charles Mobley would serve as a mentor to me, and it wasn't long before we became almost inseparable.

In a matter of months, he promoted me to the position of office manager at the campaign headquarters, and I quickly became his right-hand man.

Charlie was connected in the music industry as well. The most popular black female group at that time was The Ronettes. Ronnie was the lead singer of the group and was managed by the legendary music producer Phil Spector, ultimately becoming his wife. Charlie was Ronnie's uncle, and when he found out that I could sing, he allowed my group and me to use the office after hours to rehearse. He would often sit in on the rehearsals, and I could see that he was impressed with us.

One evening in the winter of 1969, Charlie took me to the Top Club on 125th Street and introduced me to Duke Baldwin, club owner and popular Harlem radio personality at the time.

With its location just down the street from the world-famous Apollo Theater, the *Top Club* was a well-known venue for up-and-coming singers and groups. Tuesday evenings at the Top Club were reserved for new acts to showcase their talent. Duke Baldwin, who also owned a larger nightclub in Brooklyn called Tempo Soul City, was always on the scene at the Tuesday night talent shows. If a singer or group could win three weeks in a row at the Top Club, Duke would put them on the bill at his Brooklyn nightclub. Popular black recording artists showcased their hit songs there as well. So, of course, winning at the Top Club and appearing at Tempo Soul City was every up-and-coming singer's dream. Duke told me to bring my group to his club on Tuesday night, and I assured him we would be there.

We called ourselves Black Myth, and there were four of us in the group, counting myself. I was the lead singer, followed by the background harmony of Eddie Bryant, William Davis, and Francis Leper.

Francis and I were from the same neighborhood in Harlem, and we grew up together. That was one of the reasons why I let him join the group. His vocal abilities were not great, but he was dedicated and never missed a rehearsal. Eddie and William, on the other hand, had great voices and didn't seem to mind that they had to "carry" Francis on vocals most of the time. All Francis wanted to do was smoke weed and sing. He was funny and always kept us laughing. So, basically, I guess you could say that he was more of a "mascot" than anything else.

For our Top Club debut, we picked the new song by The Moments, "Not on the Outside." It is a slow, tender love song with a soft tenor lead, and we were as ready as we would ever be. We had rehearsed the song until we had every nuance and inflection down pat. As the house band played the song's opening chords, the club patrons clapped in recognition but were clearly waiting to see if we would do the song justice. When I started to sing, "So you think my heart's made of stone…," the ladies in the audience went wild. I continued with confidence: "And when you're near me…there's no reaction…well, you're wrong." Now the ladies were crowding around the stage, screaming their approval. The background harmony was smooth and tight—even Francis sounded good! We smiled as we exited the stage to continued applause and shouts of approval. I was pleased to see Duke Baldwin himself nodding his head and smiling. It was then that I actually thought we had a chance of winning.

Judging was by audience applause, and although the rest of the show's acts were good, we were clearly the crowd favorite. When Duke Baldwin held his hand over our heads for audience response, they went absolutely wild. There was no question about it—we had won! We were excited, of course, but we knew that we had to win two more times before setting our sights on Tempo Soul City.

Rehearsing feverishly after our Tuesday night's win, we took the next two shows easily. We sang "Not on the Outside" each week, so we didn't see the need to change it for our upcoming show at Tempo Soul City. As a matter of fact, since we would be on the show with professional recording artists, it was important to make a good impression. I only wish that Francis had kept that in mind. He, however, was in love with the new song by The Temptations, "Cloud Nine," and wanted us to sing that. Since we were not familiar with the song, we rejected that suggestion immediately. Also, as already stated, we wanted to go with the song that got us there in the first place. Francis used every argument he could think of to get us to change our minds, but our decision was firm. Besides, I told him, we were getting paid for that night's performance, so we definitely had to be at our best.

When it was time for us to go on, Duke Baldwin took the stage and introduced us as the latest Top Club talent show winners.

Pointing in our direction off stage, he shouted, "Ladies and gentlemen, let's have a big round of applause for…Black Myth!"

We ran onto the stage to wild applause as the band—to our total dismay—began to play the opening chords to "Cloud Nine"! Before we could get the bandleader's attention, Francis stepped to the microphone and began to sing: "The childhood part of my life wasn't very pretty." I was fuming and silently vowed that when I got him backstage *another* part of his life wasn't going to be very *pretty* either!

We stumbled through the song, unsure of the words or the harmony, and I could make out the puzzled look on a few faces in the audience. Add to this the fact that Francis was singing *lead*, and you can imagine how we must have sounded. Needless to say, we were a total disaster that night, leaving the audience to wonder how we were able to win one night at the Top Club, never mind three.

At song's end, with the roar of boos from the audience ringing in our ears, we cornered Francis backstage. We were on the verge of beating him down when Duke Baldwin stepped in to save him. Francis looked up sheepishly at us and smiled. It was then that we realized that he was stoned out of his mind on weed. He was high when he went behind our backs to the bandleader and told him we had decided to change our song. And he was still high when he actually tried to sing the song. For some reason, Duke found it amusing. Laughing, he told us to go out into the club and enjoy ourselves. He said the drinks were on him and we would still be paid for our "performance." Our anger at that point began to subside, and we just shook our heads in disgust.

Out in the club, among all the fine ladies, it wasn't long before we had forgotten about what Francis had done. We even laughed about it on our way home that evening. Francis still had some weed left, and William and Eddie shared a joint with him. I never liked marijuana because it made me feel paranoid and disoriented. So I chose not to join them. Alcohol was good enough for me; I didn't see the need for anything stronger, at least at the time, but that too was about to change.

CHAPTER TEN

A few weeks after the Tempo Soul City debacle, I received my draft notice. The Vietnam War was going strong, but I couldn't see myself in a strange country, armed to the teeth and moving cautiously through jungle brush, so I immediately looked for a way out.

I spoke to a few guys in the neighborhood who had either served in or had been rejected by the army. They told me that drug addicts were not being accepted into the armed services. Based on that information, I decided to go to the induction center with heroin in my system. A neighborhood junkie injected me with the drug hours before my physical. It worked like a charm. The heroin in my system, along with the needle mark on the arm, was enough to convince the medical personnel that I was an addict. As a result, I was immediately rejected and sent on my way. Mission accomplished.

That one shot of heroin, however, whetted my appetite. So on April 14, 1969, I celebrated my twentieth birthday with another shot that would ultimately turn into a one-hundred-dollar-a-day habit. The rest, as they say, is history.

The transition, however, from draft dodger to junkie was a subtle one. I kept up appearances in an effort to hide my growing addiction, but I wasn't really fooling anyone. I especially didn't want Charles Mobley to know about my heroin addiction, but of course there was no fooling him. Although he didn't say anything about it at the time, it was clear that he knew.

On the first anniversary of the assassination of Martin Luther King Jr., Charlie arranged for me and another campaign worker named Ray to go to Memphis, Tennessee, with him to represent Harlem at a rally. City Hall paid for our trip, and we participated in publicity photos with then New York City Mayor John Lindsey. I was excited because I had never been on an airplane before and was looking forward to the experience. I was also tired of my addiction and had decided to try and kick my habit while I was down South. I really wanted to come back to New York City drug-free. So with that goal in mind, I took a single shot of heroin the morning of our flight but held nothing in reserve for later.

Arriving in Memphis, we immediately checked into the Lorraine Motel, the same motel where Dr. King had been murdered a year earlier. I could feel the presence of the slain civil rights leader quite strongly as we unpacked our bags.

Later, at Operation Breadbasket headquarters, the Reverend Dr. Ralph Abernathy formally welcomed us to Memphis. He ushered us into his office and asked about our work with the campaign in Harlem. We ate lunch, took a lot of pictures, and then headed outside, where throngs of reporters and local townsfolk waited. As Dr. Abernathy spoke to the reporters, I started to feel the onset of withdrawal symptoms. My nose was running, and I was experiencing hot and cold flashes. Charlie leaned over and asked if I was okay. I shook my head and asked for the motel room key. He gave me the key, and I immediately took a taxi back to the motel. *What have I done?* I asked myself on the ride back. I had to be completely out of my mind to come all the way to Memphis, Tennessee, with a one-hundred-dollar-*a-day* drug habit and no drugs!

I marveled at the fact that I was able to get through that weekend in Memphis, because it was one of the worst experiences of my life. Charlie and Ray wanted to take in the Memphis nightlife and wanted me to go along. Since I was in no condition for "partying," I was relieved when the mayor imposed a dusk-to-dawn curfew. Just one year after Dr. King's assassination, the tension in the white and black communities was still strong. The police didn't want to take any chances, and since the curfew was in effect the entire weekend we were there, Charlie and Ray did not get the chance to experience Memphis the way they wanted. As for me, I just wanted to get back to Harlem so I could get a shot of heroin. And almost as soon as we arrived in New York City, that's exactly what I did.

Shortly after the Memphis trip, I was closing the campaign headquarters late one evening when a girl from the neighborhood walked by. Her name was Luvella, and she was new to the neighborhood. I had noticed her from time to time, but I wasn't attracted to her or anything. On this particular evening, though, I felt like having sex, so I decided to try my luck with her. She had a rented room between Amsterdam and Convent Avenue across the street from our office.

"What's up, Luvella?"

She smiled. "Not much, just on my way home."

"Mind if I walk with you?"

"That would be nice," she said. "I'd like that."

I quickly locked the office and held her hand as we walked.

"You know I've had my eyes on you for a while, girl."

She laughed. "Oh, *really?*"

"Yeah, *really.*" I liked the way things were going.

"I've had my eyes on you too, Teddy."

"Well then, it looks like it's going to be a pleasant evening for us *both.*"

She smiled and clenched my hand tighter. Clearly she was looking forward to my company that night. By the time we reached her door, I knew that Luvella was going to let me *inside*—in every sense of the word.

As she unlocked the door, I made a gesture as if to leave, and she quickly grabbed my hand. She pulled me inside and locked the door. The room was dark, and I asked her to put on some slow music. She lit some candles, put on some romantic music, and slowly pulled me down on the bed. As we kissed and caressed, I asked if she wanted me to make love to her. She nodded, staring deeply into my eyes.

We made love twice, the second time slower and much better. When we were finished, I reached for my clothes, and she asked me to stay the night. I told her that I had some things to do in the morning and I needed to be at home to change my clothes. I promised that I would see her again, and she reluctantly released me from her embrace.

The next evening, Luvella came by the campaign storefront and asked if I would join her for a drink. We went to the Hamilton Bar on the corner of 141st and Amsterdam. I didn't realize it at the time, but there was a new barmaid at the Hamilton, and Luvella had made friends with her.

I sat there on the barstool, completely mesmerized by the new barmaid's beauty. I tried to act nonchalant, but I was struck by her almost identical resemblance to the singer Tina Turner. She had the same facial and physical features, right down to Tina's famous legs. Her name was Sylvia Canztlow, and she was fine…fine…fine!

Luvella introduced me as the guy she had told her about. She offered me her hand, and I gripped it softly. It was soft and warm, and she smelled like wildflowers. She said she was pleased to meet me, and I told her that the pleasure was all mine.

Little did she realize it, but introducing me to Sylvia was the worst thing that Luvella could have done. If she wanted to keep me to herself, she should have left well enough alone. Love at first sight? Yes, it really does happen, and I found it out that evening. I couldn't wait to see Sylvia again and let her know how attracted I was to her. I wasn't going to be satisfied until I did. The three of us conversed a little while, and then I excused myself. I was determined to see Sylvia again—minus Luvella.

I made it my business to see Sylvia again as soon as possible. I had sensed that the attraction was mutual, and I wanted to confirm it. As soon as I entered the Hamilton Bar, her eyes told me all I needed to know.

"Well, fancy seeing you again so soon," Sylvia said with raised eyebrows.

"Not soon enough, as far as I'm concerned," I replied with a smile.

"Are you close by?" she inquired.

"Three doors down," I gestured with my head. "I'm the office manager for the Harlem Poor People's Campaign."

I told her about my recent trip to Memphis, Tennessee, and also let her know that I was an aspiring singer. I told her about my group, Black Myth, and that I was the lead singer. Her eyes lit up as I told her about our recent performances.

"I love to sing myself," she said, "but I'm afraid to stand in front of an audience."

I nodded my head in understanding. "Oh, you're a *shower* singer, huh?"

She laughed. "Something like that. Do you have any of your performances on tape?"

I had made a tape during one of our performances at the Top Club, so I let her listen to that. I brought a tape player into the bar, and as she listened to the tape, I could see that she was impressed, which made me feel good. After all, my goal was to impress her.

"You sound good, baby!" she said as the song came to an end.

"Thanks, I'm glad you like it," I replied, not letting the fact that she called me "baby" escape me.

"Can I have it?" Sylvia squealed.

"Can you *have* it?" I echoed.

"Yes, I want my girlfriend Dinah to hear my *baby* sing!"

I had to smile at that—her "baby." There it was again. I nodded my head, gave her a quick kiss on the cheek, and left the tape on the countertop. I told her I'd be back soon and then exited the bar with a big smile on my face.

Luvella still tried to act as if she and I were going together, but it soon became clear that my focus was now on Sylvia. I'm sure she regretted having introduced Sylvia to me, but as far as I was concerned, Luvella was never my girlfriend in the first place. So I did not feel any guilt for my pursuit of Sylvia. Eventually Luvella simply stopped coming around, soon dropping completely out of the picture.

Since I was working for Charles on a volunteer basis, I was not receiving a paycheck, only what money he would give me every now and then. As a result, I made it my business to hang around the bar every chance I got. Sylvia was ten years older than me, but her age didn't make a difference. We were meant for one another, and it showed. Also, because she was so attractive, all of the "fly" guys in the neighborhood were after her—the pimps, the players, and the hustlers. They all were trying to get her.

Normally I would wait for Sylvia to finish her shift at the bar—usually between 3:00 and 3:30 in the morning—then hail a cab, see her safely into it, and give her a gentle kiss, and she would ride home alone. After about two months of dating, though, she finally took me home with her for the first time.

On this particular night, when the cab arrived, Sylvia gestured for me to get in with her. Needing no further prompting, I was inside the cab in a flash. She smiled, grabbed my arm, and leaned her head on my shoulder. We rode the short distance to her apartment on 138th between Seventh and Lenox Avenue. Her apartment was on the top floor of a five-story building, and I navigated each landing as if walking on a cloud.

Sylvia told me that I could stay the night but that I would have to sleep on the sofa. I was so eager to be near her—I would have slept in the bathtub if necessary. I immediately agreed to the sleeping arrangements. Besides, I didn't want to seem too eager to sleep with her. She was that special to me.

After making up the sofa for me, Sylvia kissed me good night and then retired to her bedroom. Just the thought of her being so close interfered with my ability to fall asleep. I tossed and turned repeatedly on that small, uncomfortable sofa. When I heard her softly call my name, I thought I was just imagining it. I got up and peeked into her bedroom. She was lying there in bed looking directly at me. I asked if everything was okay, and she said that she was cold. Being the "gentleman" that I was, of course, I told her that I would be glad to warm her up. She held the bedcovers back, inviting me into her bed. It took all the self-control I could muster to keep from leaping into the bed. My heart was beating a mile a minute.

We made passionate love in those early-morning hours and then fell asleep in each other's arms. Before drifting off, however, I made a promise to myself that I would make a real effort to kick my heroin habit before Sylvia found out. There was no way I could let that happen. It would ruin everything.

I opened my eyes to sunlight streaming through the bedroom window, causing me to squint and turn away from the brightness. Sylvia was in the kitchen fixing breakfast, and I smiled contently. My ears perked up as I heard her talking to someone, because I knew we were alone when I brought her home. Then I remembered that she had a nineteen-month-old daughter. I continued to lie there, listening, anticipating my first meeting with Sylvia's daughter.

All of a sudden, this little ball of pure energy burst into the bedroom and came to a complete stop just inches from my face. I was transfixed as I looked into the eyes of the prettiest little girl I had ever laid eyes on. Her name was Nya, but Sylvia's nickname for her was "Tutu." I found that to be most appropriate because she looked just like a little ballerina. She stared at me nervously, and then a big smile covered her little face. I smiled back, and she turned and ran from the room. I laughed and settled back under the warm covers. I was pleased that Nya liked me. She was a friendly child, and we took to one another right away.

I started taking Nya around with me, introducing her as my daughter. It was really amazing how much we actually resembled one another. So much so, in fact, that people would have already made the assumption that she was my daughter. They would tell me that it looked as if I had "spit her out." I was proud of Nya in a way I had never experienced before, and as far as I was concerned, she *was* my daughter. Once that had been established, my goal was to make her mother my wife. I wanted to marry her as soon as possible.

One evening, as the three of us were relaxing at home, I called Sylvia into the bedroom. As we lay together on the bed, I looked deeply into her eyes.

"Will you marry me, baby?"

I could tell that the question came as a complete surprise, because Sylvia began to cry as she held me closer to her warm body.

"Are you sure you want to get married, Ted?"

"I've never been surer about anything in my life, Sylvia."

"The ten-year age difference doesn't bother you?"

"Not at all," I whispered, holding her even closer. "I want the three of us to be a family."

With tears in her eyes, she accepted my proposal, and we started making wedding plans immediately. Being basically unemployed, there was little I could contribute financially. Sylvia rented the church, the reception hall, and even bought our wedding bands. All I did was sit back and let it happen. The wedding was set for June 29, 1969, and would be held at the

Convent Avenue Baptist Church on the corner of 145th Street and Convent Avenue.

My parents loved Sylvia and absolutely adored Nya, so they had no problem signing the consent form for me to marry her. I was twenty years old at the time, and Sylvia would turn thirty on June 26, 1969—three days before the wedding. My parents, probably assuming that Sylvia would help me get my life in order, were pleased that I was marrying her. Charles Mobley agreed to be my best man and was happy for me as well.

Not everyone, however, was happy that I was marrying Sylvia. There were those who couldn't understand what Sylvia saw in me, and our wedding was the talk of the neighborhood. I knew it was nothing more than jealousy and envy, for the most part, because the ones doing the talking wanted Sylvia for themselves. The fact that I was the one who had her was something they couldn't understand or accept. A few even went so far as to tell Sylvia about my drug habit, but she refused to believe it. The fact that we had only been dating for two months worked to my advantage in hiding my addiction. I was careful not to let Sylvia see me high, and I took pains to act normal around her and Nya. I desperately wanted to kick my habit and resolved to do it after we were married. It was important that I change my life and be a good husband and father.

I spent the night before the wedding at Charlie's house while Sylvia stayed at our apartment. Her girlfriends were helping her prepare for the wedding, while friends of mine dropped by Charlie's house to help ease my growing anxiety.

The morning of the wedding, I was determined not to have any drugs in my system. I had plenty of opportunities to get high, but I didn't. When Charlie and I arrived at the church, friends and family were already there. My parents were seated in the front row, along with my three sisters, Retie, Lou-Lou, and Dee-Dee, as well as my two brothers, Danny and Marvin.

Sylvia's sister, Caroline, sat in the front row on the opposite side, along with her husband, Bernie, and their kids. As the sanctuary began to fill, the only person missing was the bride.

Then, from the back of the church, she appeared—a vision of loveliness, in a beautiful white gown. As the opening chords of "Here Comes the Bride" began to play, my eyes followed my bride-to-be all the way down the aisle. Nya followed her mother, happily throwing flower petals to the floor. I smiled, along with the wedding guests.

Finally, Sylvia was at my side, and we turned toward the minister. I felt like the luckiest man alive. The ceremony went off without a hitch.

After the wedding, my parents took Nya with them while Sylvia and I returned to Charlie's apartment to change. We also wanted to rest up a bit before heading out to our wedding reception.

Our reception was held at a club on 126th Street, between Park and Lexington Avenue. I hadn't had a shot all day and was beginning to feel slight withdrawal pains. Anyone with an eye for the symptoms of heroin withdrawal would have recognized them easily. I was experiencing hot and cold flashes, and my nose was beginning to run. Thinking I was coming down with a cold or something, Sylvia asked if I was okay. I nodded my head and made a beeline toward the open bar, requesting a double shot of Bacardi rum. It helped a little bit, but I knew I was going to have to get a shot of heroin soon. Finally, I pulled my new wife to the side of the room.

"Can we leave now," I asked, desperately needing a fix.

"Can't wait to get the *honeymoon* on?" Sylvia teased.

"You must be reading my mind, Mrs. Harris," I said, faking a smile.

We had reservations at a Midtown hotel, and I wanted to get there as soon as possible so that I could sneak away and get a shot of dope. Sylvia agreed to leave early, so after a few more drinks and the obligatory dance with my new bride, we headed for the hotel.

After checking in, I left Sylvia to unpack while I used the excuse of going to the drugstore for some cold medicine to cop some drugs.

"I'll be right back, baby," I said, kissing her deeply.

"You *better*," she replied, holding me close.

I headed immediately for the Uptown subway. When I arrived in Harlem, however, my regular dealer was nowhere to be found. Reluctantly, I set out in search of another dealer. I had absolutely no time to spare and needed to make a connection as soon as possible. After all, not only did I need to purchase the drugs, I also needed to find a place where I could shoot up.

Three hours later, I was on the subway once again, headed back to the hotel. I really didn't know what to expect when I arrived, but of one thing I was certain: Sylvia was going to be furious!

My heart was beating rapidly as I entered the darkened hotel room. I was hoping that Sylvia had fallen asleep during my absence, but when I tiptoed into the bedroom, I found her stretched out on top of the bed, wide-awake and fully clothed. It was clear that she had been crying. I really didn't know what to say. I just stood over the bed, staring down at her.

Without a word to me, she got up, turned on the light, and started packing. I continued to stare at her, still not knowing what to say or do. We had not been married twelve hours, and our marriage was already over. I knew that I had to say something. I just didn't know what.

"I'm addicted to heroin, Sylvia," I finally blurted out.

Sylvia stiffened but continued to pack. I could see that this bit of news was a terrible shock to her.

"I wanted to tell you, but I was afraid I'd lose you," I continued. "I promise you, I'll find a drug program—just don't leave me, baby," I pleaded. Tears welled up in my eyes. I loved her and Nya dearly and didn't want to lose them.

Sylvia stopped packing and turned slowly toward me. She stared at me for a long time. I could see the hurt in her eyes but also the love that she had for me. I held my arms out to her, and she came to me, still crying. We returned to the bedroom and melted into one another.

Our lovemaking was more passionate that night than it had ever been. I felt as if a heavy burden had been lifted from my shoulders. My wife still loved me and was going to stand by me. I was determined not to let her and Nya down. As soon as our honeymoon was over, I was going to find a drug program and kick my habit. We were going to live happily ever after—as a family. Such were my thoughts as my wife and I drifted off to sleep, locked in a warm embrace.

CHAPTER ELEVEN

At the beginning of 1970, my heroin habit was costing me about $150 a day. I honestly intended to keep my promise to my wife and go for treatment, but my habit was more in control of my life than I was. As a result, my marriage—if you could call it that—suffered greatly. Sylvia and I argued constantly, which only served to drive me further from home and deeper into the streets. I chose to feed my habit rather than make an effort to become the husband and father that she and Nya deserved. Consequently, from the early part of 1970 until the beginning of 1973, I was in and out of Riker's Island as well as the Manhattan House of Detention—better known as "The Tombs."

The Tombs is a concrete fortress located in lower Manhattan and is connected by a tunnel to the criminal courts building at 100 Centre Street. On the fourth through ninth floors, the inmates are housed in maximum-security cellblocks. The cells themselves are six feet by nine feet in dimension, complete with sink, toilet, and bunk bed. The cells were originally designed to hold two people at a time, and even then the living arrangements are cramped, to say the least. So one can imagine my shock when, after one of my latest arrests for burglary, I approached my assigned cell—well after midnight—to find four men already inside! Thinking a mistake had been made, I turned to the guard at the end of the cellblock and told him there were four men inside the cell already. He looked at me as if to say, "And?" then opened the cell door electronically and hollered, "Lock in!"

From experience I knew it wouldn't do any good to argue with him, so I reluctantly stepped inside the cell. Although I was exhausted, I had absolutely no idea where I was supposed to sleep. Of the four men inside the cramped cell, one was sound asleep on the top bunk, another on the bottom, a third on the floor directly in front of the cell door, and the fourth under the bed. That left the toilet bowl for me.

I made my way carefully over to the filthy stainless-steel commode, shaking my head in disbelief. I was careful not to step on anyone because it probably would have led to a physical confrontation, and I was definitely in no shape for that.

I sat down, grateful for the darkness and dreading the dawn. I slept with my head in my lap, and my ears tuned to the slightest movement from my cellmates, which unfortunately occurred when they had to use the toilet. I was already beginning to experience the onset of withdrawal, complete with hot and cold flashes and a runny nose. I knew it wouldn't be long before my body would be screaming for relief. I watched as the latest person to interrupt my already restless sleep finished relieving himself, and then I headed back to the toilet bowl, determined to clean up my act. *Now's the time to take advantage of the situation*, I thought. *I need to return to Nya and Sylvia drug-free.*

Using my wife and daughter as motivation, I kicked my habit in about two weeks. Three months later, I felt like a new man. I was exercising on a daily basis, eating three meals a day, getting proper rest, and actively working on getting my life together, none of which would have happened had I not been arrested. All that remained was to get the judge and district attorney to send me to a drug program and allow me to get back to my family as soon as possible.

Since my crime was drug related, I was a good candidate for the drug program at Phoenix House. I wrote and asked them if they would accept me. A few days after mailing the letter, my cell door opened, and in walked a short, elderly Italian man. When my new cellmate arrived, I was enjoying the luxury of having the cell to myself, a direct result of a class-action suit concerning the overcrowded living conditions at The Tombs.

Normally, the man with the least seniority in a two-man cell was required to take the top bunk, but since this man was obviously older than me, I decided to offer him the bottom bunk. It just felt like the right thing to do. He protested at first, but I insisted that he take the bottom bunk. I looked at it this way: since we had to live together, we might as well be cordial to one another. I asked him his name, and in a brisk, raspy voice, he said, "Joe." I noticed that he had a deep hole in his throat—the result of throat cancer, he told me.

After moving my mattress to the top bunk, I proceeded to help him get settled in.

I lit one of the few cigarettes that I had. "Want me to save you a couple of drags, Joe?" I asked in an attempt to put him fully at ease.

"Nah," he replied, getting his things situated on the bottom bunk. "I only smoke cigars."

"Well, no problem getting those. As long as you've got money on the books, you can order them from the commissary."

"Money's the *least* of my problems, kid," he said with a smile.

The commissary sheets were passed out the following day. Since I didn't have any money in my account, I didn't receive one. Joe did, though, and was clearly having a problem with the order form.

"Let me help you with that, Joe," I said, reaching for his commissary sheet.

"Thanks, kid," he said, handing the sheet over.

"What do you want me to order?" I asked. "You can spend up to fifty dollars."

"Just get me about ten dollars' worth of cigars," he said heading for his bunk.

"That's it?" I asked.

"Yeah, that's it. Get what you want for yourself."

"You have forty dollars left, Joe. How much of that do you want me to spend on myself?"

"Spend the whole forty, kid," he said, stretching out on his bunk.

I couldn't believe my ears. From that day on, I never ran out of food or cigarettes. Each week Joe would get a commissary sheet, and each week he would just by cigars. He would always tell me to spend the rest on myself. I was so caught up in my good fortune that the printed name, "Joseph Bonnano," at the bottom of the commissary sheet didn't ring a bell.

One morning during our recreation period, I was teaching Joe to play chess and noticed that he was finding it difficult to concentrate. I asked what was on his mind, and he said he was wondering what was taking his "family" so long to come up with the bail money for him and his son. They were charged with conspiring to steal millions in copper tubing from Con Edison, and their bail was a million dollars each. Both had been locked up for about a month at the time, and Joe was getting impatient. He spoke of the two million dollars bail as if it were no problem at all. My own bail of thirty thousand dollars cash might as well have been a million dollars like Joe's, and I couldn't imagine anyone putting up that kind of money to get me out of jail. It was then that I came to realize that I was in the presence of someone with a lot of power.

Since Joe confided in me, I decided to tell him about my own case and what my bail was. I left out the part about my drug abuse, of course, telling him that I would work for him in any capacity if he got me out on bail. He said to give him a call when he got out and he would see what he could do. He wrote his name and phone number on a small piece of paper then handed it to me. The large bold signature scrawled at the bottom of the paper read "Joe Bananas." I was stunned. My cellmate was the infamous mob boss himself.

A few days later, Joe and his son were released on bail. I waited a week or so and then called the number he had given me.

"Can I speak to Joe?" I said to the woman who answered the phone.

In a matter of minutes, the familiar raspy voice came on the line. "Yeah, this is Joe. Who's this?"

"It's Teddy Harris, Joe—your cellmate from the Tombs. You told me to give you a call about helping to get me out on bail. How's it looking?"

"I'm gonna be straight up with ya, kid," he said. "That two million for me and my son put a strain on my finances." My heart sank as he continued. "But I'll tell you what. See if you can get your bail lowered to something manageable—say around ten or fifteen thousand—and I should be able to help you out."

"Yeah, okay, Joe," I said with little enthusiasm. "I'll see what my lawyer can do."

I hung the phone up with a heavy heart. Although I didn't say it to Joe, I didn't put much stock in getting the district attorney or the judge to agree to lower my bail.

I called Joe a few more times after that, but since I was unable to get my bail reduced, it wasn't long before I stopped calling him altogether. We simply lost touch after that, and I never spoke to or heard from him again.

My next cell partner was a friend from my neighborhood. His name was Everett Cruise, but everyone called him "Chubby." I always wondered where that nickname came from, since he was far from being overweight, but I never asked him about it. Chubby and I had done a robbery together once, but he was too cold-blooded for me, so I was afraid to do anything with him again. I didn't want to end up with a murder charge.

As he made up his bed, we talked about the neighborhood, and then I asked what he was in for. He said the charge was robbery, and his bail was fifty thousand dollars. I told him I had a burglary, and my bail was thirty thousand cash. We sat in silence, resigning ourselves to the fact that neither of us would be going anywhere anytime soon.

A few days later, while Chubby was still sleeping, I sat at one of the recreation tables on the gallery, staring in the direction of the bank of telephones at the end of the cellblock. Unlike today, at that time, we were able to make direct local phone calls free of charge. A civilian phone aid would dial the number given and then pass the telephone through the bars to the person making the call. The aid would then move down the line to the next caller, and the process would be repeated.

As I sat at the table staring at the relatively few men waiting to make a call, a plan began to slowly take shape. When I had worked out all of the details, I approached the phone aid and told him that I wanted to make a call. He asked what the number was, and I told him that I couldn't remember. I told him to just connect me with directory assistance then hand me the phone. He nodded, dialed directory assistance, passed the phone through the bars to me, and walked away. When I was certain he was out of hearing range, I asked to be connected to Kennedy Airport.

A woman's voice came on the line. "Kennedy airport, how may I help you?"

"Listen closely," I whispered into the phone. "I'm only going to say this *once*." I was whispering because I didn't want those around me to hear what I was saying, especially the civilian phone aides.

"Excuse me?" the airport agent said. "Can you speak up, sir?"

"There's a *bomb* on one of your 747s!"

A sharp intake of breath convinced me that I had her complete attention. She asked me to hold on a moment while she got her supervisor. When he came on the line, I got straight to the point of the call.

"Get a pen and paper, because I'm only going to say this once. There's a bomb on one of your 747s. I want Everett Cruse and Theodore Harris out on bail by noon tomorrow, and I'll call back then with the exact location of the bomb."

"Just a moment," the supervisor said nervously. "Where are these men at?"

"They are at the Manhattan House of Detention, 125 White Street. Got it?"

I could almost hear him nodding his head on the other end of the line. "Yes," he said, "Everett Cruse and Theodore Harris, out on bail by noon tomorrow. I got it."

When I returned to the cell, Chubby was sitting on his bed, playing a hand of solitaire. Observing my jubilant mood, he asked what I was so happy about. I told him that if everything went as planned, we both would be out of jail by noon the following day. He laughed and asked how that was possible. Hesitantly, I told him that I called in a bomb threat to Kennedy Airport.

Chubby stared at me as if I had an eye in the middle of my forehead. A large vein on the side of his neck began to throb, and I braced myself for what I knew was coming. He was absolutely livid, and I knew that I had better start explaining—fast!

"Look, Chubby," I said calmly, in an attempt to put him at ease. "There's nothing for you to worry about."

He continued to stare at me as if I had completely lost my mind. "Nothing to worry about?" he shouted. "Tell me what you did, man!"

"I spoke with the supervisor at Kennedy airport and told him there was a bomb on one of his 747s."

Chubby grabbed his head in hands, shaking it from side to side.

"Listen, man," I quickly added. "I gave him our names and said I wanted them out on bail by noon tomorrow. The *worst* that can happen is that we don't get bailed out, Chub, but what if we do?"

"That what I'm worried about, Teddy," he said. "What if we *do*? You know the FBI is gonna follow us, right?"

"*And*?" I said. "Let them follow us. It's not like we're gonna *lead* them to anything or anyone. All we know is that the bail was posted for us, and that's that."

Chubby continued to shake his head in disagreement, but I still felt that we had a 50/50 shot at being released. And from where I stood at the time, those odds were good enough for me. I stretched out on my bunk, put my arms behind my head, and fantasized about our freedom. Soon I was sound asleep.

When I awoke the following morning, I stripped my bunk and proceeded to gather up all of my personal belongings. When inmates are released on bail, all issued blankets, sheets, and pillowcases are required to be turned back in. So when I had everything packed and ready, I sat on the edge of the bed, waiting for our names to be called over the loudspeaker.

Chubby was still sleeping when the voice over the loudspeaker blared: "Everett Cruise…Theodore Harris…step out!" I smiled, shook Chubby awake, and grabbed my things, waiting for the cell door to open. I told Chubby this was it; we were headed for freedom. When the cell door opened with a loud clang, we rushed to the front of the gallery. The guard at the gate looked at us strangely and asked why we had our property and bed linens with us.

"We're being bailed out, right?" I asked, nervously.

"No," said the guard, "an FBI agent is here to see the two of you. So take your things back to your cell and get back up here."

We walked dejectedly back to our cell. As soon as we were inside, Chubby spun on me.

"I told you, man!" he shouted. "It's the FBI! What we gonna do now?"

"Calm down, man," I said. "I done already told you. As far as we're concerned, we don't know anything. That's what I'm going to tell the dude. I'll go in first. All you have to do is follow my lead."

In the interview room, a young FBI agent greeted me politely with a badge and a handshake. He opened the interview by asking if I knew anyone on the street who wanted me out badly enough to call in a bomb threat. Without realizing it, he had just given me my out, so I ran with it. I told him that I was a drug addict who had done dirt to a lot of people, so it was a real possibility that someone would do that.

"It wouldn't surprise me at all," I told him, "if someone wanted to hurt or even kill me."

He asked if I could think of anyone in particular, and I said no. After a few more questions, the interview was over. The agent handed me his card, shook my hand again, and told me to call him if I could think of anyone. I smiled and assured him that I would.

Exiting the interview, I caught Chubby's eye and gave him the thumbs-up sign. I wasn't worried about him; he could handle himself, especially since we went over our story earlier in the cell. As the guard unlocked the gate for me to return me to my cell, the FBI agent came out and extended his hand to Chubby in greeting.

Twenty minutes later, Chubby was back in the cell. He said the agent asked him the same questions that he had asked me, and his answers were just as we had rehearsed them—he didn't know anything. We both agreed that there was no harm done and that it was worth a try. Still, Chubby insisted that I discuss any new ideas with him first. I laughed and told him I would definitely do that. We quickly settled back into our normal routine, counting the days until our court appearance.

I had forgotten all about the letter I wrote to the Phoenix House drug program. Therefore, when it came time for me to appear in court, I was shocked to see that the judge and district attorney each had a copy of the letter. When I entered the courtroom, my court-appointed attorney was in conference with the both of them.

"Is anyone here for Mr. Harris from Phoenix House?" the judge inquired, directing his attention to the spectator section.

"I am, Your Honor," said a timid voice from the back of the courtroom.

I turned to see a young white woman, who looked to be in her early twenties, approaching the bench. She handed some papers over, along with her identification, and the judge carefully reviewed them. He then looked in my direction and told me that before releasing me to Phoenix House I would be required to plead guilty to the charges, as well as successfully complete the drug program. Failure to do so, he continued, would result in my serving a three-year prison term instead. I told him that I understood and agreed to the conditions.

I pled guilty to the burglary charge and was given a suspended three-year sentence. I was then released to the custody of the young woman from Phoenix House. I could hardly believe it— after more than six months in The Tombs, I was free! Well, not totally free, but if everything went according to plan, I soon would be.

As the young woman and I exited the elevator, I headed immediately for the bank of telephones near the courthouse exit. I told her that I wanted to call my mother, just to let her know that I was out. It was probably obvious that I was up to something, because she stuck to me like glue. I entered the telephone booth, and she positioned herself directly in the doorway, blocking my exit.

"Yo, Teddy, what's up? Where you been, man?"

Black Freddie was a pimp, drug dealer, and hustler from my neighborhood, so I wasn't surprised to see him in the lobby of the criminal court building. *He must have a court appearance or something,* I thought. Totally ignoring the woman from Phoenix House, he moved closer to the phone booth.

"I just got out, man," I said. "The judge released me to Phoenix House." I nodded my head in the girl's direction. "She's taking me."

Looking the nervous young woman up and down, Freddie turned his attention back to me. He started to laugh. I knew what was coming, and I tried to give him the signal to be cool, but he either didn't pick up on it or simply didn't care.

"Phoenix House?" he asked, still laughing. "Man, I'll see you uptown tonight."

He then turned and walked away, chuckling softly to himself. I could have murdered him right then and there. Now the girl was more nervous than ever. She hustled me out of the phone booth, not even letting me complete the call to my mother.

On the short walk to the subway station, I feigned interest in the drug program, and that seemed to relax her somewhat. As she talked about Phoenix House, I nodded my head when appropriate, but my thoughts centered on getting away from her as soon as possible.

Inside the subway station, a train was already at the track with its doors open. As we entered, I was careful to take a seat next to the sliding doors. The doors closed, and the train pulled slowly out of the station. At the next station, she was still talking about Phoenix House. Instead of listening to her, however, I was trying to gauge the exact length of time it took the sliding doors to start closing once they were opened. As soon as the train doors slid open, I began to count slowly in my mind. After a few stops, I had determined the doors would start to close when I reached the number twelve. I decided to make my move at the next stop.

The doors slid open at the next station, and I began my mental count. The girl talked…I counted…she talked…I counted, gradually moving toward the magic number twelve. Suddenly, I stood and turned, sliding smoothly through the narrow opening of the closing train doors. The girl jumped up quickly, but it was too late. I had timed my escape perfectly.

The train doors closed softly in her face, leaving her stranded inside. The look on her face was a mixture of shock, hurt, anger, and betrayal. To add insult to injury, I waved good-bye mockingly as the train pulled slowly out of the station. Just as my friend Black Freddie had predicted, I was back in Harlem that very same night.

CHAPTER TWELVE

Clearly, my time in The Tombs was nothing more than a drying-out period. Before long, I was back to using heroin, bringing my habit to over $100 a day in a matter of months. That meant, of course, that I had to resume a life of crime in order to support it. Some of the things I did during this period bordered on the insane. This brings to mind one particular act of insanity that I will remember for as long as I live.

In an attempt to maintain a one-hundred-dollar-a-day heroin habit, my friend Alfred and I were on the roof of a thirty-story housing project, casing apartments for a possible break-in. Peering over the side of the roof, I could see none that were appealing. All of the apartments had closed and locked windows. Making it even more difficult, the building had no fire escape, so any entry from the roof had to be made by dangling from a rope. Not very appealing, considering that it was a thirty-story fall from the roof to the sidewalk below.

I was about to give up and look for another building when I spotted a partially opened window, off to the side, about two floors below where I was standing. I thought about it for a moment, weighing my chances of successfully swinging over to the window.

"Al, you see that window down there?" I asked, pointing to a window two stories below.

Alfred looked over the roof at the window I had indicated. He nodded his head.

"I can get inside that apartment, man" I said confidently.

"How are you going to get down there?" he asked. "And, even more importantly, how are you going to get *over* to the window?" The window was about fifteen or twenty feet away from where we were standing.

"That's easy," I said without hesitation. "I'm going to *swing* over."

Before he could respond, I quickly entered the rooftop stairwell and went to the fire hose box. I ran with the hose back to the rooftop and threw it over the side of the building. The hose was extremely long, so I had no doubt that it would reach over to the targeted window.

"I need you to swing me over to the window, Al," I said, holding on to the hose as I climbed over the side of the building.

"Man, you got to be *crazy!*" he shouted. "I'm not gonna *swing* you over to the window."

"You have to do it, Al," I insisted. "I need you to help me get the momentum to launch myself through the air when I let go of the hose."

"I'm not gonna do it, Teddy," he said adamantly. "If you miss, you're dead!"

"That's why I'm not gonna miss, man." I smiled as I climbed further down the hose.

As I slid down the fire hose, Alfred again tried to talk me out of it, reminding me that there was no room for error or miscalculation. Actually, I needed no reminder because the dizzying height made all that very clear—I could definitely not afford to miss the window. When I reached the level of the intended window, I looked over to see just how far away it was. From that height, what appeared to be miles was actually only about fifteen or twenty feet away. Alfred was waiting for me to give him the go-ahead to start swinging the hose. I took a deep breath and nodded for him to begin.

He started slowly, and as the momentum of the swing continued to build, I tried to calculate the best time to let go of the hose. I felt like a trapeze artist, only this was no circus act and there was certainly no safety net to catch me if I missed. I had one chance and one chance only to grab that windowsill. As Alfred swung the hose faster and faster, my heart began to race. Finally, taking the position that it was now or never, I let go. Sailing through the air toward the window, I executed the flight path perfectly. I came in hard and fast, hitting the windowsill with outstretched hands and grabbing it with my fingertips. Dangling twenty-seven stories above the ground, I held on for dear life. I had done it! All I needed to do now was pull myself up and scramble inside the apartment. That's when a most disturbing thought entered my mind: *What if someone was home?*

As if to confirm the worst, a huge black man immediately appeared at the window. Paralyzing fear rushed through me as he shook his head in disbelief. All he had to do was pry my fingers from the window, and I would be history. We stared at one another but with different intentions. His stare conveyed anger and amazement, while mine was silent and pleading. Realizing that he literally held my life in his hands, I was at a complete loss for words. We maintained eye contact as he continued to shake his head from side to side. I didn't know what his head shaking indicated, but my fear suddenly shifted to panic. I didn't want to die! I was unable to convey that, however, because I was frozen with fear. With tears streaming down my face, I silently willed the man to spare my life. It was all up to him.

Huge hands moved suddenly toward me. Fearing the worst, I shook my head. Grabbing my arms roughly, the man's grip was like a vice. *This is it*, I thought, resigning myself to my fate. *He is going to fling me thirty stories to the concrete below.* However, to my surprise and great relief, I was snatched through the open window and flung to the living room floor. I was so grateful that my life had been spared that I actually looked forward to the beating I thought was coming. Instead, without a word, he pointed to the door. I understood immediately and made a mad dash for it. Opening the door as fast as I could, I zoomed out of the apartment and ran down twenty-seven flights of stairs. I didn't even bother to try and find Alfred. I just kept running.

When I finally did meet up with Alfred and told him what had happened, he listened closely, shaking his head in disbelief. He said that what had happened was nothing short of a miracle and that I needed to thank God for saving my life. I nodded my head half-heartedly, not really giving God credit for saving my life. A few weeks later, however, as if to confirm His intervention, God literally brought me back from the dead.

———————

I opened my eyes and knew immediately that I was in the hospital. I also knew why. This was not my first heroin overdose. Because of my low tolerance for the drug, I had been there, done that. I didn't know, however, that this time I had actually been pronounced dead and that my parents had been called to the hospital to identify my body.

With a tube running through my nose, down my throat, and into my stomach, I was quite uncomfortable. I turned my head and saw a middle-aged black nurse staring at me. She began to cry when I opened my eyes, then jumped up and ran out of the room to get the doctor. I was puzzled by her strange behavior but just shrugged it off.

The doctor removed the tube, and shortly after, I was able to sit up and talk.

"How are you feeling?" the doctor asked.

"Still a little groggy," I mumbled.

"Well, your parents are in the waiting room," he said. "So when you're ready, I'll sign your release." He looked at me for what seemed like an eternity before turning and leaving the room. I thought that was strange, but not as strange as the sight of this black nurse sobbing as she stood off to the side of the room. My throat was dry, and I wanted a drink of water, but my curiosity was stronger.

"Excuse me, ma'am," I said, turning to her. "Why are you crying?"

She looked at me with piercing eyes before responding. She was obviously trying to get herself together. "Because you were *dead*," she said finally.

"Yeah, I know what you mean," I replied, thinking she was just being dramatic.

"No," she said firmly. "You *don't* know what I mean. Why do you think your parents are in the waiting room right now? They were called here to identify your *body*."

Now she had my full attention. She went on to explain that when I was brought into the emergency room, my heart had stopped beating. The medical team used a defibrillator in an attempt to get my heartbeat back, but to no avail. After numerous tries, the doctor placed a sheet over my body and pronounced me dead.

"I'm a Christian, son," she went on to say, "and I've been at this hospital for over twenty-five years. It just seemed like the Holy Spirit moved me to ask the doctors to try one more time to revive you. I asked them to do it for *me*, and they did."

I was crying now, marveling at the thought of a complete stranger caring that much for me that she would use her clout as a senior nurse to intervene on my behalf. It was really starting to sink in—I was *dead*! I wanted to hug this nurse so badly, but I just sat there, tears streaming down my face, listening.

"On that final attempt to get your heart beating," the nurse continued, "I began to pray like I have never prayed before. God is truly with you, son, because as soon as the doctor hit you with the defibrillator, your heartbeat jumped right on the monitor!" She began to cry once again.

As the gravity of what she had just told me began to sink in, tears rolled in huge, heavy drops from my own eyes. I had just been brought back from the dead! And all because a nurse—a total stranger—pleaded for my life and then prayed for me.

"I know you're using them drugs, son," she sobbed. "But God done gave you a second chance, and you need to promise me that you'll leave them drugs alone from now on."

"I promise, ma'am," I whispered through my tears.

Just then the doctor returned and told me that I could be discharged if I felt up to it. I told him I was ready to leave, and he signed my release right then and there.

"Don't forget your promise, now," the nurse said, giving me a hug.

I hugged her back and told her that I would definitely turn my life around.

My parents jumped up when they saw me coming toward them. They hugged me excitedly, and my mom began to cry. I told them to go home and I would be there shortly. I said I wanted to go and see Nya and Sylvia to let them know that I was okay. They both gave me a piercing look, wanting to believe me but not fully able to. They seemed to sense that I had something up my sleeve. Still, they agreed to wait for me at home then turned and walked away. As soon as they were out of sight, I headed straight for the dealer who sold me the heroin I had overdosed on earlier. Once I knew how potent it was, I wanted some more, and I wanted it right away. This time, though, I would make sure I took just the right amount.

Less than an hour later, I was back in the emergency room with another overdose. Thankfully, the nurse who pleaded for my life was no longer on duty. There was no way I could have faced her. The same doctor *was* there, though.

"When you get yourself together, I want to see you in my office," the doctor said after saving my life a second time.

I was not really looking forward to facing him, but there was really nothing I could do to avoid him. After all, he had to sign my discharge papers. So when I felt that I was ready, I walked into the doctor's office.

"You wanted to see me, Doc?" I said.

"Close the door," he said in a voice too calm for my liking. "If you repeat what I'm about to say, I'll deny it."

I looked at him, puzzled.

"My shift is over in another hour," he began. "If you come in again tonight while I'm still on duty, I'm going to *let* you die."

I stood there shocked. I could not believe what I had just heard.

"It's obvious that you're trying to kill yourself, son," he added, "so there's no reason for me to go out of my way to save you again. Do I make myself clear?"

I nodded, shrugged my shoulders, then turned and walked out of the hospital. I kept on walking until I reached my parents' apartment. To my surprise, they were still waiting up for me. I did not return to the hospital emergency room—at least not that night.

My addiction had taken control of me to the point that my marriage didn't really mean anything to me. I would stop by and see Sylvia and Nya from time to time, but my wife would not allow us to live together while I was still using drugs. She told me to let her know when I was ready to get help for myself. I had no idea when that would be because I had a habit to support. It made a real hustler out of me. As a result, I was always on the prowl for my next victim.

CHAPTER THIRTEEN

It's been said that the best hustler in the world is a drug addict. This is because an addict will take full advantage of every opportunity to make a dollar. I can relate to that because my habit kept me on the offensive. I was always thinking ahead, and whatever my habit had me do, that's what I did. If I had to act crazy, I would do that. If I had to be bold, I would do that. If I had to think quickly to take advantage of a given situation, I could do that as well. That being said, one scam in particular sticks out for me.

I was leaving my wife's apartment on 138th Street between 7th and Lenox Avenue, after having spent one of my rare nights with her and Nya. It was early morning, and I was in desperate need of a fix. Normally, I would have headed downtown to the white neighborhood, where the real money was. However, since withdrawal symptoms had already set in, I needed to confine my hustle to the neighborhood.

On this particular morning, I arrived at the corner of 145th Street and St. Nicholas Avenue and was staring at the hill leading up toward Convent Avenue. I was on the same side of the street as the Convent Avenue Baptist Church, where Sylvia and I had been married. Across the street from the church in the middle of the block was a bar that was open for business, even at that early hour. Looking for a possible victim, I watched as bar patrons entered and left. Seeing nothing of interest, I began the slow walk up the hill.

Directly in front of the church, a telephone repair truck was double-parked with its side doors wide open. I could see the driver, a young black man, poking around inside, gathering up his tools. Had I not spied a ring of keys inside the lock of the door, I would have walked on by, not giving the truck a second thought. The driver was still rummaging through his toolbox with half his body inside the truck as I passed. I deftly extracted the keys from the lock and put them in my pocket.

I continued on to the corner of Convent Avenue and then turned to see if the man had noticed his keys missing. He was still gathering his tools inside the truck. I lit a cigarette, still undecided as to what my next move would be. Whatever it was, I knew that I had to approach the driver correctly. I didn't want this opportunity to backfire on me, leaving me with nothing but a set of keys. Finally, I threw the cigarette down and walked back to the truck.

"Yo, my brother," I said, tapping the side door.

"What's up?" he asked, turning to look at me.

"Look, man," I began, "it's probably none of my business, but a dude just took the keys from your truck and walked away."

He jerked his head toward the side door so fast that I thought he was having a seizure. It took everything I could do not to laugh. Homeboy was in extreme panic mode. His job was on the line, and I knew he would do anything to get those keys. He turned back to me, clutching my arm and shaking nervously. For a moment I felt a little sorry for him, but this was business, and I had a habit to support.

"Which way did he go?" he shouted.

"Across the street," I said calmly. "Toward the bar."

He dashed madly across the street, stopping at the bar's entrance. As he stared through the window, it dawned on him that he didn't know who he was looking for.

He bolted back across the street in my direction. "Can you come and point the guy out for me?" he asked. There was a controlled desperation in his voice.

"Man," I said, shaking my head, "I'm not trying to get involved." I turned to walk away, and he desperately clutched at my arm.

"C'mon, brother," he said, "you *gotta* help me out. My job's on the line, man!"

Acting as if I was giving it some thought, I said, "Okay, man, wait right here."

I ran over to the bar and disappeared inside. After relieving myself in the men's room, I crossed the street again and met him at his truck. He was anxious for whatever information I could provide concerning the stolen keys.

"Okay, listen, man," I began. "I spoke to the guy, and he wants a hundred for the keys."

At this bit of information, it became clear to him that this was a con job, and he started looking at me in a different light. I knew what was coming next, and I was prepared for it.

When he threatened to call the police, I turned and walked further up the hill toward Amsterdam Avenue. I could feel his eyes on me, knowing what was coming next. Realizing that I was his only hope to get his keys, he called me back. He had to go along with the program, and he knew it. He asked me to see if "the guy" would accept $50. He said that was all the money he had on him.

I walked back to the bar, staying inside just long enough to make it convincing. When I returned to the truck, I had the keys in my hand, holding them out for him to see. I told the driver that the "the guy" had agreed to the $50. I could see the relief in his eyes as we made the exchange.

I walked back to the bar one last time and peered through the window, watching as the man got in his truck and drove off. When he was no longer in view, I made my way toward Amsterdam Avenue, willing myself not to run. I could already taste the dope.

When experiencing withdrawal symptoms, such as I was at the time, an addict's biggest fear is of being ripped off. And although it didn't happen to me that particular day, such was the case the night Alfred and I were arrested by detectives from Manhattan's 26th Precinct. We had just copped what we thought was heroin, but it turned out to be baking powder.

Alfred and I were coming out of a building on 140th Street between Broadway and Riverside Drive when, all of a sudden, we were surrounded by police and placed in handcuffs. One of the detectives had my picture in his hand, and I knew immediately why I was being arrested. I was wanted by City College security guards for a number of burglaries on its campus, and there was an outstanding warrant for my arrest. Alfred had had nothing to do with any of this, but since he was with me, he was taken into custody too.

We rode in separate cars to the 26th Precinct, a brand-new building located on 126th Street between Amsterdam Avenue and Old Broadway. With its state-of-the-art security measures and high-tech operations, "The 26th," as it was called on the street, was the pride and joy of every cop who worked there.

Alfred and I were taken to the second floor detective division and locked inside of a high-security holding cell. We were both in advanced stages of withdrawal—a result of the baking powder we thought was heroin—so Alfred stretched out on the floor and curled up in the fetal position. I knew it wouldn't be long before I broke out in cold sweats and hot flashes myself, but there was nothing I could do about it.

Suddenly, a call came in concerning a shooting that had just occurred on 126th Street and Eighth Avenue. Every detective in the room grabbed their coats and made a dash for the door. The last one out the door switched on the alarm to our cell, telling us, in an attempt at humor, not to go anywhere. *Funny guy*, I thought as he ran out the door. *A real comedian!* But what would be even funnier, I fantasized, would be if we were both gone when the cops got back. A *fantasy* was all it was, however, because there was absolutely no way to get out of that cell, at least none that I could see. The bars were solid steel, and they ran from the top of the cell into cinder blocks. Still, there was something about those cinder blocks that sparked my interest. Alfred was asleep on the floor, but my attention was on those cell bars. Then it dawned on me: the *cinder* blocks! That was our way out. I was no MacGyver, but I knew enough about cinder blocks to know they were easily broken. And, once one was broken, the rest would follow suit.

Positioning myself on the floor directly in front of the bars, I began kicking one of the cinder blocks as hard as I could. I kicked faithfully, full force, for about ten minutes. I was wearing ankle-length boots, but they didn't seem to have any effect on the cinder blocks. I was just about to give up but decided to give it one last try. I kicked with all my might and a crack finally appeared. That was all that I needed—that one crack. A few more well-placed kicks and the cinder block crumbled to pieces. I could hardly believe it. I had done it. All we had to do was remove the rest of the blocks and squeeze through the opening.

The remaining blocks came out easily, leaving about a six-inch space to crawl under. Of course, now we had no choice but to leave, because there was no telling when the detectives would return. We certainly couldn't be there when they got back. With the condition the cell was now in, I didn't even want to think about what they would do to us. I removed the thick sweater I was wearing and began the tight squeeze through the opening. The space was so small that I literally tore flesh.

Once outside the cell, I put my sweater back on and reached through the bars for my coat. My heart was beating wildly as I called out to Alfred. He opened his eyes and jumped up at the sight of me *outside* the cell. He started with the questions, but

I told him there was no time to talk—he was either coming or he wasn't. Without another word, Alfred removed his coat and began the tight squeeze through the opening.

I quickly searched the desk drawers, taking evidence related to other cases the detectives were working on. I found three guns and a small quantity of heroin and cocaine. I put everything into my pockets and then ran over to the door leading to the hallway. I opened it and peered out cautiously. To my relief, the hallway was empty. With Alfred close on my heels, I cautiously navigated the staircase leading to the closed door at the bottom. Not knowing what was on the other side of the door, I took a deep breath and pulled it open. The precinct desk sergeant sat directly in front of me, freezing me in my tracks.

"Can I help you guys?" he asked, looking up from his paperwork.

"Uh, yeah," I stammered. "My brother was arrested about an hour ago, and I'm trying to find out if he's here or at the Thirtieth Precinct."

The desk sergeant asked my brother's name, and I made up one on the spot. He checked his logbook and then said that my brother wasn't there. He suggested that we try the 30th Precinct and pointed toward the lobby exit. I thanked him, and then Alfred and I walked out into the cold winter evening. We were free.

We ran to the subway station on 125th and Broadway and took the train downtown. Alfred said that his girlfriend would put us up for the night, so that's where we headed. She did let us stay the night, but when she found out what we had done, she insisted that Alfred turn himself in. I could see the logic in that. After all, before our breakout, he was not wanted for anything, so there was a good chance that the cops would let him go if he turned himself in. I told him to blame everything on me. If they released him, I reasoned, he could provide me with inside information. I wanted to know what the mood was at the precinct. Reluctant at first, Alfred finally agreed to follow our advice and turn himself in.

In the morning, he and his girl headed for the 26th Precinct while I went to my parents' apartment. My parents had no idea, of course, that I was now a fugitive, and I certainly didn't volunteer that information. I quickly changed clothes and went out into the streets to see if I could sell the guns I had taken from the police station. In a matter of hours, all three guns were sold, and I was glad to be rid of them. I now had a wad of cash to go with the drugs still in my possession. All that remained was to hear from Alfred.

He was released late that afternoon and didn't waste any time getting right down to the nitty-gritty.

"Man, those cops want you bad, Teddy."

"What happened, Al?" I said, eager for information. "Tell me everything."

"They got a shoot-on-sight order out for you," he said. "All those detectives got busted down in rank. You need to get out of town, bro, and that's on the *real* side!"

"Get out of town?" I said. "I'm a drug addict, man. Where the heck am I gonna go?"

"I'm tellin' you, Teddy," he said excitedly, "they gonna kill you if they see you!"

I told him that I would think about leaving town, but I didn't really mean it. After all, like I said, I was a drug addict with a one-hundred-dollar-a-day heroin habit. So where in the heck was I going? At the moment, I needed a fix, so Al and I went to get high, soon forgetting—or at least not caring—that every cop at the 26th Precinct was looking for me with "unofficial" orders to shoot on sight.

CHAPTER FOURTEEN

The Hudson Hotel takes up the entire block between 141st and 142nd Street and Amsterdam Avenue. At the time, the majority of its tenants were alcoholics, drug addicts, welfare recipients, or all of the above. The rooms the drug addicts occupied were called "shooting galleries," and it is where I went from time to time to shoot up.

There were quite a few rooms in the Hudson Hotel designated as "shooting galleries," all of which were known by most of the junkies in the neighborhood. The hotel was a seven-story, shabby, rundown-looking building, with an old-fashioned, lever-operated elevator. The elevator operator and I—a junkie himself—had gotten high together on a number of occasions, and he would always warn me if the police were in the building. Since my escape from the 26th Precinct, I had been successful at evading the police and was trying to keep it that way.

I entered the Hudson Hotel one evening, with a pocket full of drugs and money, on my way to one of the "shooting galleries." The person I was going to see was a junkie herself who only wanted a shot of dope for the use of her room.

"Man, what in the hell did you do?'" the elevator operator said as I stepped inside.

"What you talkin' 'bout, man?" I said.

"There was two detectives in here not too long ago, lookin' for you."

"How you know they was lookin' for me?" I asked

"Because they had your *picture* in one hand and their *gun* in the other!"

"Well, I appreciate the information, but ain't nothin' to worry about," I said with little conviction.

The situation was to the contrary. The message was clear: I was a dead man.

I left the hotel immediately after shooting up and went to another location to enjoy my high. As the drug took possession of my mind and body, I slipped serenely into the land of the walking dead. I didn't care about anyone or anything. I was at peace.

About a month later, on a brisk winter evening, my friend "Black Butch" and I were walking down the hill on 144th Street and Amsterdam Avenue toward Convent Avenue on our way to cop some drugs. No sooner had we turned the corner on Convent, heading toward 145th Street, than a black car drove slowly toward us. Since I was still on the run, warning bells went off immediately.

Butch and I continued on our way, talking and walking at a normal pace. As the car slowly passed us, I was able to make out two black men inside the car. The man on the passenger's side was staring intensely at me.

Suddenly, the car sped toward us in reverse, coming to a stop directly in front of me. Both men jumped out with their guns drawn, yelling for me to put my hands up. Not knowing what was happening, Butch threw his hands up too. One of the men told Butch that they only wanted me, gesturing with his gun for him to leave. Butch took off running. I just stood there, hands high, trying to get my thoughts together. I knew this had something to do with my escape from the 26th Precinct, and I had to keep my cool.

The guy on the passenger's side walked over to me and placed his gun in the lower part of my back. He identified himself as a security guard from City College. He then told me to walk slowly toward the car and get in the backseat. The backdoor was already open, and the driver was leaning over the hood of the car, his gun on me as well. Thoughts of what was waiting for me at the 26th Precinct ran through my head. I decided at that moment that I would rather die than go back there willingly.

With the gun still pressed into my back, I leaned over as if to get into the backseat of the car. Then, without any real thought on my part, I turned and made a mad dash toward the corner of 145th Street. I was in point-blank range, so I closed my eyes as I ran, waiting for the bullets to tear through me. When the expected gunshots never came, I careened around the corner on 145th and Convent, past the church where Sylvia and I were married, and headed straight for St. Nicholas Avenue.

I turned the corner at the subway station at the bottom of the hill and dove beneath a parked car. I was out of breath and my heart was pounding as I lay underneath the car in a pile of snow. I still couldn't believe that I wasn't shot, but I figured that they would at least be looking for me. I remained curled up in the snow until a sufficient amount of time had passed, then crawled from my hiding place, copped my drugs, and headed back to Black Butch's apartment.

When Black Butch opened the door, he couldn't believe his eyes. He quickly ushered me inside and began to tell me what he had witnessed.

"Yo, they had you dead in their sights, Teddy," Butch said. "All they had to do was pull the trigger."

"Why didn't they shoot, man?"

"You caught them off guard," he said. "That's why."

"What you mean?"

"I heard the one guy tell his partner that anybody who wanted to get away that bad deserved to get away. Neither one of them could believe their eyes."

"I hid under a car on St. Nicholas Avenue for about half an hour."

"You didn't even have to do that, man," he said. "They didn't even bother to go after you. As a matter of fact, they drove off in the *opposite* direction. Somebody *up there* sure must like you, Teddy."

I nodded my head, concentrating more on getting that shot of dope in my veins rather than on Butch's last comment. I really didn't know who or what to credit for escaping with my life, but I can tell you that God was the furthest thought from my mind at the time. I injected the heroin slowly, slipping into a state of ecstasy in a matter of seconds, thoughts of my recent ordeal already ancient history.

Two detectives from the 26th Precinct arrested me two weeks later without incident. I never saw them coming. I was at the corner grocery store across the street from my parents' building when they entered. I told the store clerk to contact my stepdad and tell him to come to the 26th Precinct immediately. I said it loud enough for the detectives to hear, just in case they had unpleasant plans for me. My fears were unfounded, however, because I learned on the ride to the station that they were both new to the 26th Precinct. They said I was lucky it was them who arrested me, because there were still cops at the station who had it in for me. I listened to them in silence, gazing thoughtfully out of the window. Once I arrived at the station, I had to be prepared for anything.

We stopped at the precinct's booking desk, and then I was taken upstairs to the detective division on the second floor. They locked me inside the cell from which I had escaped months earlier. I had to smile at the renovations. Instead of cinder blocks, the bars were now imbedded in concrete. Occasionally, a few detectives would walk over to the cell and look in on me. I didn't know if they had anything planned or not, but I was very much relieved to see my stepdad walk through the door a short time later.

To my surprise, I was only charged with criminal trespassing, stemming from the City College complaint. I guess bringing up the escape from a brand-new, high-security police station was too embarrassing, so it wasn't even mentioned. I was happy about the whole thing, of course. Instead of multiple felony charges, I was only charged with a misdemeanor—punishable by a maximum of one year at Riker's Island.

During the court proceedings, I instructed my court-appointed attorney to tell the district attorney that, if he would agree to a sentence of ninety days, I would plead guilty to the charge. I knew that Riker's Island was overcrowded; I also knew how the system worked. The only thing that the district attorney was concerned about was a conviction at minimal expense to the taxpayers. Therefore, although it shocked my lawyer, it came as no surprise to me that my plea deal was accepted. Still, I had to shake my head at the thought of all of the running, ducking, and hiding I did while the police were looking to kill me. All of that for just ninety days in jail!

Just before I was sentenced, the judge asked the arresting officers why it took so long to bring me before the court. One of the detectives smiled and said, "Mr. Harris is fleet of foot, Your Honor." At that, the courtroom burst into laughter. Even I had to laugh at the detective's reply. *If they only knew*, I thought as I was led to the bus headed for Riker's Island.

I have to say, though, I was relieved that it was all over. I had reached the point where I was determined to use the jail time to my advantage, clean up my act, and get my life in order, once and for all. Or at least I thought I had reached that point.

CHAPTER FIFTEEN

Almost as soon as I was processed in at Riker's Island, I appeared before the program committee to determine where I would be assigned to work. I was pleased that I would be getting a work assignment so quickly, because working made the time pass faster. And it got even better—I was assigned to work at the Women's House of Detention!

The day after seeing the program committee, I was transferred to The Tombs, where inmates working in Manhattan from Riker's Island were housed. Besides the Women's House of Detention, other work sites included Bellevue Hospital's prison ward, Potter's Field Cemetery on Ward's Island, and The Tombs itself. However, of all the work assignments just mentioned, the Women's House was the most sought after. And, for reasons that should be obvious, it was also the hardest to get. I know guys who would have sold their soul to the devil to get that assignment, and I got it without even asking for it.

The Women's House of Detention at that time was located in the West Village. Ten of us were driven there at 7:00 a.m. each weekday, and we would work until 3:00 p.m. Our work assignments included unloading supply trucks, emptying and cleaning garbage cans, and any other heavy labor that the women inmates could not do. One of my jobs was to take the garbage from the kitchen and empty it into the Dumpster outside in the transport yard. The transport yard was where the Department of Corrections vans and buses made their daily runs, picking up female inmates who were scheduled for court appearances and dropping off those who had been remanded by the court.

Working the transport yard, I witnessed the arrival of Joan Bird, a ranking member of the Black Liberation Army, as well as the highly publicized arrival of Angela Davis. Both were brought in under heavy guard, but Angela Davis had the tightest security. Angela was picked up in a midtown Howard Johnson motel on an interstate flight to avoid prosecution warrant and was on the FBI's "Ten Most Wanted" list at the time. She was charged with aiding and abetting the escape of Jonathan Jackson (George Jackson's brother) from the Los Angeles, California, courtroom of a judge who was murdered in the escape attempt. Although I witnessed the arrival of other famous—or infamous—woman prisoners while working the Woman's House transport yard, Joan Bird and Angela Davis were the most celebrated and notorious by far.

Since I only worked at the Women's House on weekdays, I volunteered to help friends working the transport yard at The Tombs on weekends. It gave us a chance to sing, goof off, talk about girls, and basically just hang out together. Some of the assigned duties in the transport yard were garbage disposal; grounds work; and washing vans, buses, and cars belonging to the Department of Corrections. Stan was the name of the officer in charge of The Tombs transport yard crew. He was a decent white guy who pretty much let us do our own thing.

One Saturday afternoon, a friend of mine was busy washing the warden's car. Bus and van traffic was almost nonexistent on weekends, so I was sitting on the loading dock with Stan and the rest of the guys, just making general conversation. It was a warm summer day, and we were all just chilling out.

On either side of the transport yard were two electric gates, one on the Centre Street side of the building, the other on the White Street side. A small garage was located inside the yard, almost flush with the Centre Street gate, and at the White Street gate there was an even smaller supply shed. The distance from the garage to the supply shed was about thirty feet. My friend was finishing up the warden's car just inside that garage. When the car was finished, my friend yelled over and asked me to move it so the next car in line could be washed. As I ran to the car, my friend told Stan that he needed to get something out of the supply shed. They walked over to the shed together as I slid smoothly behind the wheel. The keys were in the ignition, and the car was idling. I took it out of park and stepped on the gas.

Assuming that I knew how to drive, no one paid any attention to me. After opening the shed for my friend, Stan leaned against the wall near the White Street gate. I exited the garage on the Centre Street side. Well, to be more precise, I shot out of the garage like a cannonball. That would describe more accurately the car that Stan—who was now frozen against the wall in shock—saw coming his way! I didn't merely step on the gas—I *floored* it. And, to make matters worse, the car was headed straight for Stan.

With the pedal to the metal, I panicked and pressed down on the brake pedal with the other foot. I had one foot on the gas and the other foot on the brake. That—and divine intervention—is probably what saved Stan's life. Mercifully, the car stalled mere inches from Stan's rigid body.

There was total silence in the yard. Stan was as white as a sheet, and the rest of the guys stared in disbelief.

"Get out of the car," Stan said, slowly regaining his composure.

I quickly exited the vehicle and stood face-to-face with Stan.

"Have you ever driven a car before?" he asked.

I shook my head no, and he stared at me for what seemed like an eternity.

"Then what possessed you to get behind the wheel of the *warden's* car without knowing how to drive?"

"I just thought that I could do it," I answered, lowering my head.

He stared at me a moment longer, and then without another word, he took all of us back inside. Work was officially over.

My life was saved that day as well. Had the car slammed into Stan at the speed that I was traveling, it would have certainly crushed him to death. To this day, I shudder every time I think about what might have happened to me had I killed a Department of Corrections officer in The Tombs yard.

I continued to use drugs while serving my ninety-day sentence. Drugs were prevalent at The Tombs, and I was able to get almost anything I wanted. I had developed a close relationship with a major drug dealer from the neighborhood who was a few beds down from me. His name was Alan Lyons, but everyone called him "Heads," and he was serving a one-year sentence. "Heads" and his girlfriend, Doloree Mapp, had most of the heroin on Sugar Hill at the time. Doloree's claim to fame was from the Supreme Court decision *Mapp vs. Ohio*, a Fourth Amendment issue in which the court ruled against the use of evidence in criminal prosecutions obtained as the result of an illegal search and seizure. It was a landmark case affecting criminal prosecutions and convictions nationwide. I had copped from them from time to time, but that was the extent of my relationship with them.

When I met "Heads" on a personal level in The Tombs, I was kind of surprised that he pulled me into his inner circle. He controlled the drug supply, so of course I exploited our relationship to the hilt. I stayed high so much during my time at The Tombs with "Heads" that it was almost as if I wasn't even serving time.

As my release date drew near, I realized that I had acquired another drug habit. I was going to be released with no money, no job, and probably no place to stay once my wife found out that I had not changed my ways. So I talked "Heads" in to letting me have some heroin on consignment upon my release. He was hesitant at first because he knew that I had a drug habit. Therefore, the odds were that I would take his "package" and *use* it rather than sell it. He was right, of course, but I assured him that I would sell the drugs and bring all of the proceeds to Doloree. After much persuasion on my part, he reluctantly agreed to start me off with a small "package."

On the day of my release, I headed immediately to a prearranged meeting with Doloree at a grocery store on 111th Street, near the entrance to Central Park. She was leery of me and really didn't want to give me the drugs, but "Heads" had authorized it. So when I got there, she handed me a "bundle" of heroin and told me to make sure she got her money. I told her she could count on it and that I would be back for another "bundle" in no time. She never saw me again.

I was an addict, not a dealer, so selling those drugs never entered my mind. Fifteen five-dollar bags gave me a three- or four-day supply, so I was all right for a while, but as the saying goes, "All good things must come to an end." So when the drugs ran out, it was back to the streets for me.

I was on the prowl late one evening in desperate need of a fix. Actually, it was about two a.m., and I was walking the deserted streets of midtown Manhattan. I was on the east side, near the Copacabana nightclub, when I spotted a Lincoln convertible idling near the club's entrance.

As I walked slowly past the car, I glanced inside and saw a huge white guy fast asleep behind the wheel. It looked as if he was waiting for someone inside the club and had fallen asleep. I circled the block a couple of times as I tried to formulate a plan of action. The third time around, I tried the passenger side door and found that it was not locked. My heart was pounding fast as I eased into the passenger seat next to the sleeping giant. The guy looked as if he weighed about three hundred pounds. He would definitely be hard to handle if he woke up. I also knew that whatever I was going to do needed to be done in a hurry, because whomever he was waiting for could come out at any moment. The guy reeked of alcohol and garlic, so I immediately pegged him for an Italian. That only served to compound my fear and anxiety. *Maybe he's a mobster,* I thought. And if that were the case, I reasoned, the person he was waiting for was probably a mobster too. Still, I had a habit to feed, so I reached for his pockets.

He was so big that I couldn't budge him; I could only pat his back pockets. I was able to feel the bulge of a wallet in one of them, but getting to it was all but impossible. The only visible item of value was the watch on his left wrist. I fumbled with it but couldn't get it off. I was starting to get nervous. I had been in the car much too long and needed to get out before the guy woke up. I reached for the door handle, and that's when he opened his eyes.

I froze in the seat as he straightened up and stared directly at me. Shifting from park to drive, he asked if I was ready to go. His speech was slurred, and I could smell the alcohol on his breath. In the dim interior of the car, I probably resembled the person he was waiting for. Besides, it was dark in the car, and he was still somewhat drunk, so I decided to go with it. Without missing a beat, I nodded my head.

He pulled away from the curb and stopped at the corner for a red light. My mind was racing, and I knew I had to think of something quick.

"Make a right at the light," I said, testing my control over him. He immediately did as I instructed. *That was easy,* I thought. Apparently the person he was waiting for back at the club was in a position of authority. That being the case then, I decided to play it to the hilt.

"Pull over at the curb," I instructed, "and check your pockets."

Without hesitation, he pulled the car over and idled at the curb.

"I saw some guys hanging around the car when I came out," I said.

He just looked at me with a blank stare, still quite intoxicated.

"Let me see your wallet," I said, holding out my hand.

He removed his wallet and handed it to me.

Going for the brass ring, I decided to push the limits of my authority over him. "Now, let me see your watch."

He removed the watch without question or hesitation and handed it to me. *This is unbelievable*, I thought. *Now all I have to do is get out of the car.* I reached for the door handle, and something seemed to click in his inebriated brain: a total stranger was in the car with him, and he had just given him his watch and wallet!

Flipping a switch that locked all four doors, hands the size of ham hocks reached for me. I punched him squarely in the face with every ounce of strength I could muster. It was like hitting an elephant with Ping-Pong balls. He grabbed me, and I began to fight for my life. Thankfully, the window on his side of the car was down. I fought my way over to the window, climbing on top and over of him. With a knee in his chest, I threw a barrage of punches at his head that had little or no effect. Inching closer to the open window, I pitched myself through it. He managed to grab my legs and hold on tightly as I dangled halfway out of the car. He began to pull me back through the window, but there was no way I was going to allow that. I jerked one of my legs from his grasp and kicked him squarely in the face. He screamed, grabbed his face, and let go of my legs. I fell headfirst into the street. I was fortunate that a police car hadn't happened by during our struggle. That would have been all that I needed. Still, I needed to get out of the area—fast.

I jumped to my feet and ran all the way over to the west side. I didn't stop until I reached the subway station. I rode the train to 145th Street and St. Nicholas Avenue and smiled at the wad of one hundred-dollar bills inside the wallet—twenty-five of them to be exact.

As I exited the 145th Street station and headed up the hill toward Amsterdam Avenue, I gave absolutely no thought to how close I had just come to losing my life. The only thing that was on my mind was getting high. The watch didn't excite me all that much either. It was some brand that I had never heard of. I mean, after all, how much could a *Rolex* be worth?

CHAPTER SIXTEEN

E ven in my addiction, I had dreams of a singing career. So when Lloyd Price opened his new nightclub, Lloyd Price's Turntable, in midtown Manhattan, I decided to audition for him. Besides rising to fame with hit songs like "Personality" and "Stagger Lee," Lloyd Price was also responsible for talking Don King, the fight promoter, into combing his hair in the sweeping mane that has now become his trademark. It was during the Ali/Foreman fight when he and Don King were business partners. Lloyd told Don that since his last name was "King," he should comb his hair straight up to resemble a crown. Don King took his advice, and the rest is history. Now he has one of the most recognizable hairstyles in the world.

Someone told me that Lloyd was holding auditions for his weekly "Talent Showcase" at the Turntable, and I went to see if I could get on the bill. While waiting to audition, I went into the men's room to relieve myself. As I stood at one of the urinals, the door to the men's room opened, and in walked a sharply dressed black man. Just as I was finishing up, he approached the urinal next to me. We nodded a greeting to one another, and I walked over to the sink to wash my hands. *I recognize that face,* I thought as I turned the tap water on.

"How you doin'?" the man said, joining me at the sink.

"I'm good," I replied, still trying to place the face. "I'm here to audition for a spot on Lloyd's show."

Hearing that, he smiled and proceeded to give me some tips on stage presence, showmanship, and microphone control. He spoke as if he knew what he was talking about.

"You sound like you're in the entertainment business," I said. "Are you?"

"I got *decades* in the business, son," he answered with a broad grin.

"Well, you *do* look kinda familiar," I said. "I just can't put a *name* to you."

"You ever heard of Wilson Pickett?" he asked as his smile got wider.

"*You're* Wilson Pickett?" I asked incredulously.

"The one and same," he replied.

I could hardly believe it was true. Standing before me was Wilson Pickett, the legendary R&B singer, or the "Wicked Pickett," as he was known in the industry. With such songs as "6-3-4-5-7-8-9" and "Mustang Sally" in his long list of hits, Wilson Pickett was an industry legend indeed.

Noticing that I was somewhat skeptical about his identity, he took out his wallet and showed me his driver's license. Yes, he was indeed Wilson Pickett. My interest now, however, was on the thick wad of bills in his wallet. I no longer cared who he was. My first impulse was to snatch the wallet and hit the door running.

Thankfully, however, that impulse was just a passing one. The moment the thought entered my mind, the biggest man I ever laid eyes on opened the men's room door.

"Everything okay?" asked the man.

"Yeah, Tiny, everything's good," Wilson replied. "I'll be out in a minute."

Tiny? I thought as the giant stood in the doorway.

I don't even want to think about what would have happened had I snatched the wallet and tried to get past King Kong at the door!

"Good luck at the audition," Wilson, offering me his hand.

"Thanks, Wilson," I said, truly grateful that I had not tried to rob him.

I turned back to the sink as Wilson Pickett's bodyguard held the door open for him to pass. Telling a friend about this later, I was informed that had I snatched the singer's wallet, his bodyguard would have been the *least* of my worries. My friend told me that Wilson Pickett had been a semi-professional boxer before becoming an entertainer. In other words, the "Wicked Pickett" would have "mopped" that bathroom floor with me!

I auditioned for Lloyd Price, and it went well. He told me to come back the following Tuesday evening and he would put me in the showcase. I told him I would definitely be there. And I would have too—had my addiction not had other plans.

A few days later, I was in the process of breaking in to an apartment two blocks from where my parents lived. I was "sick" and needed a shot of dope fast. I was on the roof, attempting to enter the apartment through the skylight. It was evening, and I had just removed the skylight from its foundation, which left a gaping hole. A broad sheet of metal covered the opening, preventing me from hanging and dropping into the apartment. This, of course, was nothing new for me. I had burglarized other apartments in the same manner and had encountered the same problem from time to time. The remedy was simple. All I had to do was climb onto the metal covering, jump up and down on it until the bolts came loose, and the covering would fall off. This always worked, unless the metal covering was uncommonly thick. I just needed to test the strength of the covering, and the rest would be easy.

I got on my hands and knees in the darkness, leaned over with my palms pressing the metal covering, and plunged headfirst into a porcelain bathtub fifteen feet below. The metal covering was actually black construction paper! I fell hard and fast into the tub, busting my head wide open. I lay there in shock, with blood streaming down my face. It took every ounce of willpower I could muster not to slip into unconsciousness. I had the presence of mind to know that I had to get out of there immediately. It took a few minutes to get my bearings, but I managed to stagger to the door. I know now that it was only through the grace of God that I was able to remain conscious.

I unlocked the door and stumbled down the stairs leading to the street. With blood flowing down my face and into my eyes, I can only imagine how I must have looked to the people I passed—most of who knew me, as well as my family. My focus, however, was on getting to my parents' house. I needed immediate medical attention.

Climbing the five flights to their apartment was a struggle, but somehow I managed it. My sister Retie opened the door and let out a scream that brought everybody in the apartment running. Blood flowed profusely from the gaping wound in my head, and my mother became hysterical. My stepdad, who had been drinking, thought that was a good time to lecture me. Mom turned on him immediately, however, telling him that *now* was not the time. She told him to get me to the hospital right away.

He half carried me back down the stairs and hailed a passing taxi. When the driver saw the blood, he tried to prevent me from getting into the cab. My stepdad threw the door open and pushed me inside anyway.

When I regained consciousness, I was in Knickerbocker Hospital, stitched up and heavily bandaged. The doctor who treated me wanted to keep me overnight for observation, but my drug habit would have none of that. I told him that I was leaving and signed myself out immediately. I headed out into the night, a semi-mummy, looking for a fix. If I thought that injury was bad, the next one almost got me killed—literally.

A couple of black gangsters had just opened a nightclub on Sugar Hill called Noah's. The club sat adjacent to my parent's building at 1634 Amsterdam Avenue, so I was there on opening night. In fact, I knew "Noah" personally, having met him and his wife, Ruth, while the club was being renovated. What I didn't know was that Noah was mob connected and that the nightclub was backed by gangsters. I broke into the club shortly after its grand opening, taking everything of value.

Two weeks later, I was walking past 1642 Amsterdam Avenue and noticed a black guy standing on the top step leading into the building. The entrance door was closed, and he was just standing there, smoking a cigarette. I had never seen him in the neighborhood before, so I didn't pay him much attention.

"Yo, Teddy!" he called to me as I passed by the stoop.

I stopped and turned to look at him. "What's up?"

"Let me talk to you for a minute."

As I walked toward the guy, the entrance door opened, and another black guy jumped out at me, swinging a lead pipe at my head. I turned to run, but he caught me full swing in the back of my head with the pipe. My head split open like a ripe melon, making the same squishing sound as the pipe connected. Amazingly, I did not lose consciousness. I tried to run once more, but he swung the pipe again, hitting me flush on my kneecap, causing me to fall to the sidewalk. I didn't know who these men were or why I was being assaulted, but I was soon to find out. It was broad daylight with many people witnessing the attack. So to get me off the street and away from prying eyes, the two men dragged me by the collar across the street to the Hudson Hotel.

"I'm gonna blow your brains out!" one of them said, pointing a gun to my head.

I just stared up at him in silence, still not knowing what this was all about. At that point, however, I no longer cared. I was tired of everything—how I was living; being away from Sylvia and Nya; and, most of all, I was tired of my addiction. At that point, I didn't care if he pulled the trigger or not.

"You got *three* seconds to tell me where my shit is at," the man with the gun said.

Little did he know that, as far as I was concerned, death at that point would have been a relief. "Go ahead an' shoot, man," I said weakly. "I don't even care no more."

At that very instant, almost as if on cue, the lobby door opened, and a friend of my stepdad's walked in. I don't know if he had witnessed what had happened out on the street or if God just placed him there at that moment. All I know is that the two men knew him and seemed to have some respect for him. He looked at them, nodded in greeting, and called them by their names. They nodded back, calling him by his name. To this day, I don't remember his name, but I *do* remember hearing him say, "That's Danny's boy. Don't shoot him."

The man with the gun seemed to be thinking it over. "You got *one* week!"

I just lay there staring up at him. "Get my stuff back to me or you're a dead man." His face was inches from mine. "You understand me?"

I nodded my head slowly.

"Thanks, man," my stepdad's friend said. The two men nodded at him, and the three of them exited the hotel.

It was while lying there on that filthy hotel floor that I decided that enough was enough. If I didn't get my life together, it was possible that my wife and daughter would get hurt because of me or I would be found dead somewhere. I had to get Sylvia and Nya out of the city and clean up my act once and for all.

Someone called an ambulance, and I was again taken to Knickerbocker Hospital. This time, however, after being stitched up, I stayed there long enough to heal. I told the doctor that I was a drug addict, hoping he would give me some methadone, a synthetic form of heroin, to help ease the withdrawal pains. However, rather than methadone, he gave me some other medication to help me sleep.

Sylvia and Nya visited me in the hospital. She was happy that I had finally decided to do something about my addiction and was just as anxious to leave the city as I was. All that remained was for us to decide where to go.

I had family in Binghamton, New York. Gram was living there, as well as some uncles, aunts, and cousins on my mother's side. I didn't know anything about Binghamton; I just felt that it had to be better than New York City in terms of raising a child. Besides, it would be good to see Gram again. So Binghamton it was.

CHAPTER SEVENTEEN

My wife and I welcomed in the New Year of 1973 at the homes of various relatives in Binghamton. We were, however, finally able to move into our own house a couple of weeks later on Dickerson Street. I was down to my last few methadone tablets by that time, but I was determined to remain drug-free once they were gone—which, at the rate I was taking them, wouldn't be long.

I had brought a number of methadone tablets with me to help with my withdrawal. However, instead of taking the tablets in small doses to ease the withdrawal pains, I took them in large doses to get high. Methadone is really nothing more than synthetic heroin, so I was simply replacing one addiction for another. Little did I realize, however, that kicking a methadone habit was ten times more severe than kicking heroin—a little trivia that I would learn the hard way.

One evening, after taking my last methadone tablet, I headed out to the corner store. There was a Mayflower moving van parked directly across the street with two white guys inside.

"Say!" the guy behind the wheel yelled, calling me over to the truck. "You interested in making some money?"

"Doin' what?"

"We're moving an IBM family down to Kentucky tonight," he answered. "We could use an extra hand." As if to make my decision easier, he added, "The van's loaded and ready to go."

"Give me a minute," I said, "I wanna talk it over with my wife first."

Although reluctant to ride down to Kentucky on such short notice, Sylvia and I felt that the work would be good for two reasons: one, we would be making some much-needed money, and two, the trip would give me an opportunity to kick my methadone habit. So it was settled. I was on my way to Kentucky.

The first leg of the journey went smoothly, but I soon started to experience hot and cold flashes, and my nose began to run. I was sitting in the middle of the cab, pressed between the driver and the other passenger, sweating profusely.

By the time we pulled into an all-night rest area for truckers, I was in agony. The other two guys settled in for a couple hours of sleep with me between them. There was no way I was going to be able to sleep. I just suffered in silence.

By the time we reached Kentucky, I was totally out of it. My bones ached, and I felt weak and disoriented. My traveling companions asked if I was okay. I told them that I was sick, which wasn't a lie. They just didn't know what the "sickness" was. They thought I had come down with the flu or something. Still, they expected me to live up to my commitment and help unload the truck.

I had no idea that a full-size Mayflower moving van could hold so much stuff. When the truck's rear doors were opened, I let out a slight moan. It was packed to the brim. There was no way I was going to be able to help unload the van—not in my condition.

I walked over to a chair on the back porch of the house and sat with my head in my hands. I was so weak that I could barely move. The guys were clearly upset with me. They mumbled and grumbled as they went about unloading the truck themselves, but their complaints didn't faze me in the least. I was hurting so badly death itself would have been a relief. It seemed like it took them forever to unload the van. And the longer they took, the weaker I got. At that point, I would have sold my soul to the devil himself for a shot of heroin. When they finally finished unloading, I was delirious.

On the trip back to Binghamton, it felt like worms were running relay races underneath my skin. My body temperature fluctuated wildly. I was either extremely hot or extremely cold; there was no in between. Still upset with me, my traveling companions didn't talk the entire trip back. I was grateful for that, however. I was in no mood for small talk. I just wanted to be left alone.

When I finally made it home, I could hardly find the strength to climb the stairs to the apartment we were renting. Sylvia knew the deal as soon as she saw the condition I was in. I told her to go to the liquor store and get me a bottle of wine. I needed something to get me through my withdrawal. She was reluctant at first, but my condition was so bad that she felt sorry for me. She bought a fifth of Wild Irish Rose, and that helped to take the edge off. As a result, however, I started drinking every day, and it wasn't long before I became a full-fledged alcoholic.

It was during one of my drinking binges that I experienced my first blackout. I came out of it to find myself in a locked cell at the Binghamton Police Station. While in the blackout, I had broken into somebody's house and was arrested for carrying some of their property down the street. I was charged with burglary and really didn't remember anything of the crime. Still, I was offered three years in prison and accepted the plea bargain rather than taking my chances at trial. There was no way I could prove to a jury that I was in a blackout. So in the fall of 1973, I was sent to Attica Correctional Facility, just two years after the uprising that had cost thirty-nine inmates and two civilian hostages their lives. Needless to say, I was scared to death.

Attica lived up to its billing as one of the most fearsome maximum-security prisons in New York State. A concrete fortress with forty-foot walls and massive steel gates, Attica was something right out of my worst nightmare. The atmosphere was so thick with tension and hostility that it virtually assaulted the senses.

I was twenty-four years old, but I knew enough to keep my mouth shut and observe my surroundings. I was sitting inside of a holding cell, waiting to be assigned to a cellblock, and I could sense the hostility of the guards toward the inmates. I didn't want to give them any reason to jump on me and beat me up. So I just sat back and kept quiet.

My first weeks at Attica were spent going through an orientation period consisting of interviews by medical staff to determine if I had any ailments or diseases and a counselor to determine what programs would best suit my needs. Compared to the majority of the inmates at Attica, my sentence was extremely short. As a result, I was given a "minimum security" classification, which meant that I could work outside the prison walls. I was also eligible for a transfer to one of the minimum-security work camps.

In the meantime, since I could type, I was assigned as a clerk in the central office trailer just outside Attica's walls. I would leave the prison each morning and return late in the afternoon. I was pleased with the job and looked forward to going to work each day. On the weekends during my free time, I would sing with a group of guys in the prison yard. As a result, time passed quickly for me.

Attica's four main cellblocks are A, B, C, and D blocks. A fifth cellblock, E block, was annexed to the four main ones. Given a choice, most inmates preferred to lock in E block because the cell doors were solid instead of the steel bars found in the main cellblocks. That meant that it was quieter and more peaceful at night. E block also had its own small fenced-in recreation yard, eliminating the need to go to the main yards, where it was more crowded, more hostile, and more dangerous.

I was assigned to E block because of my "outside clearance" status, but because members of my singing group locked in the four main cellblocks, I chose to spend my recreation time in one of the four main prison yards. Also, going to the main yards gave me a chance to see friends of mine from the neighborhood and walk the yard with them.

In the early seventies, Attica's yards contained a virtual "who's who" of notorious and infamous inmates. The inmate Imam for the Nation of Islam was Norman Butler, one of the three men convicted of killing Malcolm X. I also walked the yard with the black militant H. Rap Brown, sharing some of my poetry with him and listening to his views on black consciousness and awareness. Winston Mosely, the serial rapist and murderer, was there at the time as well. When he was finally arrested for the murder of Kitty Genovese in 1964 in front of dozens of eyewitnesses, the press had a field day. His hunt and capture is also detailed in the book *Chief*, memoirs of the New York City chief of detectives who orchestrated the investigation leading to Mosely's arrest.

After three months at Attica, I was transferred to a minimum-security work camp in Horseheads, New York. I didn't stay at Camp Monterey long, because I wanted to get as close to home as possible to make it easier for Sylvia and Nya to visit. I learned that Camp Pharsalia was closer to Binghamton and requested a transfer there. So almost as soon as I arrived at Camp Monterey, I was transferred to Camp Pharsalia.

Immediately upon my arrival, I called Sylvia and asked her to visit me that weekend. My Aunt Lil agreed to drive her and Nya up, and I anxiously anticipated the visit. I couldn't wait to see them. I missed them so much.

When they arrived that weekend, we had an enjoyable visit—or at least Nya and I did. Sylvia, however, seemed distant but worked hard to act as if she was glad to see me. I asked if everything was okay, and she said everything was fine. It was obvious, though, that something was on her mind, something she clearly didn't want to discuss—at least not face-to-face.

A week later, I received a "Dear John" letter from her. In the letter, my wife said she was tired of waiting for me and wanted a divorce. Although the letter hurt me deeply, I couldn't really blame her for being tired of my nonsense. After all, my family deserved better than what I was putting them through. I had to face the reality of the situation. We had been married four years, and during that time I had not been a husband to her or a father to Nya.

I didn't even bother to answer the letter. There was no point in it. There was nothing I could say to convince her that I would change. She had certainly given me more than enough chances at that. So I simply took the "Dear John" letter in stride, accepted my wife's desire for a divorce, and moved on with my life.

CHAPTER EIGHTEEN

As my date to see the parole board drew near, I was transferred to Elmira Correctional Facility. Although Elmira was a maximum-security facility, I didn't mind being there. My "outside clearance" status was still in place, so I was assigned to an outside work crew. Since it was early summer, most of our work consisted of grass cutting and shrub trimming. Time passed quickly on the work gang, and I utilized my free time to sing in a group at Elmira called "The Black Jewels."

The Department of Correctional Services implemented a furlough program around that time as well. The furlough program allowed eligible inmates to go home for three to seven days and then return to the facility. At first I didn't believe it. No way was an inmate going to be permitted to leave a maximum-security facility and trusted to return. Still, I had nothing to lose by applying. At worst I would not be approved, and at best I would. So I filled out the application and submitted it to my counselor. Two weeks passed without a response, so I assumed I had been denied and simply forgot about it.

The leader of our singing group was a guy by the name of Jewel Powell, but everyone called him "Coke." We had become close friends, so after one of our rehearsals, I asked him if he knew any girls that might be interested in corresponding with me. I was getting kind of lonely and longed for regular correspondence with a female. Coke, to my surprise, told me that I could write his niece, Deborah. Her full name was Deborah Powell, and I immediately wrote and enclosed a picture of myself. She responded favorably, and our friendship blossomed. After just a few weeks of writing to one another, Deborah said she wanted to visit me.

At the time, the procedure for inmates to receive visitors was to have their named placed on an approved visiting list. The prospective visitor's name was submitted to the inmate's counselor, and he or she would either approve or disapprove it. I quickly wrote to my counselor, asking for an interview. It was the beginning of the week, and I wanted to get Deborah's name on my visiting list before Saturday came around, the day of her intended visit.

That Thursday afternoon, I was called to my counselor's office, and I gave him Deborah's name. It only took him a few minutes to put her on my visiting list, so after exchanging a few pleasantries, I thanked him and turned to leave.

"Oh, Harris, by the way," he said before I could complete my exit, "how was your furlough?" That stopped me dead in my tracks. I turned and looked at him.

"Furlough?" I asked, puzzled. "What furlough?"

He called me back inside the office and reopened my folder.

"I applied for a furlough about a month ago," I said, walking back to his desk.

"Well, according to the information in here," he began, reviewing my folder, "your furlough request was approved a week ago."

I sat there in stunned silence.

"You should have been notified so that a furlough date could be arranged," he added.

I sat there in shock, dumbfounded by the news. He snatched the phone from the receiver and dialed the office of Mr. Gallagher, Elmira's temporary release coordinator. They talked for a few minutes, and then my counselor cupped the phone with one hand and asked me when I wanted to go on my furlough. That completely floored me. What kind of a question was that? "Now!" I wanted to scream. "Right now!"

"Whenever possible," I said calmly.

He turned back to the phone and conversed a few minutes more. Then he cupped the phone once more and said, "Gallagher wants to know if you want to go home this Monday."

I could no longer speak. I nodded my head and walked back to the cellblock in a daze. I couldn't believe what had just happened. I had gone to my counselor to get Coke's niece on my visiting list and came back with a furlough.

"Everything good?" Coke asked, sitting outside his cell, getting his hair braided.

"Yeah," I replied, wanting to have some fun with them. "A change of plans, though." I smiled.

"A change of plans?" he said, clearly puzzled. "What's that s'posed to mean?"

"It means that I'll be seeing your niece this coming Monday rather than Saturday."

"What's she comin' up on a *Monday* for?"

"She not *comin'* up on Monday." I smiled. "I'm *going* to see her on Monday!"

Coke looked at me like I was crazy.

After explaining what happened in the counselor's office, Coke immediately called his niece and told her to meet me at Port Authority on Monday morning. Deborah was extremely excited by the news, assuring her uncle she would be there.

That Monday morning, the bus ride to New York City was almost surreal. It was a bright, sunny day, and I was seated next to a cute black girl who happened to live in the town of Elmira. She was on her way to the city to visit relatives. When I told her that I was on a furlough from the prison, her interest in me really seemed to pique. She asked how long I had been in. When I told her I hadn't so much as kissed a girl in almost two years, the invitation in her eyes was clear. I spent the remainder of the bus ride enjoying warm, tender kisses with a lot of heavy petting.

We exchanged contact information before the bus pulled into the Port Authority and agreed to stay in touch. She told me she would visit me when I returned to Elmira, but I didn't think that Coke's niece would allow that. I quickly scanned the crowd for Deborah, and then I felt a gentle hand on my shoulder. I turned and looked directly into the eyes of an attractive medium-brown-complexioned girl.

"Teddy?"

I nodded.

"I'm Deborah," she said, smiling.

We hugged briefly and then walked hand-in-hand toward the uptown Broadway subway line. It was hard to imagine that only a few hours earlier I was inside of Elmira prison. I pulled Deborah close as we entered the subway station. I was determined to cram a month of fun and pleasure into my seven-day furlough. It was good to be home.

Deborah proved to be a gracious hostess, and I mean that in every sense of the word. We hung out every day, and she even took me to Brooklyn to meet Coke's parents. It was clear that she was falling for me harder than I had expected. I mean, she was a nice girl and all, but my feelings for her were not that deep. I just wanted a female companion to party with and make love to. And Deborah fulfilled both of those desires.

The day of my departure, I took an early bus to Elmira because I wanted to make sure I got back well before my 3:00 p.m. deadline. If I were even a minute late, it would blow my chances of getting another furlough. And I wanted another one as soon as possible.

I arrived at the front gate of the prison at around 2:00 p.m. and reported directly to the officer on duty. I told him that I was returning from a furlough. He looked at his pad, found my name, and told me that he couldn't let me in because I was too early. The shifts were changing for correction officers entering and leaving the facility, so I couldn't get in until exactly 3:00 p.m. I couldn't believe it. I sat on the front steps of the prison, *waiting* to be let in. Most of the correction officers entering and leaving the prison found it amusing.

I sat there on the prison steps, daydreaming about the past seven days and my time with Deborah. Also, because Coke and I were such close friends, it was good that I met his parents and would be able to provide him with information concerning them. I knew he would really appreciate that.

Interrupting my thoughts, the officer at the front gate told me that I could now enter the prison. I stood, took a final glance at the "free world," and strolled back into the belly of the beast. As the steel door clanged shut behind me, I couldn't help but think about my upcoming parole board appearance. My furlough had given me a small taste of freedom. I now I hungered for the full course.

I was granted parole that same year, 1974. With my release date just two months away, I was told to pack my belongings. I and some other friends who had also made parole were being transferred to Bayview Correctional Facility in lower Manhattan. We were so excited about the transfer that the night before we were scheduled to leave, we continued to talk after the "quiet bell" had rung. That was a definite no-no at Elmira.

Most of the guys I worked with on the outside crew were on the Bayview draft with me. I had become friends with three guys in particular: Al, Shala, and "Fat Tony." Now as his name suggests, "Fat Tony" was, well, fat! Weighing in at just over five hundred pounds, Tony was our "recreation" on the gallery that night.

The guard in charge of the gallery had already told us once to be quiet. However, since we were being transferred in the morning, we kept right on ribbing Tony about his weight. So when the guard yelled to us a second time to be quiet, Al laughingly screamed out, "You heard what the guard said! Knock off the talking, *Tony!*"

Angry with Al for yelling his name loud enough for the guard to hear, Tony screamed, "Why you wanna call me by my *name*, man? Why you can't call me 'Heavy' like everyone else?"

"You weigh five hundred pounds," Al hollered back. "You *really* think the CO don't know who Heavy is up here?"

The entire gallery shook with laughter, including the CO who had told us to be quiet. We decided to end the evening on that note.

The following day, we were on our way to Bayview Correctional Facility. When we arrived, we were immediately informed that we must first undergo a two-week orientation period before being allowed to go home on weekends. We would, however, be allowed day passes, but only for the purpose of finding a job.

The following morning, I learned that there was a typing class in the building. I quickly located it and immediately offered my services to the female instructor. She handed me a blank sheet of typing paper and pointed at one of the typewriters. I was typing around sixty-five words per minute at the time, and my fingers flew across the keyboard. She and the rest of the class looked on in amazement. It was a five-minute speed test and, after checking for accuracy as well as speed, she said that I had done well. So much so, in fact, that she left the room and came back with one of the job counselors at Bayview.

The counselor said he knew of an office in midtown that was looking for a typist and asked if I was interested. I told him that I was, and he took me for an interview that same afternoon.

I returned to the facility later that day with the job. As a result, the two-week orientation period was waived for me. To the envy of Al, Shala, and Tony, I began work the following day. I had to rub it in, of course, telling them about all the fine women I was working around. I wasn't kidding either—there were a lot of fine women in that office, which kind of cooled the relationship I still had with Deborah. I also failed to mention that I was now in touch once again with my wife.

Sylvia's sister, Caroline, had passed away the same month that we moved to Binghamton, and she took her death hard. Caroline was in the hospital in the final stages of cancer when we left New York City. So when we received the news of her death, Sylvia felt guilty about not being there for her. Now she and Nya were staying with Caroline's husband, Bernie, and her nieces and nephews in the Wagner Projects on East 124th Street.

We were not officially back together, but we were maintaining a dialogue. I would visit her and Nya from time to time and spend the night whenever asked. Sylvia and I enjoyed those intimate moments, and I also enjoyed being able to spend quality time with Nya. I would take her to the park, push her on the swings, and play catch with her. Nya loved it when I would sing to her too. She always asked for "My Cheri Amour" by Stevie Wonder, and I was happy to oblige. Unfortunately, I was too immature to appreciate the treasure that God had given to me in her. I was too busy enjoying my newfound freedom and trying to make up for lost time.

CHAPTER NINETEEN

I was paroled from Bayview just before Christmas 1974 and was staying at my parents' apartment on Amsterdam Avenue. I introduced Al and Shala to my sisters, Retie and Lou Lou, and we would all hang out together on a regular basis.

Al liked Retie the first time he met her, and she liked him too. I can't say the same for Lou Lou. It was clear that Shala liked her more than she did him. I would find out from Lou Lou later that Shala was obsessed with her to the point of possessiveness, and she was afraid of him. In the beginning, however, it seemed that everyone was happy, and we had some fun times together.

I had also regained an interest in pursuing a singing career. My brother Danny had formed a band, and they were looking for a lead singer. Lou Lou sang lead from time to time, but they were looking for a male vocalist.

When I took over as lead, it was a perfect fit. We covered R&B songs of the day and some original material as well. Danny was on lead guitar, Tooch was on rhythm guitar, Randy was on bass guitar, and Pepe was on drums.

We started out with local gigs and would undoubtedly have gone on to bigger venues had I not started using drugs again. As a result, it wasn't long before I started arriving late to rehearsals and then missing them altogether. As usual, my drug habit took complete control of my life. So when I was ultimately kicked out of the group, I didn't put up much of a protest. I was more concerned with supplying my growing drug habit.

The group continued in their quest for fame and fortune, however, with two of its members reaching great heights in the music industry. Danny became Kurtis Blow's lead guitarist, touring, recording, and producing with him. Pepe went on to drum for such legendary entertainers as Ashford & Simpson, Roberta Flack, and Luther Vandross, but I'm getting ahead of myself. Bottom line, I had a drug habit to feed and was out of the group—case closed. And almost no one was immune to my brand of larceny, not even friends, family, or family friends.

A friend of the family owned and operated a barbershop two buildings over from where my parents lived. His name was Jimmy, and he lived in a ground-floor apartment in the back of his shop. On this particular day, Shala and I were standing in the hallway of Jimmy's building, drinking wine, and decided to break into his apartment. I walked to the back of the hallway and knocked on Jimmy's door to see if he was home. After a number of knocks with no response, I assumed he wasn't there. I gave Shala a nod, and he produced a long screwdriver from his back pocket. He then proceeded to remove the apartment door from its hinges.

We didn't know it at the time, but Jimmy *was* at home and was calling the police at that very moment. It took about fifteen minutes of working on the door to remove the final bolt from its hinge, and just as we grabbed hold of the door to remove it, the door to the building flew open. Suddenly, the hallway was overflowing with cops, guns at the ready. We had absolutely nowhere to run. And if that wasn't bad enough, Shala reached inside his waistband and removed a .38 revolver.

I prayed he wouldn't do anything stupid like fire at the approaching cops. I knew if he did that, we would both be dead. To my great relief, however, he listened to me and laid the gun on the staircase leading to the basement.

We then came from behind the staircase, hands high in the air. The cops rushed us, handcuffed us tightly, and then directed us to lay flat on the ground. After being jerked to our feet, we were taken back to Jimmy's apartment, where the door was still hanging off the hinges. Jimmy peered out at us from behind the door, but his eyes were locked on me. I hung my head in shame, unable to look him in the eye. He asked how I could do such a thing to him. I had no answer.

I was praying that the cops wouldn't find the gun on the basement staircase, but that, of course, was too much to ask for. One of the cops shined his flashlight directly on the gun, asking who it belonged to. To my surprise and relief, Shala said the gun was his.

After two weeks on Riker's Island, Jimmy dropped the attempted burglary charges against Shala and me, and I began to look forward to my release. Shala, however, still had the gun possession charge, so he wasn't going anywhere. I told him not to worry, that I would look out for him once I was back on the streets. As fate would have it, though, just as I was being processed for release, the warrant from Phoenix House surfaced, and that ended that. It seemed like ages since I left the woman from Phoenix House on the train, laughing as the train pulled off without me. Now it looked as if she was going to have the last laugh.

I had just served a three-year sentence, gotten a furlough, and was paroled without the warrant showing up. Now, as a result of this arrest, here it was. Still, I wasn't all that worried. I figured there was no way a judge would send me back to prison on a three-year-old warrant, especially after just serving three years. I couldn't have been more wrong.

The judge who released me to Phoenix House three years earlier wasn't trying to hear anything. He clearly stated at the time that if I didn't live up to the conditions of my release and successfully complete the drug program, he would sentence me to the three years I had hanging over my head—and that's exactly what he did. I couldn't believe it. I had not been out of prison two months, and I was already headed back Upstate with a brand-new sentence.

Me and my little "Tutu"—my daughter Nya. (1969)

Me, Nya, and Sylvia at our wedding reception. (1969)

Me as NAACP President—
Auburn Prison. (1979)

Me and my brother Marvin—Groveland Correctional
Facility (1991)

Me with my brother Marvin, Mimi, and Phyllis after a successful production of my play "Soul Food"—Wallkill Correctional Facility (1994)

Me, Stan Lucas, and my brother Marvin—Wallkill Correctional Facility (1994)

Me as lead singer for the Wallkill Band—Wallkill Correctional Facility (1995)

My sisters: Retie, Dee Dee, and Lou Lou—Binghamton, NY (1996)

Me and Phyllis on our Wedding Day—|Wallkill Correctional Facility (1994)

Mom on her way to Wallkill for my marriage to Phyllis. (1994)

The "Anointed Two"—Gospel Starseek Competition, Nashville, TN (1996)

Me and the legendary Patti LaBelle—Westbury Music Fair (2000)

Studio time with Kurtis Blow, my brother Danny, and my nephew "Dan-O" (2000)

Me and Harold Washington as paralegals for Prisoners' Legal Services of New York—Poughkeepsie, NY (2001)

A proud Mom and Siblings at my daughter Tamika's graduation—Dutchess Community College (2006)

A visit from Phyllis as my release date draws near—Fishkill Correctional Facility (2009)

Returning to prison in my capacity as Prison Partnership Associate for the Hudson River Presbytery: with Samuel Hamilton and Nigel Lawrence (Hudson Link Graduation)—Fishkill Correctional Facility (2011)

I was sent to Clinton Correctional Facility for testing and facility placement. During the two months I was there, I asked to see the prison psychologist. I wanted to find out what, if anything, was wrong me. I couldn't understand what caused me to continue using drugs, knowing it would lead me back to prison or even death. After a number of sessions, the psychologist told me that I had a "fear of success." He said that I was running from the responsibility that came with success, content to let the chips fall where they may.

I didn't understand what he meant at the time, but now I think I do. Because of my immaturity, I don't like people expecting more of me than I am willing to give. I want to be free to do my own thing. Therefore, the psychologist noted, whenever I came close to success, I would sabotage it, choosing rather to operate on the "pleasure principle"—if it feels good, do it.

I was sent back to Attica a few weeks after our sessions started, so I never got the opportunity to discuss his observations in detail. Accurate or not, they did give me something to think about.

Not long after my return to Attica, I enrolled in the "consortium" college program. The program consisted of professors from Canisus College, Rosary Hill (now Damien College), Niagara, and Buffalo State University teaching at the prison. These schools offered courses toward a BA in Liberal Arts. I enrolled initially just to get out of my cell. Then, to my surprise, I began to enjoy the classes. As a matter of fact, it was during my first semester as a freshman that I learned of my aptitude for writing.

My first assignment in Creative Writing 101 was a short story. Since it was easier to write about something I knew, rather than try to make something up, I decided to write a brief autobiography.

As soon as I put pen to paper, thoughts and memories came together, and the words just flowed. And although we had one week to turn it in, I wrote the paper in one sitting and only one rewrite. I turned it in with a mixture of confidence and expectancy.

I had to wait an extra week for my paper to be graded and returned, but it was worth it. When I got my paper back, I was pleased to see an *A* at the top of the paper. Then, looking a little closer, I noticed a faint dot right next to the *A*. That aroused my curiosity.

"Are there any questions concerning the grades?" asked the professor.

"Yes," I said, raising my hand. "I notice that my paper has a *dot* next to my A."

"Ah yes," he said smiling, "the *dotted* A!"

It was clear that the rest of the class was interested, so the professor proceeded to explain.

"In all my years of grading papers," he began, "I have never graded higher than an A." He looked at me with a piercing gaze. "But I was so impressed with your paper, Mr. Harris, that I *started* to put a plus sign next to your A but then had to catch myself. So, you see, the dot is simply the beginning of a plus sign."

As the class listened to his accolades, I could feel myself swelling with pride. I was honored that my writing had moved him to that extent, and at that moment I decided to concentrate on really learning the craft and developing my writing skills. As a matter of fact, it was his encouragement that day that motivated me to go on to write poetry, plays, and even a television documentary, produced by Public Broadcasting station WCNY-TV24, videotaped and televised from behind the walls of Auburn Prison—a documentary that would ultimately be my ticket out of prison—but again, I'm getting ahead of myself. That would be years down the road.

About six months into my schooling, I applied for school release. Under the conditions of that program, eligible inmates were permitted to leave the facility during the day, attend classes on campus, and return to the facility in the evening. Since my criminal history was nonviolent at the time with no escapes, attempted escapes, absconding, or bail jumping on my record, I was approved.

Albion Correctional Facility was the designated "school release facility" at the time, and I was transferred there in the spring of 1976. I was one of seven inmates leaving the facility each weekday to attend classes and the only one attending Rosary Hill College (now Damien College) in the Buffalo suburb of Amherst, New York. The six other school-release inmates were divided among Canisus College and Buffalo State University.

We were dropped off in downtown Buffalo each weekday morning in an unmarked prison van. We would then take public transportation to our respective campuses, returning to Albion by Greyhound bus at the end of the school day. It was our individual responsibility to get to the designated bus stop at the appointed time each evening in order to catch the departing Greyhound bus. Unlike the six inmates who were able to catch the bus at the downtown terminal, because my school was in the suburbs, I was the last pickup on the route. I had to wait at the corner of Bailey Avenue and Main Street for the bus to arrive—a distance of about five miles from the Rosary Hill campus. It was imperative that I make it to Bailey and Main on time. If I missed the bus back to Albion, I would be charged with absconding, and a warrant for my arrest would be issued. Needless to say, I certainly didn't want that. Therefore, I always made it a point to be at the Bailey and Main bus stop well ahead of the Greyhound's arrival. At least until the day I got sidetracked talking to some girls and watched in horror as the public bus pulled away from the curb in front of the school—the very same bus that would take me to Bailey and Main to catch the Greyhound!

I was in panic mode. All I could think of was being kicked out of the school release program and sent back to Attica. I had exactly fifteen minutes to reach Bailey and Main to catch the Greyhound back to Albion, and I didn't have a clue as to what to do. The two girls I had been talking with didn't have a car, and there was no time to try and locate someone with one. For a split second I thought of trying to flag down a passing car, but how realistic was that? I was in the "lily-white" suburb of Amherst, New York. Besides, even if I were able to get a car to stop for a total stranger, which wasn't very likely, I would have to waste precious time trying to explain the situation. And even then there was no guarantee that they would give me a ride. So resigning myself to my fate, I turned back toward the school's administration building, dreading the phone call I would now have to make to Albion Correctional Facility.

Suddenly, almost out of nowhere, a mail truck pulled quickly to the curb, and a young black postman jumped out. I watched as he went to the corner mailbox, opened it, and began shoveling mail into a large canvas bag. *Maybe*, I thought, *just maybe*.

"Excuse me, *brother*," I said excitedly, trying to make a racial connection. "I need to get to Bailey Avenue with the *quickness!*"

Having absolutely no idea what I was talking about, he looked at me as if I had clearly lost my mind. I realized that I needed to explain myself—*fast!*

"I'm on a school-release program from Albion Correctional Facility," I said. "If I miss my bus back to the facility, I'll be kicked out of school and returned to Attica to finish my time."

"I feel for you," he said, "but what are you asking *me* to do?"

I took a deep breath. "I need you to give me a ride to my bus stop."

"In my *mail* truck?" he shouted.

I nodded my head.

"Absolutely not!" he continued. "I'll lose my job if I let you ride in my truck."

"Well, how about if I ride on the *outside?*" I offered as a solution.

Clearly, that suggestion was so preposterous that it rendered him speechless. However, to this day, I don't know if it was the tears in my eyes, my pleading, or a combination of both, because he reluctantly agreed to let me ride on the outside of the mail truck.

Holding on for dear life, I hopped onto the truck's running board, and he took off toward Bailey and Main. I can only imagine what the pedestrians and drivers were thinking as the mail truck sped down the street with me clutching the open window with one hand and holding a stack of books in the other. The trip seemed to take forever, but when we finally approached the intersection of Bailey and Main Street, I never beheld a more beautiful sight. The Greyhound bus was just turning the corner toward the bus stop.

I thanked the mailman profusely, then hopped off the truck and bolted up the stairs of the bus. When I told the guys on the bus my story, they shook their heads in disbelief, and we all had a good laugh. I was careful, however, to never play it that close again. From that day on, I was always ahead of schedule, even if I had to leave class a little early.

Oh yeah, I almost forgot. After such a close call, I wasn't taking any more chances. Since then I only dated girls with cars.

CHAPTER TWENTY

I was paroled from Albion to the Rosary Hill campus in the summer of 1976. I had just received my grades from the previous semester and was pleased to learn that I had achieved a 4.0 grade-point average. Unfortunately, now that I was on parole and did not have to return to Albion each evening, my focus began to shift.

The girls on campus were so plentiful it was like shopping at the mall. They would throw themselves at me, and I loved the attention—what guy wouldn't? I began to party hard and strong, trying to make up for lost time. And that, of course, meant returning to alcohol and drugs.

There were other parolees on campus besides me. One of them, a white guy named Chuck, had served time at Attica with me. I saw him at campus parties from time to time but never really hung out with him. That's why I was surprised when he came to my room one afternoon, clearly excited and out of breath. After calming him down, I asked what was up. He said that he had just broken into the safe in the business office and wanted to know if I would act as his lookout. I visualized the safe sitting there wide open and wondered why Chuck needed me. After opening the safe, why didn't he simply take the money and leave? I decided to see for myself what he was talking about.

The business office was closed for the day, and the hallway was devoid of students and faculty. Chuck and I entered the office, and he showed me the safe. When I saw that it had not been opened as he had said, I turned angrily on him. I certainly was not in the mood for any games, especially the kind that could send me back to jail.

"Why'd you lie to me, man?" I said through clenched teeth.

"'Bout what?" he asked.

"About having the safe already open," I whispered.

"I never said I had it opened," he whispered back. "I said I broke into the office and needed you to be a lookout while I opened the safe."

We certainly couldn't stand there all day arguing back and forth, so I asked if he even knew how to crack a safe. He said he could open it with one of the acetylene torches from the maintenance building. I told him I would stay there while he went to get one but he needed to hurry.

He returned in about ten minutes with an acetylene torch and immediately went to work on the safe. I kept lookout in the hallway but peered in on him every now and then, just to see if he knew what he was doing. He did.

In a matter of minutes, Chuck stuck his head out of the door and gave me a thumbs-up. He had the safe open! I wanted to see it for myself, so I asked him to change places with me while I went inside the office. To my surprise, he agreed.

I dashed inside the office, quickly removing cash and other valuables from the safe. I stuffed a bunch of cash into my underwear—all large bills—and removed a rare coin collection along with a metal cashbox. All in all, it took about five minutes to clean out the safe.

Chuck and I rushed back to my room. I quickly closed the door and spread everything out on the bed—everything, that is, except the money I had stashed in my underwear. Chuck was not interested in the coin collection; he just wanted to know how much money was in the cashbox. It came to a little over three thousand dollars, and we split it down the middle. Chuck watched as I stuck the coin collection into a duffel bag. He was completely satisfied with the fifteen hundred dollars he now had in his pocket. I was anxious to get rid of him now so that I could count the money in my underwear. I started packing my bags.

"What are you doing'?" he asked.

"What's it look like? I'm getting outta here," I replied.

"Why?"

"Think about it, man. We're both on parole. Who do you think the main suspects are going to be?"

He gave that some thought, then nodded and headed for the door.

"I'll be back," he said, making his exit. "I'm gonna pack too."

"Hurry up, man," I said, closing the door behind him.

As soon as he was gone, I removed the money from my underwear and was shocked to find that I had a little over twenty-five thousand dollars! Now there was no doubt that I was leaving. I was just sorry I told Chuck to hurry back. I felt that way for two reasons. First, I didn't want him finding out about the money I had stashed. Second, a white guy and a black guy traveling together would draw undesirable attention. Still, I didn't know how I was going to get rid of him.

"Where are we going?" Chuck asked, returning to my room with his bags packed.

"Harlem," I said with conviction, figuring that would give him room for pause. No such luck.

"Well, as long as I'm with you, I should be okay, right?" he asked.

"I can't guarantee anything, Chuck," I replied, still trying to get him to change his mind.

"I'll take my chances," he said, then waited for me to finish packing.

That settled it then. We flew from Buffalo to New York City that same afternoon.

My parents had moved from 141st and Amsterdam to 150th Street between Amsterdam and Broadway. When I introduced Chuck to my parents, they looked at me suspiciously. My mother even came straight out and asked what in the world I had done now. I told her that I hadn't done anything. I was on a school break and just wanted to see the family. Rather than come right out and say she didn't believe me, my mother just gave me *the look*. I decided then and there to cut my visit short.

After shopping for some new clothes, Chuck and I boarded a train at Pennsylvania Station for Albany, New York. Fortunately, we were able to purchase fake identification as soon as we arrived, because we were stopped and questioned by Albany detectives shortly after. They said they stopped us because we were acting suspiciously as we checked our bags into the train station lockers.

The check on our phony IDs came back clean, and we were allowed to go on our way. As far as I was concerned, however, that was too close of a call. So with Chuck in tow, I headed immediately for the airport and caught a direct flight to San Diego, California. There was really no thought behind that particular destination. It was simply the next flight out, so that's what we took.

We didn't really find San Diego to our liking, so we only stayed a couple of days before heading by Greyhound to Los Angeles. En route, I almost panicked when the bus pulled onto the marine base at Camp Pendleton. The military police boarded the bus, checking for illegal aliens from Mexico, but I assumed they were looking for Chuck and me. I had completely forgotten that San Diego and Mexico were so close to one another. With my Hispanic features, my biggest worry was that I would be mistaken by the military police for a Mexican. Much to my relief, one of the MPs simply *asked* if I was an American citizen, and I told him that I was. Finally, after checking a few more passengers, the bus was allowed to continue on its way. My sigh of relief was audible, causing Chuck to smile, as the bus pulled off the base. *Another close call*, I thought as I settled back in my seat. I wondered how long my luck would hold out.

Los Angeles was not what I expected at all. The police presence in the downtown area was so heavy that Chuck and I spent almost an entire week in our hotel rooms without coming out. What made us paranoid was that the police were stopping people at random, asking for identification. Chuck and I knew that we couldn't stand an intensive identity check, so we simply stayed off the street, but that created another problem—at least for me.

Chuck's money was beginning to run drastically low. At my insistence, we had taken separate rooms, and now he was beginning to feel the financial strain. Of course, my funds were holding up nicely, but he didn't know that. In all honesty, I wanted Chuck's financial situation to deteriorate to the point that he would have to head out on his own. I wanted to be rid of him so that I could freely spend the extra money I had.

Chuck's money finally ran out, and he asked me to give him enough to take the bus back to New York. I was more than happy to. It wasn't just the money either. I also realized that it wouldn't be long before we started raising some eyebrows simply by being together. So again, I was more than happy to pay Chuck's fare back to New York.

CHAPTER TWENTY-ONE

About a week after Chuck's departure, I returned to New York myself. I had grown tired of having to stay in my hotel room, tired of eating in, tired of not being able to socialize—in other words, tired of being on the run.

I was hiding out at my sister Retie's house in Binghamton, along with her three children, Robin, Jacquetta, and Rasheim. I knew that there was a parole warrant out for me, so I figured it was just a matter of time before I was taken into custody. Not once did I consider simply turning myself in. That would have been the best decision I could have made, but then that's what the benefit of hindsight does for you. Instead, needing to feed my growing drug habit, I returned to a life of crime.

Somewhere between hiding out and my criminal activity, I met a girl named Susan Williams. I saw her from across the room in a dimly lit nightclub and couldn't take my eyes off her. I introduced myself and then asked her to dance. She declined. Instead, we just sat at a table in the corner of the room and talked. The chemistry between us was so strong that we made love that very night. We were together every day from that point on, and I even took her to New York City to meet my parents. Those trips became quite frequent—especially since drugs were cheaper in the city—until I was arrested one evening during a Greyhound stop in Scranton, Pennsylvania.

Sue and I were sitting in the bus terminal around one in the morning, and I began to get restless. I needed to stretch my legs, so I stepped outside for just a moment. That was the last that Sue saw of me that night.

Exiting the terminal, I saw a large office building across the street. Figuring I could use some extra money when I got to the city, I went directly to the rear of the building, looking for a way inside, and discovered an unlocked door. I looked around to make sure I wasn't being watched and entered the building.

Once inside I took the stairs to the second floor, where I came upon a row of locked offices. Each of the office doors had small windows in the center, so I was able to look directly inside. One office had a number of desks with IBM electric typewriters on top of them. I quickly removed my jacket, wrapped it around my arm, and used my elbow to break the window on the door. I then reached in, opened the door, and headed for the closest typewriter. I unplugged it as silently as possible, picked it up, and walked out of the office with it under my arm.

Heading back downstairs, I somehow missed the landing on the main floor from which I had entered. I continued down to the basement, where there was an unfamiliar door at the end of a long hallway. I figured the door would probably lead outside, so I moved quickly toward it.

Yanking the door open, I received the shock of my life—I was looking at a room full of cops! I didn't find out until it was too late that the office building I had chosen to break in to contained a police station as well. I stood frozen in the doorway, unable to believe what I was seeing. All eyes were on me.

I backed slowly out of the door as one of the cops shouted, "Hold it right there!" I dropped the typewriter, bolted toward the staircase, and ran back to the main floor exit with the police in hot pursuit. I crashed through the door at full speed, looking back over my shoulder to see how close the cops were. They were gaining on me, so I attempted to run even faster. The next thing I knew—*WHAM!* I ran headfirst into an iron lamppost on the side of the walkway. Everything went black. When I regained consciousness, I had been handcuffed, searched, and hauled back inside by a bunch of angry Scranton police officers.

I had the presence of mind, though, to think of Sue waiting across the street in the bus terminal. I used my one phone call to have her paged. When she came to the phone, I told her that I was under arrest without going into detail. I had given the cops the alias "Joseph Phillips" and whispered that she should use that name when inquiring about me. I told her that I would be in court in the morning. I could hear the anger in her voice, but she assured me that she would be there.

My only worry after talking with Sue was whether or not I would get away with the alias I had given to the booking officer. My fingerprints would be checked through the FBI database, and since no two sets of prints are the same, it is almost impossible to escape detection. Only through the rarest of errors does a mistake occur. So when my fingerprints came back clean, I was in total shock. Even more important was the fact that, according to the information provided by the fingerprint check, "Joseph Phillips" did not have a criminal record. My alias was going to stand up.

That mistake helped immensely when I appeared in court the next morning. I was looked upon as a first-time offender, so the judge gave me a one-hundred-dollar cash bail. Sue had to return to Binghamton in order to get the money together, assuring me that she would be back to bail me out. I told her to hurry because if my real identity were found out, a parole warrant would be lodged against me, and then she wouldn't be able to get me out. I would be headed back to prison in New York State.

My worries were unfounded, however, because Sue was back in two days with the bail money. After being given a date to appear in court, I was released and headed back to Binghamton. Needless to say, I never returned to Scranton for my court appearance.

As 1976 drew to a close, I was still a fugitive. Sue and I were staying in my sister Lou Lou's apartment, directly above where my sister Retie lived. Although a Binghamton parole officer came to Retie's house looking for me from time to time, he never looked for me at Lou Lou's apartment.

My financial status was shaky. The little money I was getting from the occasional burglary was gone as soon as I got it, so I decided to take my criminal activities to the next level. I found a starter's pistol during an earlier burglary and was amazed at how much it resembled an actual gun. Now I was ready to use it and make some real money.

I needed a partner in crime, someone I could depend on if things got shaky during a robbery, so Sue and I went to New York City to pick up my youngest brother, Marvin. Sue would be meeting Marvin for the first time, and that was the pretense on which I had brought her with me to the city. She had no idea that I had a gun or that I had come to ask Marvin to get down with me on some robberies.

Marvin wasn't home when we arrived, but as soon as he walked through the door, I introduced him to Sue. "I need to talk with you in private, Marv," I said.

"All right," he said. "Let's go into my bedroom."

Once in his bedroom, I showed him the starter's pistol. "I want you to come back to Binghamton with me," I said, brandishing the fake gun. "We can do some robberies and get some money."

"I'm with that," Marvin said, "but we need money for our bus tickets."

"That's easy," I said, waving the starter's pistol, "we can do a quick robbery here."

As we exited the bedroom, Sue looked at me questioningly.

"Wait here," I said to her. "We'll be right back."

Marvin and I headed to a Puerto Rican bodega a few blocks away. We walked in without hesitation, pleased to find it free of customers. It was early evening, and there were just two store clerks—a man and a woman.

"All right," I yelled, pulling the starter's pistol out. "This is a stick up!"

As I went through the man's pockets, relieving him of a large wad of money, Marvin went behind the counter and emptied out the cash register. We were back out on the sidewalk in a matter of minutes, running back to our parents' apartment.

We stopped just inside the building, counted the money, and split everything down the middle. We had a little over two hundred dollars each—not much, as far as I was concerned, but Marvin was grinning from ear to ear. I told him to get a taxi while I went upstairs to get Sue. We had to get back to Binghamton—fast!

When Sue and I exited the building, Marvin was already inside of the taxi. I told the driver to take us to the Port Authority bus terminal. He headed down to Broadway, passing the store we had just robbed, which was now swarming with cops. Marvin and I ducked down as the taxi made its way slowly past, not taking any chances on being spotted. Sue looked at us curiously but didn't say anything. We made it safely to the bus terminal and were back in Binghamton a few hours later.

Our money didn't last long, however, so we robbed a convenience store on the north side of Binghamton about a week later. As soon as I told Marvin that the robbery would be in the newspaper and on the television news, he headed back to New York City that same evening. I, however, was picked up the next day in a downtown Binghamton bar and taken in for questioning.

I had foolishly robbed the store sporting a huge Afro hairstyle and failed to change my appearance after the robbery. How crazy was that? My Afro was the first thing the robbery victim described. And with Binghamton being such a small town with almost no one with the size Afro I had, I might as well have gone to the police station and turned myself in.

Sue and I were on our way to the Greyhound bus station when I was arrested. She had no idea that I had committed a robbery the previous evening and wanted to stop at a Main Street bar to play a quick game of foosball. I didn't want to arouse her suspicions, so I agreed to it. As fate would have it, however, a cop in a patrol car spotted me as I entered the bar. In a matter of minutes, Binghamton police detectives had me surrounded.

"A grocery store on Robinson Avenue was robbed last night," one of the detectives said.

"I don't know *nothin'* about no robbery," I replied.

"Well, that's quite an Afro you got there," said another detective. "One of the robbers had one just like that."

I kept silent.

"We need you to come to the station with us," the first detective said.

"Am I under arrest?"

"No, but you can be *placed* under arrest—if that's what you want."

It didn't take a rocket scientist to see that, either way, I was going to the police station for further questioning whether I wanted to or not.

Sue followed me out to a waiting unmarked police car. "What's this all about?" she asked.

"Don't worry, baby," I said in an attempt to reassure her. "This is just some kind of mistake. I'll meet you back at Retie's house in an hour, okay?"

She nodded her head as I gave her a quick kiss. I was then placed inside the police car, and we headed for the police station.

I was taken to an interrogation room at the police station and was joined almost immediately by two detectives. They began to question me in depth about the convenience store robbery. I was tired but continued to deny any knowledge of the crime. I was tired of everything—tired of being on the run, tired of how my life was going, and tired of how I was living. Oddly enough, at that moment, I wanted to confess and get it all over with. So I did. It took the detectives completely by surprise.

My statement was recorded and then typed up for my signature. I not only signed the confession but also told them that my real name was Theodore Harris. I knew they would find that out anyway once my fingerprints came back, but I wanted to exhibit at least the *spirit* of cooperation. After all, in a bid for leniency, every little bit helps.

Apparently, as far as Broome County district attorney, Patrick Monserrate, was concerned, I didn't *help* enough. Angry that I would not identify the other robbery suspect, he offered me ten to twenty years as a plea bargain. That meant that, if I accepted it, I would have to serve a minimum of ten years before I would be eligible for parole consideration—no guarantee, mind you, just *consideration*. If denied parole, however, the maximum term of my incarceration would be twenty years! (Actually, with time off for good behavior, it would come to sixteen years and eight months, but still too close to twenty years for my liking.) If convicted of the first-degree robbery charge at trial, I knew that the most I could receive would be twelve and a half to twenty-five years, by law. So by simply reducing my minimum time by two and a half years and my maximum by five years, the district attorney wasn't giving me much of a break. The way I saw it, after doing ten years straight, two and a half years more would be a piece of cake. Still, he was adamant about not going any lower unless I gave up my partner in the robbery. On that subject, however, I was adamant—there was no way I was going to give up my brother. So I rejected his offer right there on the spot. As far as I was concerned, there was nothing more to talk about.

Thankfully, when arraigned on the robbery indictment, I stood before a judge who also failed to see the incentive in the district attorney's plea offer. Wanting to avoid a costly and totally unnecessary trial, the judge leaned over the bench and asked if I would be willing to take seven and a half to fifteen years. Although the district attorney was clearly upset by the judge's plea offer, there was nothing he could do about it. I definitely could not afford to go to trial—especially after *confessing* to the crime—so I quickly agreed to the judge's offer. After all, I didn't want to press my luck.

A few weeks later, with Sue and Retie in court on my behalf, I was sentenced to seven and a half to fifteen years in prison. The sentencing was over in a matter of minutes. Sue and Retie gave me an encouraging smile. I managed a brief nod and a smile of my own as the court officers led me from the courtroom. *Here I go again*, I thought as tears welled up in my eyes.

CHAPTER TWENTY-TWO

I went to Attica for the third time in my life in February 1977. Although it was a new year, it was hardly a cause for celebration. Rather than a fresh start or a change for the better, the reality was that it was more like déjà vu.

Two months later, I was transferred to Auburn Correctional Facility. At that time, if an inmate truly wanted to better himself, Auburn was the place to be. The emphasis at Auburn was on education and rehabilitation rather than punishment. So when I arrived there in April, I was determined to use my time wisely— to let time serve me rather than the other way around.

I was still interested in writing, so my first few years at Auburn were devoted to correspondence courses from the Writers' Institute of America. I learned how to write commercials, as well as how to write and develop scripts for radio, television, and screen. My instructors were encouraging but also demanding. They wouldn't settle for anything less than my best effort. I am grateful for that, because I learned a lot as a result. Little did I realize that I was sowing the seeds for my parole board appearance seven and a half years away.

Auburn also had a fantastic music program with top-notch singers and musicians. The prison band would play before the weekly movie started, and some of the better singing groups in the facility would get an opportunity to showcase their talents. As the inmate population filed into the auditorium, the show would already be in progress. Fifteen or twenty minutes after everyone was seated, a rapid flicker of the lights would signal the start of the movie. Once that happened, I don't care how good the singers were, they moved quickly off the stage.

I witnessed quite a few groups attempt to finish their song at the start of the movie, only to be heckled and jeered off the stage. It never failed to amaze me how fast the band and singers removed their equipment from the stage and took their respective seats in the audience. They had that down to a science.

The prison yard had an abundance of singing groups, so it wasn't hard to find good entertainment. Some groups were better than others, with those groups drawing the biggest crowd. I sang with the better groups at Auburn, harmonizing with such fantastic voices as "Heavy" from Buffalo; Charlie Hall and Danny Singletary from Rochester; and Ray "Shakim" Barnes, "Black Bucky," and Julius "Ju-Boy" Walker from New York City. Whenever we came together to sing, that particular section of the yard would be packed.

Auburn also had many talented musicians, like lead guitarist Henry McNeil and drummer Charlie Hall. And the band's horn section, under the direction of civilian music instructor Jim Vicarro, was absolutely out of this world. I had the distinct privilege of serving as master of ceremonies for the prison's musical shows—a position that gave me the opportunity to showcase my talent as a solo singer. I was able to tailor my vocals around the band with such selections as "You'll Never Find" and "Lady Love," both by Lou Rawls. I was also writing quite a bit of poetry at the time and would recite some of my work at the family day events. Sue and I were still together, and she would come to visit every chance she got. I would let her know well in advance of the upcoming family events, and she would attend, if able. However, there was one family event she was unable to attend, and our relationship was shattered because of it.

Renice Major lived in the town of Auburn. She was the guest of an inmate named Elijah Tillery, but everyone called him "Powerful." Ronnie Agee—also from the town of Auburn—introduced him to her when she came to the event with Ronnie's girlfriend, Kat. Renice and I made eye contact as I was reciting my poem, "Tribute to a Black Woman." I saw her smiling and nodding her head at me, but I didn't think anything of it at the time. I just thought she was "feeling" the poem and was hoping she could fix me up with one of her girlfriends. Besides, I didn't want Powerful to think I was flirting with her, so I was careful to limit my glances in her direction.

Elijah Tillery bore a remarkable resemblance to Muhammad Ali. As a matter of fact, just before his arrest, he was cast to play the legendary boxer in the movie *The Greatest*. Not only was Powerful an accomplished boxer, he was an imposing figure in top physical shape. If not in the gym working out, he would be in the yard doing roadwork for hours on end. We knew one another casually and had a measure of respect for one another, but that's as far as our relationship went. One thing was for sure, I definitely didn't want any problems with him over a girl—or anything else for that matter.

I could tell that Renice was impressed with my poem. That was fine with me because, as already stated, I was hoping she would hook me up with one of her girlfriends, and I wanted her to be able to say good things about me.

At the end of the event, as the guests were leaving, I called Powerful over. I handed him a slip of paper with my name and identification number on it. With Renice standing off to the side, I asked him to see if she had a friend I could correspond with. He glanced at the paper, nodded his head, and said he would do that for me. I thanked him, smiled at her, then turned and walked away.

Two days later, I received a letter with an Auburn return address. *Wow*, I thought, *that was fast!* I couldn't wait to let Powerful know that his girl came through for me—that is until I opened the letter. The letter began: "It has come to my attention that you are looking for a friend. Well, allow me to introduce you to your newfound friend!" Renice went on to say that she was attracted to me as soon as we made eye contact. She also told me that Powerful was not her boyfriend and that she had just met him for the first time at the event. She made it crystal clear that she was interested in getting to know me better. She ended the letter saying that she couldn't wait to see me again and that she would visit me that weekend. My immediate concern, however, was how Powerful was going to take the news. Not for a moment did I consider *not* telling him. I had to give him that courtesy. I just wasn't looking forward to it.

Powerful was very emotional, and that made him dangerous. I really didn't know what to expect when I handed over the letter that evening in the gym. I watched closely as he read the letter in silence, praying that he didn't flip out on me.

"It looks like she chose *you*, Theo," he said, somberly handing the letter back.

I was still on my guard, but it looked as if he was taking the situation like a man. I really didn't know what to say. "I didn't mean for this to happen, man."

"Well, I respect you for coming to me like a man," he replied, offering me his hand.

I shook his outstretched hand. "Thanks, Powerful, I appreciate that."

He nodded his head and returned to his workout. As I made my exit, I was both relieved and excited. I couldn't help but smile, excited at the thought of seeing Renice that weekend. I ran down the stairs, making my way out into the yard.

I told Renice about Sue on our very first visit. She asked if I was willing to give Sue up for her, and I told her that I was. At the time, I hadn't seen Sue in a couple of months, so it was easy to give all of my attention to Renice.

She spoiled me right from the start, visiting me as much as three times a week, and she even brought her mother and stepfather to meet me. Her stepfather, Jimmy Smith, sang tenor for the gospel group The Bells of Harmony, and they sang at our prison church services from time to time. Since I too was singing with a gospel group at the time, Jimmy and I hit it off right away.

Renice's mother, Velma Smith, had a wonderful sense of humor. She kept me laughing from the beginning to the end of our visit. I could tell that she liked me as a person and possible son-in-law, and our relationship grew stronger with each visit. Velma even came to see me alone from time to time, and I was always happy to see her. She made me feel like I was part of the family, causing my feelings for Renice to grow even stronger. Then one day, without warning, Sue showed up.

Renice and I were hugging and kissing at a table in the back of the visiting room when I looked over her shoulder and saw Sue approaching the visiting room officer's desk. I told Renice that Sue had just walked in, and we were both fairly calm about it. I felt that it would be best to talk with Sue alone. I asked Renice to go the ladies' room, and she did. Sue saw me sitting alone at the back table and smiled as she made her way toward me. My smile, on the other hand, was strained, causing her to sense that something wasn't right. I decided to give it to her straight—no chaser.

"Listen, Sue," I began hesitantly. "You need to know that I met a girl who lives here in the town and that it's pretty serious."

Sue stopped dead in her tracks. It was if I had slapped her across the face. I needed to continue as quickly as possible.

"Her name is Renice."

"Is she here?" Sue said finally.

"Yes, she went to the ladies' room so that you and I could talk alone."

"Well, I want to talk with *her*." Sue turned toward the ladies room.

"Sue," I started as she placed her hand on my arm reassuringly. "I only want to *talk*, Theo," she said. "Nothing more."

I looked had her closely and saw that she was being truthful. I nodded my approval, following her with my eyes as she made her way to the ladies room.

After what seemed like hours, Renice and Sue emerged from the bathroom. Renice came back to the table, while Sue headed for the visiting room exit, waving in my direction and blowing me a kiss. That was the last time I ever saw her.

"That woman really loves you, Theo," Renice said as she sat back down. I asked what made her say that. "Because," Renice continued, "after we had our woman-to-woman talk, she told me that you were her baby and to make sure that I take good care of you." I sat there completely stunned. It was then that I realized just how much Sue loved me. I stared at Renice, hoping that I had not made a mistake.

Two years later, Renice stopped visiting and writing all together. At the time, I had five years to go before parole consideration, and it was simply too long for her to wait.

So there I was, without Renice and without Sue. Although my gamble didn't pay off, I wasn't going to let it get me down. After all, I had no one to blame but myself. I could either dwell on the past or focus on the future. I chose the latter.

The president of the prison's NAACP chapter, James "Checkmate" Wenstley, told me that if I ran for the position of branch secretary, he could assure me that I would get it. The last thing I wanted to do was get involved in prison politics, so I politely declined. However, after pointing out that the position would look good on my record, as well as at the parole board, I decided to reconsider. And just as Checkmate predicted, with him as my campaign manager, I won easily.

The national office of the NAACP chartered Auburn prison's chapter under the name of the Inner-City Branch. Executive board meetings were held in the school building. As branch secretary, my job was to take minutes and work closely with the president. I performed my duties well, earning the respect of the executive committee, and was asked to run for branch president a year later. Since I had recently enrolled in the Syracuse University college program, I was hesitant. I was bogged down with schoolwork and didn't think I could give my all to the position, but again, Checkmate reminded me how it would look at the parole board. So I ran and won the election by a landslide.

Besides the Inner-City Branch NAACP, the United States Jaycees had a chapter at Auburn prison called the Logan Jaycees. At the time of my presidency, the Logan Jaycees had drafted a *Good Time* proposal intended for the state legislature in Albany. The proposal was designed to persuade state lawmakers to change New York's archaic system of good time credit. The proposal asked them to look at the benefits of offering time off for good behavior from the minimum, rather than the maximum, portion of an inmate's sentence.

Under the system of good time at the time, there was no incentive for inmates to better themselves. All they had to do was refrain from being a disciplinary problem and the good time was credited to them automatically. The Jaycees' proposal for time off the minimum would assure an inmate's participation in educational, vocational, and self-help programs, simply because it would be the only way they could get the good time credit. It was a good proposal, well researched and well written. The only problem was that it was too long, making for tiresome and boring reading. It needed to be brought to life so that the intended audience—the lawmakers and the taxpayers—could "see" the disparity of the present good time system for themselves. That task fell to me.

My friend and mentor, Manuel Ramirez, was chairman of the Logan Jaycees' Community Awareness committee. This committee was comprised of inmate leaders from every segment of the Auburn prison population. So as president of the prison's NAACP chapter, I was invited by Manuel to sit on the committee to assist in the good time efforts. It was he who requested that I take a look at the proposal and offer my feedback on it.

Even though he was serving a life sentence, Manuel had the respect of prison guards and inmates alike. He also had the unprecedented distinction of being the first and *only* inmate to attain the position of Jaycee International Senator. Manuel was sharp and had an uncanny knack for leadership and delegation. So when he brought the good time proposal to me, asking for my opinion, I was honored. I suggested to him that a television documentary based on the proposal would be the best way to spark the interest of the legislature, as well as the public.

Utilizing the format of a three-act play, I told him I would create believable characters representing each area of disparity in the present good time system. He liked the idea and told me to start working on the script.

I called the documentary *Good Time* and, for the next two weeks, worked right out of my cell. I was constantly writing and rewriting until I had what I thought was a workable script. Manuel and I locked on "Honor Company" and were just cells apart from one another. I gave the script to him upon completion, and he started reading it immediately. Although I tried to act nonchalant, it was clear that I was anxious for his response. Manuel smiled and said he would get back to me as soon as possible. I nodded my head and left him alone with the script.

As I stretched out on my bed with my arms behind my head, I thought about how far I had come since Manuel had taken me under his wing. He was really the one responsible for rescuing me from the traps and pitfalls of prison and got me to thinking about bettering myself. I don't know what he saw in me, but I am grateful he decided that I was worth his time and personal investment. Manual was observant enough to see that, during my first few years at Auburn, I was on the road to destruction.

The people I was hanging out with in my early years of incarceration were into gambling, drinking, and getting high. Although I was not doing hard drugs, I was drinking and gambling. I was playing chess for money and drinking on Saturday mornings in the prison barbershop with the guys—activities that resulted in two of my "hang out" partners becoming victims of contract hits. One was outright murdered; the other was assaulted to the point of death.

Moe was a janitor in the school building, and one of his jobs was to keep the barbershop clean. Since the best time to clean that area was on Saturday mornings, Moe would make a batch of wine and invite a few of us over to drink and keep him company.

On the Saturday in question, Moe had just made a batch of wine for Mack, a connoisseur of jailhouse "hooch," as prison wine was commonly called. Mack supplied all of the ingredients. Moe's job was to mix them and stash the wine while it fermented. In return, Mack would split the batch with Moe. Instead of keeping to the terms of the agreement, however, Moe got greedy. He kept the majority of the brew for himself and watered down the rest. Now, as I've already stated, Mack was a *connoisseur* of prison wine. Therefore, the plan was doomed from the start.

On that fateful Saturday morning, Moe was playing the big shot, passing around giant cups of wine to me, Checkmate, and a guy by the name of Stacks Edwards. Stacks, a master impressionist, had us rolling on the floor as Howard Cosell and Muhammad Ali. We all encouraged him to pursue a stand-up career upon his release; he was just that talented. Instead, a few months after being paroled, Stacks took part in the six-million-dollar airport robbery made famous in the movie *Goodfellas*. He wound up paying with his life for his participation—the victim of a mob hit.

On this day, though, we were all feeling the effects of the wine when Mack showed up in the barbershop doorway. I could sense that something wasn't quite right because Moe immediately became nervous. Mack said he wanted to taste Moe's "stash," and Moe said there wasn't any wine left. We knew that wasn't true because Moe had just poured us a round of drinks before Mack showed up. There was plenty left. Mack just stood there staring at Moe. Then, as abruptly as he had appeared, he turned and walked away. The mood wasn't the same after that. Each of us made excuses as to why we had to leave and quickly made our exit.

That afternoon, while relieving himself in the south yard bathroom, Moe was stabbed in the heart and was dead before he hit the floor. Checkmate and I were standing on the wall in the center yard when Moe was rushed out on a stretcher. We could see clearly that it was Moe, and that was my wake-up call. He had lost his life over a batch of jailhouse wine. I stopped drinking immediately after that.

I was still gambling on the chessboard, though, and was one of the best players in the prison. My regular opponent was Eddie "Mad Dog" Parker. Eddie was a professional hit man serving a life sentence. And as the nickname Mad Dog implies, he was extremely dangerous.

Eddie and I played chess every day, without fail. And since we were gambling, our games were intense, so we would usually have spectators around the table. In terms of "prison wages," the stakes were high—about five dollars a game. So since I couldn't really afford to lose, I read books on chess, studying the openings and defenses. Eddie, on the other hand, was well-off financially, so he played just to pass the time. That, however, didn't mean he was an easy mark. Quite the contrary, Eddie had a very good chess game—he just couldn't beat me consistently. As a result, every time his commissary day came around, he would drop off bags of groceries in front of my cell.

Ron "Rotten Ron" Davis, a wannabe chess player, was a regular spectator at our games. I had played him on a number of occasions, sociably, and found him to be a fair chess player. He certainly wasn't in the same league as Eddie and me. No one could tell him that, however. And thinking that he could play at our level was his first mistake. His second mistake, because he witnessed my large winnings, was thinking that Eddie was easy prey. It was that mistake that nearly cost him his life.

Eddie and I were playing chess in the school building one afternoon. Ron was there with his wine-drinking crew: "Hop," "Buzz," and Arnold Catten. They had a stash of brew somewhere in the building. After consuming the wine, they gathered around the table to watch Eddie and me play.

They entered the room just as I had won the first game and were setting up the pieces for the next one. Before the opening move on the second game was made, Ron asked Eddie if he wanted to play for a carton of cigarettes a game. Without looking up from the board, Eddie told Ron that he and I were already gambling. Normally, that would have been the end of it, but Ron had just consumed a large portion of wine and therefore couldn't leave well enough alone.

"I'll tell you what," he said to Eddie. "We'll play a series of ten games—a carton of cigarettes a game. If you win just *one* game, you've won *all ten* of them!"

Everyone in the room looked at Ron as if he had just lost his mind. Finally, Eddie himself broke the silence.

"You want to repeat that, Ron?" he asked.

And Ron did—word for foolish word.

Eddie asked me if I minded the interruption. He definitely wanted to take Ron up on his offer. I, of course, wanted to see this, along with everyone else in the room. It was definitely a fool's bet. Eddie only had to win *one* game to get paid for all *ten*. The psychological pressure on Ron was going to be tremendous. Arnold and Buzz tried to talk him out of it, but Ron was certain that he would win. Eddie won the first game with ease. And, just like that, Ron owed him ten cartons of cigarettes.

"Bet back," he said, trying to appear calm.

"Same bet?" Eddie inquired.

Ron nodded his head.

Eddie won the second game with the same ease as the first. Now Ron owed him twenty cartons of cigarettes, all within a matter of fifteen or twenty minutes. Ron asked to bet back once more. Eddie shook his head and told Ron that when he paid the twenty cartons, they could play again. Eddie set the pieces back up, and we resumed our competition.

Ron stared hard at Eddie, then, without another word, got up from the table and left the building.

Three months later, Ron was rushed to the "outside" hospital with both sides of his head bashed in. The attack was so vicious that his skull was the consistency of raw ground beef. The fact that he survived at all was a miracle in itself. Ron would remain in the "outside" hospital for almost another three months.

Word was that Ron attempted to pay Mad Dog on the "installment plan"—offering him five packs at a time of the two hundred that he owed. Eddie refused to accept the payments. Ron then told Eddie that either he accepted the installments or he wasn't going to get paid at all. Informed sources say that Eddie just stared at Ron and then left him standing in the middle of the yard, cigarettes in hand. No one was ever prosecuted for the assault, but it didn't take Sherlock Holmes to figure out who was behind it. It had no effect on our chess games, though. Right after the assault, Eddie and I resumed our chess matches as if nothing had happened.

I was so caught up in my "good thing" with Eddie Parker that I didn't recognize the inherent danger involved in gambling with a man who went by the name of Mad Dog. I mean, let's face it, I was gambling with a professional killer who was, at best, unpredictable and, at worst, psychotic. And on top of that, I was mixing gambling with drinking. So at some point, I might have ended up like Rotten Ron or even worse.

Again, I don't know why Manuel Ramirez decided to mentor me, but I thank God that he did. He molded me, shaped me, and pointed me in the right direction, but even though I was NAACP president at the time, I was not living up to my full potential. That's because I only agreed to run for president because it would look good on my record and might help when I came up for parole consideration. Also, the prestige that came with the position appealed to me, but my heart wasn't in it. All of that changed, however, when Manuel asked me to work with him and his Community Awareness Committee.

Manuel was very impressed with the *Good Time* script. He told me to start casting for it. I selected three of the four men the script called for from inside the Logan Jaycees. I picked Mike Massarin, Jimmy Harris, and Manuel himself. They would portray characters representing each segment of the prison population: the first time, nonviolent offender who makes his first parole board; the inmate who simply stays out of trouble and benefits from his good time credits; and the "lifer" who gets no good time at all because there is no end to a life sentence other than death. I would play a prison parole officer with each of these inmates on my caseload. We held weekly rehearsals in one of the school classrooms, polishing and tightening our roles.

Just before rehearsals began, I mailed a copy of the *Good Time* script to Richard Cowden, an executive producer at WCNY-TV24, a public broadcasting station in Liverpool, New York. Liverpool, a suburb of Syracuse, is only thirty-minutes from Auburn prison, so because of the station's location, I thought we had a good chance of getting media exposure. The cover letter explained exactly what we were trying to convey to the taxpayers via our proposed *Good Time* documentary and extended an invitation to attend one of our rehearsals. Richard Cowden, to my great surprise, accepted the invitation.

Rich—as he told us to call him—was impressed from the moment the action started. After watching the run-through of the script, he decided that he wanted to produce it. However, as written, the script ran just over thirty minutes, and that presented a problem in terms of programming. I was told that I would need to get the script down to something like twenty-eight minutes. Rich said he would return in one week to watch another performance—with a stopwatch.

Precisely *one* week later, the performance ran to the *exact* time specifications. Rich was so impressed with the rewrite that he decided to lengthen the documentary to one hour by including a panel of prison experts between each skit. This change proved to be a blessing in disguise.

The superintendent of Auburn was vehemently opposed to permitting a mobile television unit and crew inside the facility to videotape my script. Rich, however, came up with the idea of inviting then commissioner of corrections Thomas Coughlin to be a member of the panel, which proved to be a stroke of genius. I don't know what Rich told Commissioner Coughlin, but he accepted the invitation. Needless to say, we had no opposition from the superintendent after that.

Good Time aired statewide over most public broadcasting stations in the fall of 1981. The thrill of seeing my script brought to life and watching it on television, along with my fellow inmates, is difficult to articulate. Not only did the documentary appear on television, it was given wide coverage in newspapers across New York State as well. It was, quite frankly, a crowning achievement in my incarceration.

When I appeared in front of the parole board for the first time in February 1983, after serving seven and a half years, the parole commissioners were impressed with my apparent rehabilitation. So much so that two months later, I walked out of the front gates of Auburn Correctional Facility a free man, but unfortunately nothing had really changed. I had merely done what I needed to do in order to *get* out of prison, nothing to ensure that I would *stay* out.

CHAPTER TWENTY-THREE

The Upstate New York towns of Binghamton, Johnson City, and Endicott sit adjacent to one another, with Binghamton's Main Street running through Johnson City and into Endicott. The three towns together make up what is known as the "Triple Cities."

My stepfather passed away a few years before my release from Auburn. My mother was living by herself in Johnson City in an apartment just above my sister Retie. She permitted me to live with her until I could find a job and a place of my own. Although jobs were scarce in Binghamton, I was able to find part-time work with the Broome County Urban League as a volunteer. It wasn't long, however, before a part-time, paid position became available. The Urban League needed a recreational aide for their youth center, and I was hired immediately. After school, other aides and I would take the neighborhood kids to the park for structured play, roller-skating, bowling, and occasionally to an amusement park. I enjoyed working with the kids and was well liked by them as well as by my coworkers. So much so that when the administrative assistant to the president resigned her position, she and the rest of my coworkers recommended that I take her place.

I was called in for an interview by then Broom County Urban League president John Hall. I told him that I had just been released from prison after serving seven and a half years for armed robbery and was presently on parole. I also told him about my educational background, my communication and clerical skills, and my NAACP involvement. I told him that I had served as branch secretary and as its president. I also explained why that experience would make me an asset as his administrative assistant. I must have been convincing because I was hired without him interviewing another applicant. I couldn't believe it; I had only been out of prison a mere four months and was now administrative assistant to the president of the Broome County Urban League.

Both my coworkers and my family were happy for me. My first day on the job found me having lunch at the Broome County Rotary Club as the president's guest, rubbing shoulders with judges, lawyers, and businessmen—the "movers" and "shakers" of Broome County. Life was good, and I was looking forward to it getting even better.

A year prior to my release, my friend and mentor Manuel Ramirez had been granted clemency by then governor Hugh Carey. In recognition of his many achievements while in prison, Manuel was granted parole. He had served twelve years on a sentence of fifteen years to life. Everyone in the prison, the guards included, was happy for him. I was happy for him as well but was sorry to see him go. I owed him so much and wanted him to know how deeply grateful I was for his intervention in my life. Although he assured me that he would contact me when I got out, the prison grew a little dimmer for me the day that Manuel left.

Therefore, it was with great excitement that I received the news that he had called while I was at work. My mother gave me the phone number he left with her, and I returned his call immediately. Manuel answered the phone himself, and we had a long conversation, filling each other in on what was happening in our lives. He told me that he owned a company in the South Bronx, selling foreign language instruction tapes, and that he and his wife, Joann, were living in New Rochelle. I, in turn, told him about my position with the Urban League. He seemed pleased that I was doing so well in such a short period of time. He asked when I would be coming to New York City, and I told him that I was planning a visit with my brother Danny and his family that coming weekend. I gave him my brother's telephone number, and he said he would call me there.

That weekend was my first time seeing Danny and his family since my release from prison, and they made me feel very much at home. Although he and his son's mother were not legally married, I still considered Audrey my sister-in-law, and we were very close. I enjoyed every minute of my visit and was sorry when Monday came so quickly.

I had to report to my parole officer before his office closed at five that afternoon, so I got up early and took my time packing. During a wonderful breakfast of ham and eggs, Manuel called to apologize for not getting in touch with me sooner. He asked if we had time to get together for a couple of hours, and I told him yes. Since it was only around nine a.m. when Manuel called, I figured I would be able to catch my afternoon bus with time to spare. I gave him Danny's address, and he said he would be right over. I was really looking forward to seeing Manuel again.

He showed up about an hour later, and I introduced him to my family. Then I grabbed my bags and headed downstairs to his waiting Mercedes Benz. By reputation alone, I knew that Manuel was well connected and had access to literally millions of dollars in cash and narcotics. So not only was I honored just to be in his company, I was looking forward to being welcomed into his inner circle as well. After putting my bags into the trunk of the Mercedes, I climbed into the passenger seat, and off we went.

"Theo, you're not in a hurry, are you?" Manuel asked.

"Not really," I replied. "Why, what's up?"

"Well, I live in New Rochelle, but I need to have a suit altered at the store in Spanish Harlem, where I bought it."

"So let's do that," I said, settling back in the passenger's seat. "As long as I'm back in Binghamton before five, I'm good."

"Don't worry," he said. "I'll make sure you're back before five."

While at the store, Manuel bought me a couple of hundred dollars' worth of clothing items—things that I would need in my new position at the Urban League: dress shirts, slacks, ties, etc. I didn't ask him to do that; he just started going around the store, picking items out for me. And I accepted them gratefully.

When we arrived at his home in New Rochelle, he gave me the grand tour. Needless to say, I was impressed with how he was living, and that's when the "seed" was planted. I knew that whatever it took, I wanted to be a part of his lifestyle. We spent most of the day talking about our Auburn years.

"So what are your long-term plans, Theo?" Manuel asked.

"I would really like to work for *you*, man," I said without hesitation.

"Doing what?"

"It doesn't matter," I answered. "Whatever you can find."

"I'll keep you in mind," he said, smiling, "if something comes up."

As the day wore on, it was clear that I was worried about getting back to Binghamton in time to report to my parole officer. I had to catch my bus at the Port Authority terminal in midtown Manhattan, and we were all the way in New Rochelle. So since I only had about half an hour to catch the last bus that would get me there in time, it didn't look good for me at all, but when Manuel asked if there was an airport in Binghamton, I just stared at him and nodded my head. No problem then, he told me. He would arrange for me to fly back to Binghamton. With that statement, any hesitation I might have had about leaving my new job and joining Manuel quickly evaporated. I was hooked—it was as simple as that.

On the way to the airport, we made a stop at one of his "safe" houses, where he gave me an ounce of pure cocaine. He told me that I could do whatever I wanted with it, that it was a gift. I thanked him and stashed the package in one of my bags. We then made our way to the airport, where I caught a charter plane. In a little under half an hour, I was back in Binghamton and able to report to my parole officer with time to spare.

Because I needed the money, I sold the majority of the cocaine Manuel gave me for two thousand dollars. I then shared the rest with my coworkers and friends. Two weeks later, Manuel called me at my Urban League office and offered me a job as a publicist with his South Bronx Company. I accepted without hesitation.

By Thanksgiving of 1983, Manuel was giving me a tour of the company and introducing me to the other workers. After the tour, he surprised me by taking me to his office, where Richard "Jabbar" Taylor, a friend of ours from Auburn prison, was waiting for us. Jabbar, or "Brother Rich," as he was more commonly known, was head of the Muslim security squad in charge of protecting the civilian hostages during the 1971 Attica riot.

Shortly after the prison was retaken, Brother Rich was transferred to Auburn. A short, stocky, muscle-bound man serving a life sentence for murder, he served as security for the prison's Muslim community, and I met him through Manuel during my tenure as NAACP president.

Now here we all were on the outside—Manuel, Brother Rich, and me—each of us on parole and each of us already in violation of our parole terms simply by being in one another's company. At the time, however, that was the furthest thing from my mind. Happy to see one another, Brother Rich and I embraced warmly, and the three of us were inseparable from that point on. Wherever Manuel went, Brother Rich went as well—as his bodyguard.

Manuel had secured an apartment for me in the Kingsbridge section of the Bronx, but because it was being renovated, I was not able to immediately move in. Until then, I stayed at the "safe" house, where I was surrounded by kilos of cocaine and heroin. Needless to say, the temptation was unbearable. The cocaine appealed to me more than the heroin and was so abundant that I felt like a kid in a candy store—with unlimited credit. I was using heavily in almost no time at all.

I was so caught up in my cocaine use that I didn't even make my arrival report to the Bronx parole office as required when a parolee is transferred from one county to another—a definite no-no. By then, however, I was using so much cocaine that I couldn't even think straight. Seeing my new parole officer, therefore, was the furthest thing from my mind.

Surrounded by all those drugs, I decided to send for a girl I had been getting high with in Binghamton before I left. She was an Italian girl named Peggy, and I called her from a pay phone. She told me that she would take the next bus out and asked me to meet her at the Port Authority bus terminal. I assured her that I would be there and went back to the "safe" house to wait.

I was also involved with a woman from the Dominican Republic at the time named Monica, who worked at SUNY-Binghamton as a secretary. She and I met at a dance at the university and were immediately attracted to one another. Monica was married with three children but separated from her husband. She told me that he was abusive to her and that she was in the process of filing for divorce.

My mother fell in love with Monica the moment she met her. My sisters took to her as well, urging me not to let her get away. I was glad that my family liked Monica, because after just a few short months of dating, I found myself falling in love with her. I told her about my relationship with Manuel and was eager for him to meet her as well. I didn't tell her, however, that I was planning on moving down to the South Bronx to work for him. I decided to save that information for later.

I arranged for Monica and me to spend a weekend with Manuel and Joanne at their home in New Rochelle, and of course Manuel gave her the royal treatment. I could tell that she was very much impressed with his lifestyle, but I sensed also that she was curious as to how he was able to maintain it. That too was information I decided to save for later.

Manuel surprised us by taking us to the home of the Latin recording star Joe Quijano. Monica, a big fan, had some of his records at home but had absolutely no idea that she would meet him, much less have dinner with him and his family. Joe Quijano, to my pleasant surprise, was the perfect host, introducing us to his lovely wife, Grace, and their two children. He proudly showed us advertisement clippings from the New York *Daily News* of his young son and daughter modeling clothes for Macy's department store.

Grace prepared a delicious dinner, with Monica helping in the kitchen, and we all sat down to eat. Then after dessert, we retired to the living room to relax. Manuel asked if I would sing, and Joe, to my surprise, accompanied me on flute and backup vocals. I don't remember what I sang, but everyone enjoyed it—so much so that Joe asked if I wanted to do something with him on his next album! I said that I would be honored, and he told me that he would be in touch. He then presented Monica with a few of his albums and autographed them at her request. As we prepared to leave, we thanked the Quijanos for their hospitality. Manuel gave them a hug, and we said our good-byes, with Monica clutching the albums tightly.

After a much-needed night's rest, we headed back to Binghamton the following morning. During the drive back, I told Monica that I was planning on working for Manuel at his company in the South Bronx. She never came right out and asked what else Manuel was involved in, but I'm sure she knew. After all, it didn't take Sherlock Holmes to figure out where his money was coming from. She tried talking me out of leaving the Urban League, telling me that New York City was not the best place for someone with my history. I remained quiet, knowing she was right but not wanting to admit it. As usual, that was another bad decision I would come to regret.

CHAPTER TWENTY-FOUR

When Peggy's bus pulled into Port Authority, I was right there at the gate to meet her. As soon as we arrived at the safe house, we got right down to business—drugs and sex. When she saw the amount of drugs in the apartment, she completely forgot about her classes at SUNY-Binghamton—Peggy was with me to stay.

When my Kingsbridge apartment was ready, Peggy moved in with me. We continued our heavy cocaine use, sniffing it at first and then graduating to shooting it directly into our veins. Peggy had never taken drugs intravenously but was eager to follow my lead. Although I didn't try to talk her out of it, I should have, because exposing her to that form of drug use not only got me sent back to prison, it almost got me killed as well.

One day while visiting our apartment, Peggy's brother saw the needle marks on her arm. He promptly informed his family that she was shooting drugs, and her father put a "contract" out on my life. Also, her sister, who was still living and working in Binghamton, called the Bronx parole office and told my parole officer that not only had I influenced her sister to drop out of school, but I turned her into a junkie as well. Of course, all of this occurred without my knowledge.

One day Peggy came to me crying hysterically. "You have to leave New York, Theo!"

"Calm down," I said, cradling her in my arms. "What are you talking about?"

"My father found out that I've been shooting up," she cried. "He has a *contract* out on your life!"

"He has a what?" I asked incredulously.

"A *contract!*" she screamed. "We can't stay together, Theo."

She was certainly right about that last statement. If her dad had put out a contract on me, we *definitely* could not be together any longer. At that point, I didn't know if Peggy's father was mob-connected or not, but I wasn't taking any chances. Peggy was Italian, and that was enough to raise serious concerns.

I told Peggy that it would be best for all concerned if she returned to her classes at SUNY-Binghamton. She agreed, and I took her to the bus station that very same day.

After seeing Peggy off, I never felt so alone in my life. Climbing the stairs to my apartment, I could feel a bout of depression coming on, which made me anxious for another hit of cocaine. As I approached my apartment door, I saw a message from the Bronx parole office taped to it. It was from my parole officer, and the message instructed me to report to his office immediately. I knew at that moment that I was on my way back to prison.

Even the certainty of incarceration, however, couldn't get me to go on the run again. I had enough of that in 1976, and I wasn't about to put myself through the life of a fugitive again, which is really no life at all. I decided to report as directed to my parole officer and try to talk my way out of a violation. After all, I reasoned, my parole officer was only upset with me because I didn't make an arrival report from Binghamton. I had no idea that he knew about my drug use, and I certainly didn't factor in his knowledge of my relationship with Peggy.

Still, I didn't want to go alone to the parole office, so I called Monica and asked her to go with me. Hearing the fear in my voice, she immediately agreed, and I reserved a ticket in her name on a flight out of Binghamton that evening. I picked her up at the airport about three hours later and was very happy to see her. I could sense, however, that she was upset with me. Knowing that Peggy had been staying with me, she never forgave me for that.

The following day, with Monica by my side, I walked into the Bronx parole office and gave the receptionist my name. Her response was if I had said *John Dillinger* rather than Theodore Harris. After announcing me over the intercom, two rather large parole officers appeared almost out of nowhere. They handcuffed me as Monica stood watching, mouth wide open and in total shock as they took me away. I was glad that I had the foresight to give her my car keys on the way up in the elevator. At least she would be able to *drive* back to Binghamton.

Queensboro Correctional Facility is located in Long Island City, and at the time of my violation, in December 1983, it was where parole revocation hearings were held. To her credit, Peggy came down from Binghamton and testified on my behalf. Although her family tried to make it seem like I had kidnapped her and shot her up with drugs against her will, Peggy took full responsibility for her actions. Her testimony, however, had absolutely no effect on the parole commissioners. My parole was revoked, and I was ordered back to prison for a period of nine months.

I served most of my violation time at Sing-Sing and wrote a musical play for children while there. The play, *Transylvania Truckin'*, is about a group of kids who, with nothing to do during summer vacation, open a talent agency. In their search to find a unique act, a young runaway witch from Transylvania introduces them to a group of talented teenaged monsters who call themselves the "Boos" and "Ghouls." Frightened and intimidated by the monsters at first, the talent agency kids see great potential in them as a singing group but find that they are lacking a dynamic lead singer. That is remedied when "Funky Frank"—a young Frankenstein monster—is *made* for them by "Uncle Angry," a mad scientist. The highlight of the play is when Funky Frank comes to life, surprising everyone by rapping instead of singing. It is a play designed to tear down stereotypes, showing that no matter what someone looks or acts like, there is good in everyone—all one has to do is look for it and cultivate it.

Transylvania Truckin' was my pet project during my brief stay at Sing-Sing, and the few people that I allowed to read it were very helpful and encouraging. My biggest motivator was my good friend and bridge partner Arnold Catten. Arnold and I served time together as teenagers at Coxsackie Reformatory back in 1965. Then, thirteen years later, we were together at Auburn Correctional Facility. Now here we were again at Sing-Sing in 1984, not realizing that we were actually serving life on the "installment" plan. Arnold gave me helpful feedback on the play, and I was confident that I would have no trouble getting it produced upon release.

Writing the book and the music to *Transylvania Truckin'* consumed me, and before I knew it, my nine months were up. I was transferred to Lincoln Correctional Facility on 110th Street in Manhattan in September 1984, where I appeared before the parole board and was granted release. Two weeks later, I walked out into the bright sunshine of freedom and boarded a greyhound bus to Binghamton.

Upon my arrival, I showed *Transylvania Truckin'* to an actress friend I had met during my tenure at the Urban League. Her name was Veleria, and her father, Harris Thompson, was a former president of the Broome County Urban League. Veleria fell in love with the play and became immediately involved in its production.

We were able to assemble a talented cast of teenagers committed to making the production a success. Then, with Binghamton's largest department store as our sponsor, we performed scenes from the play for the public in preparation for a Halloween performance of *Transylvania Truckin'* at Binghamton High School. Working diligently toward opening night, everyone was excited and in high spirits—everyone, that is, except me. I was busy behind the scenes, sabotaging my own play.

Peggy had returned to classes at SUNY-Binghamton, and of course I had to let her know that I was back in town—a huge mistake of course, because once we started seeing each other again, we also resumed our cocaine use. This time, however, I no longer had my coke connection, and the small amount of coke we were able to purchase was definitely not enough. So one night, when we ran out of cocaine after a particularly heavy binge, all I wanted to do was get money for more.

Driven by a frenzied coke rush, I ended up on the fire escape of an office building in downtown Binghamton. The building was closed for the night, and I entered an office through an unlocked window. To my surprise, there was nothing more than a desk and a chair—period. I had picked an *empty* office to burglarize. That brought me to my senses, and I quickly exited the building through the downstairs lobby. Unfortunately, just as I was making my exit, a police car pulled up. I was immediately detained and questioned by two Binghamton police officers.

Then one of the officers entered the building as the other continued to question me.

"What were you doing in there?" the cop asked.

"Just looking for a job," I said. "But I left as soon as I saw that all of the offices were closed," I quickly added.

The cop nodded his head, clearly waiting for his partner to return. That wait wasn't long at all.

"Cuff him!" the returning cop said. "He came in through the top floor fire escape." The cop looked down at my feet. "He broke an office window," he added. "There are sneaker prints on the windowsill."

Of course, I just happened to be wearing sneakers. I was handcuffed and placed under arrest.

The initial charge was unlawful entry, a misdemeanor. However, upon further review of my criminal history, the district attorney elevated the charge to third-degree burglary—a felony! He knew I couldn't afford to go to trial—not with my record. So when he offered me a two-to four-year sentence as a "cop out," I immediately jumped on it.

I had only been out of prison two months and once again had thrown everything away. I was sentenced in February 1985 and didn't give one thought to the kids I had let down—the kids who were so excited about doing my play—not to mention how Veleria must have felt after all of the work she put into it. No, I wasn't thinking about any of that. I just rolled with the punches and took things as they came.

I spent the next two months in reception at Wende Correctional Facility, just outside of Buffalo, New York. From there I was transferred to Albion Correctional Facility, a medium-security facility in Albion, New York.

Albion in 1985, to my pleasant surprise, was a coed correctional facility. Women inmates were housed on one side of the compound, male inmates on the other. All that separated the two sides of the compound was a tall chain-link fence.

I was escorted to the bunkhouse where the male inmates were housed and saw a number of guys I knew from my Auburn days. Charlie Hall, my former singing partner from Rochester, New York, was among the first to spot me. He was standing a few feet from the fence talking to a female inmate.

"Yo, Theo! What's up, man?" he hollered.

"Ain't nothing, Charlie. I'll talk with you in a minute," I yelled over my shoulder.

As I headed toward the bunkhouse, I noticed other male and female inmates at the fence besides Charlie Hall. *This looks okay*, I thought, smiling as I entered the bunkhouse. Although I didn't know it at the time, I had just witnessed the "fence program" in full swing.

Although I didn't particularly care for trying talk to someone through a fence, it wasn't long before I was "invited" to the fence by more than a few female inmates. I took a couple of the women up on their invitations, but I wasn't really serious about any of them. As far as I was concerned, it was just something to do to pass the time, but others fell deeply in love—dressing up as if they were going on a hot date. I never understood that, especially since there was no possibility of physical contact. Or at least that's what I thought at the time.

My education and writing skills came to the attention of the civilian Inmate Grievance Resolution Committee coordinator, a young black woman by the name of Deborah Watkins. Her office was located on the female side of the compound, and about two weeks after my arrival, I was summoned there for an interview. Actually, my counselor, another young black woman named Linda Polk, gave Ms. Watkins my name as a candidate for the vacant grievance clerk position.

So with a pass to Ms. Watkins office in hand, I walked through the female compound—unescorted. I couldn't believe it; there were female inmates all around me, of all shapes, colors, and sizes—a virtual "smorgasbord" of sexual partners to choose from. Some of the women made kissing sounds in my direction, while other more aggressive ones yelled out their sexual desires and fantasies. Not wanting to jeopardize my job interview, I walked past them in silence, comfortable in the knowledge that I could have almost any of these women I desired. I knew once I secured the grievance clerk position, an opportunity for a sexual romp would only be a matter of time. Smiling, I picked up the pace as I basked in the glow of the catcalls and verbal advances of these sex-starved women. I was in prison heaven.

Linda Polk, my counselor, and Ms. Watkins were good friends. So the job was virtually mine for the asking. I returned to the men's side of the facility as their new inmate grievance clerk/representative. In any other facility, I probably would not have wanted the aggravation of being on the "front line" of the many grievances that came my way daily, but at Albion, I didn't mind at all. Since my supervisor's office was on the female side of the compound, all I had to do was ask my housing unit officer to phone Ms. Watkins and tell her that I needed to see her. Ms. Watkins would then direct the officer to give me a pass, and I would be admitted to the female side of the prison. Many prearranged sexual encounters took place on the way to Ms. Watkins's office. From time to time, while waiting for Ms. Watkins to arrive, the female grievance clerk and I were left alone in the office. Needless to say, we didn't spend the time discussing "grievance" business. I couldn't thank Ms. Polk enough for recommending me for the job. I was tremendously content.

Just six credits short of receiving an undergraduate degree from Syracuse University, I desperately wanted to complete my studies while at Albion. Ms. Polk assisted me in getting those credits, which resulted in a bachelor's degree in liberal arts. She was also instrumental in my enrollment in the graduate program at SUNY-Buffalo's American Studies department.

Because of my interest in playwriting, my concentration was in theater. I had just started work on my second play, an inspirational musical titled *Soul Food*, and submitted the first draft to my friend June License at the American Studies department for feedback. June knew me from Auburn prison and was familiar with my work. She was one of the panel members in the *Good Time* documentary that I wrote when I was in Auburn. June worked in the Women's Studies department at SUNY-Buffalo, and I valued her critique highly. To my delight, she was extremely impressed with my *Soul Food* script.

June sent a copy of my play to Dr. Endesha Holland, a professor in the Women's Studies department at SUNY and former recipient of the prestigious Lorraine Hansberry playwriting award, the black playwright most noted for her play *A Raisin in the Sun*.

Dr. Holland's play *From the Mississippi Delta* had just completed a successful run off-Broadway to rave reviews. She also wrote the highly acclaimed play *Ms. Ida B. Wells*, both of which were directed by Ed Smith, an adjunct professor at SUNY's theater department. June sent a copy of *Soul Food* to Professor Smith as well.

Endesha and Ed, as they later insisted I call them, were so impressed with my play that they, along with June License, came to visit me at Albion. Since Ms. Polk had arranged the visit, I insisted that she join us. June made the introductions, and I felt honored that Dr. Holland and Professor Smith thought enough of my work to not only talk with me in person but also to agree to be my staff advisors.

Surrounded by these four people who believed in me more than I believed in myself, I was determined to make them proud. I was going to be the best student I could possibly be and work hard toward my master's degree.

However, in the fall of 1987, Albion was designated an all-female correctional facility, and consequently, the male inmates were transferred to other facilities around the state. I was sent to Wyoming Correctional Facility, a medium-security facility located right next to Attica.

The change did not affect my studies, however, and I stayed in contact with Professor Smith and Dr. Holland. In the meantime, June License was working on getting me transferred to Wende Correctional Facility so I could continue my graduate studies in a classroom setting.

There were nine "lifers" at Auburn Correctional Facility—former Syracuse University classmates—who were also enrolled in the master's degree program at SUNY-Buffalo. June License had arranged for classes to be held at Wende Correctional Facility, and the logistics of getting everyone there was time consuming and frustrating, but June was determined to pull it off, and she had powerful people behind her. So all together, there were eleven of us June was trying to get transferred.

Ironically, however, I was transferred to Mid-Orange Correctional Facility in Warwick, New York, before my transfer to Wende came through—formerly known as Warwick State Training School for Boys—the same facility that I served time in as a youth. Amazingly, almost twenty-five years had passed, and here I was, still incarcerated and seemingly going in circles.

CHAPTER TWENTY-FIVE

I didn't stay at Mid-Orange long, and for that I was grateful. Having returned to the facility of my youth caused me no small measure of depression. I was assigned to C-4 cottage, the same cottage I was in twenty-five years earlier. That's when it began to sink in that perhaps I was making a career of incarceration. I was more depressed at Mid-Orange than at any other facility I had been in. I was anxious to leave and get back to my studies. June License kept in touch, telling me that she was doing all she could to secure my transfer to Wende.

Finally, in the summer of 1988, just three months after arriving at Mid-Orange, I boarded a Department of Correctional Services bus for Wende Correctional Facility. As the bus exited slowly from the facility grounds, I became pensive. I couldn't shake the feeling that incarceration was becoming a habit for me. And even more disturbing was the feeling that there didn't seem to be anything I could do about it. I settled back in my seat, staring out the window, lost in thought.

I was the first of the master's candidates to arrive at Wende, so when the others arrived from Auburn, it was a reunion of sorts for me. These were the same guys that I served hard time with seven years earlier. However, there was one major difference between them and me: they were all serving life sentences.

During my first week at Wende, I learned that Deborah Watkins, my former boss at Albion, was the inmate grievance coordinator there. She had transferred to Wende months earlier to be closer to her home in Buffalo, New York. That, of course, worked out well for me.

When Ms. Watkins learned that I was in the facility, she immediately hired me as her grievance clerk. Because of my commitment to my studies, I was not really looking forward to listening to inmate grievances on a daily basis, but the job was not without its perks. Being a grievance clerk is one of the top-paying jobs in New York State correctional facilities and came with an "institutional pass," allowing me to move around the facility without an escort. I also had my own office during the day, affording me the privacy I needed when studying or working on my school papers.

The fact that I began my graduate work at Albion helped a lot. I had only a few months of study remaining and was presently working on my third play. The new play, *Jailwise*, as well as my play *Soul Food*, fulfilled the thesis requirements for my master's degree in American Studies.

Professor Smith had previously directed a dramatic reading of my play *Soul Food* at the Theatre Loft in Buffalo, New York, and it was well received. Based on audience feedback, I was able to determine what worked and what didn't. As a result, only minimal changes were recommended in the script, with an eye toward a full stage production in the future. I was also scheduled for parole review in a few months and was therefore hopeful that I would be on the SUNY-Buffalo campus to assist in its production.

I had discussed with Dr. Holland, Professor Smith, and June the possibility of my being paroled to Buffalo and transferring to the university's theater department. They were all for the idea, but I would need an approved residence in Buffalo if paroled.

June told me about a halfway house in Buffalo named *Hope House* and said that she would talk to the director of the house about me. The director, a nun by the name of Sister Karen, became interested enough in me to approve my application for residency at *Hope House* and also wrote a letter of support to the parole board on my behalf. Based on that letter, my good prison record, and my academic achievements, I walked out of the front gate of Wende Correctional Facility in September 1988, greeted by a smiling Sister Karen.

My first few days at *Hope House* were spent trying to get adjusted to being on the "outside." There were house rules to follow, chores to do, and, of course, a mandatory curfew—none of which bothered me in the least. I was just happy to be free to come and go as I pleased, with the majority of my time spent with students and professors from the University of Buffalo's theater community.

At the time of my release, there was a visiting black female playwright from South Africa staying with my staff advisor, Dr. Endesha Holland. The Women's Studies department was producing one of her plays, and auditions were being held at Dr. Holland's home. After minimal encouragement from her and Professor Smith, I auditioned for a part in the play and got it. I was also attending theatre classes taught by Professor Smith, as well as working toward getting my plays, *Transylvania Truckin'*, *Soul Food*, and *Jailwise*, produced.

My transition from prison was going smoothly, and I made sure I stayed busy and surrounded myself with positive people. Staff and residents of *Hope House* were supportive of me, and I was meeting new and exciting people almost daily. The rehearsals for the South African play were challenging, but Professor Smith and Dr. Holland were always there for me, making sure that I stayed focused. I was finally in my element—and things were going well for me.

Near the end of my stay in Albion, I started a relationship with a female inmate. She was a very attractive Puerto Rican girl from New York City and was close to being paroled. We had maintained contact through correspondence during my brief stays at Wyoming and Mid-Orange Correctional facilities.

She was paroled to New York City a few months before my own parole to Buffalo. After talking with her on the phone a number of times, she said that Buffalo was too far for her to travel with her kids and that she needed to see me on a regular basis. Knowing that I had family in Binghamton, she said it would be easier for her to see me if I got my parole transferred there. At some point during our correspondence—I don't know exactly when—I had convinced myself that I was in love with her. So under the pretense of wanting to be closer to my family, I had my parole transferred and returned to Binghamton.

After visiting me two or three times in Binghamton, she decided to break the relationship off. I thought about returning to Buffalo, but my pride wouldn't allow it. I didn't want to admit that I had made a mistake, especially after Sister Karen, June, Ed, and Endesha tried so hard to talk me out of leaving Buffalo. So there I was, back in Binghamton, deeply depressed and without a job.

I went to an organization for ex-offenders called PROBE and talked with Mark Rogers, an employment counselor there. Mark was a character to say the least, but he did find a job for me. I was hoping to get something involving clerical or office work, certainly not the job that he came up with.

"I know a place looking for a short-order cook," he said, reaching for the phone. "Ever do that kind of work?"

"No," I said, shaking my head. "I don't have any experience doing that."

"Don't worry about it," he said, dialing the phone. "You'll be fine."

Before I could protest further, he got on the phone and called P. T. Reardon's, a popular Irish bar and grill. He spoke with the owner, Pat Reardon, and from Mark's opening statement, I knew the job was doomed.

"Yeah, Pat—Mark here," he began. "Listen, I got a guy that's perfect for that short-order job." He paused, listening. "Yeah, his name's Theo Harris...he's an *armed robber* and—" Mark held up his hand, cutting off my protest, indicating that he knew exactly what he was doing. "What's that?" he continued, leaning into the phone. "No, he's a good guy…paid his debt…yeah he's done short-order work before." Again, he raised his hand to stop me from coming out of my seat. "Right now?" he said into the phone. "Sure, I'll send him right over."

As Mark hung up the phone, I sat there staring at him as if he had just lost his mind. Not only did I not know anything about short-order work, but also—even if I did—what employer would hire me after an introduction like that? An *armed robber*! What the heck was Mark thinking? I continued to sit there, dumbfounded.

Mark assured me that I could do the job and convinced me to go over and at least talk with Pat Reardon. I reluctantly agreed.

To my utter disbelief, I was hired on the spot. I was told that I would be working the evening shift and was scheduled to begin the following day. Pat then showed me around the small kitchen as I tried to decide if I really wanted to go through with the charade. *What the heck*, I thought, paying closer attention to the kitchen tour. *I might as well give it a try.*

Thankfully, my first night was relatively slow. Pat's brother, Tim—the *T* in P. T. Reardon's—worked the kitchen with me. To my surprise, it wasn't as difficult as I expected, and before long I was in the swing of things.

Since "prep work" is such a vital part of short-order cooking, I came in early the first few weeks to familiarize myself with that aspect of the job. It wasn't long before I pretty much breezed through the food orders. However, since I was working in an Irish bar, the weekends were the hardest for me because that's when alcohol orders were at their peak. As a result, the food orders were heavy as well, but even with that, if I needed help in the kitchen, I could always count on Tim Reardon or one of the waitresses to give me a hand.

The waitresses, especially, were very nice to me, going out of their way to see that I wasn't overwhelmed by the continuous food orders. Also, at the end of each shift, they would ask if I wanted to "wind down" with a drink. I never came right out and told them that I couldn't drink alcohol, but I always declined the offers. And for that, I was quite proud of myself, as was my family. As long as I didn't return to drugs or alcohol, I felt that I was safe. However, somehow I knew that it would be just a matter of time before I succumbed to temptation. Oddly enough, that thought was always in the back of my mind.

One evening near closing time, I was at work in the kitchen when one of the waitresses told me there was a girl in the restaurant asking about me. I hurried out to the dining area and was surprised to see my cousin Robin from Harrisburg, Pennsylvania.

Robin is the daughter of my mother's sister, Aunt Sarah, and I hadn't seen her—or her brothers, Jay and Dean—in years.

"What's up, cuzzo?" I said, sliding into the booth next to her. "I haven't seen you in *years*. How's the family?"

"Everybody's good, but I really came 'cause I have some news about your dad that you might be interested in."

Might be interested in, I thought. Is she kidding? Of course I was interested!

"I'll be right back," I said. "Wait for me while I close the kitchen down."

As we walked back to my mother's house, Robin explained how she learned about my biological father's whereabouts. It seemed that her younger brother, Dean, had taken a girl to the senior prom who said she was my cousin on my *dad's* side.

"Dean told me that her dad is *your* dad's brother," she continued to explain.

I stood there in shock—I could hardly believe my ears. I had been curious about my real father ever since I learned about him. Now here was an opportunity to finally locate him and, even more importantly, *meet* him!

"Your uncle's name is William Saye," she said. "He lives in Steelton, Pennsylvania."

"*Steelton?*" I said. "Where's that?"

"Right outside of Harrisburg," Robin replied. "About fifteen or twenty minutes away."

Now I was really excited because I recalled my mother telling me that my father's last name was Saye and that I was named after him. It was too much of a coincidence to be ignored. I had to check it out.

Considering the circumstances, and since it was close to Christmas, I knew I wouldn't have a problem getting time off from work. Robin said I could stay with her, and I told her that I would contact her in a couple of weeks. I couldn't believe it. I had never been this close to locating my dad, and I was excited about the possibility of finally meeting him.

When I asked my boss for the time off, he was extremely supportive, as was everyone else at work. They were all excited for me, as was my own family—especially my mother. Although I had never questioned her about him, she knew that I was curious to see him face-to-face. So she was just as anxious for me to find him and finally meet him as I was.

The weekend I arrived at Robin's house, I didn't waste any time. I asked my cousin Dean to take me to William Saye's house so that I could talk with him. It was a Friday evening when we arrived at his house, and my stomach was churning. Dean knocked on the door, and a light-complexioned, middle-aged man answered. As soon as we laid eyes on one another, we knew we were family. The resemblance was uncanny; it was like looking in a mirror.

"Finally," my uncle said, smiling. "I've been expecting you."

"You know who I am?" I asked, shocked.

"Yes, Teddy," he said, ushering us inside. "I know *exactly* who you are."

As we entered the clean, modest home, I was unable to take my eyes off of my dad's brother—my *uncle*.

"I'm your uncle *Wiggy*," he said, conscious of my prolonged stare. "That's what the family calls me, and *you* are family, Teddy."

"Does my dad know about me?" I asked hesitantly.

Uncle Wiggy nodded, but his eyes took on a sadder look at my question. "Your dad is married with four grown children—three sons and a daughter."

I could hardly believe it. I had three brothers and a sister I never knew existed.

When Uncle Wiggy got on the phone to call my father, my heart almost stopped. I was finally going to talk to my dad and hopefully set up a meeting, but as soon as uncle Wiggy got him on the phone, I could sense that something was wrong. Uncle Wiggy's smile faded, and he began to whisper into the phone. I stared at him expectantly, but he hung up the phone without handing it to me. There was a long silence, and then he told me that my dad was not prepared for my arrival. Bottom line: he did not want to meet me.

Seeing the hurt on my face, Uncle Wiggy called my half brother David over to the house. Anxious to meet me, David came right over, and we hit it off right away, embracing warmly. After explaining the situation to David, he suggested that I meet the rest of the family first and see where that led. I nodded my agreement. If I couldn't see my dad, I at least wanted to meet his side of the family.

The following afternoon, David came to my Aunt Sarah's house with Ricky, the second of my three half brothers. David made the introductions, and Ricky gave me a big bear hug. After introducing them to Aunt Sarah and her husband, Uncle

Jim, we headed back over to Uncle Wiggy's house. From there, Uncle Wiggy took us to his sister's house down the street, where she and his brother, Uncle Donald, were waiting to meet me. Everyone kept commenting on how much I looked like my dad, but no one really wanted to talk about his decision not to see me. I tried to act like it didn't bother me, but it was obvious that it did. Someone placed bottles of alcohol on the kitchen table, and the next thing I knew, I was drinking like a lush. I spent the rest of the afternoon into early evening trying to numb the hurt with alcohol. It didn't work, but I put on a pretty good show. By the time I got back to my cousin Robin's house, I was good and drunk.

I spent the next couple of days hanging out with David and Ricky, and I even got a chance to talk with my half sister, Lana, on the phone. To my dismay, however, Lana supported my dad's decision not to see me. She felt that it wouldn't be good for their mother, who never knew of my existence. That puzzled me. I was almost forty years old, so how would knowledge of my existence be detrimental to my father's wife? Also, as far as I was concerned, she didn't have to be told about me. I just wanted to *see* my father in person. I didn't want anything from him other than that.

I returned to Binghamton with a book filled with addresses and phone numbers, but not the one that mattered most. I never attempted to contact my father again.

CHAPTER TWENTY-SIX

My job at P. T. Reardon's didn't last long after my return from Harrisburg. I had started drinking again while there and accepting the waitress's offers of drinks at the end of my shift. Soon it got to the point where I wouldn't even wait for the shift to end; I would sneak drinks in between. Then—as is so common to the natural progression of addiction—I returned to my drug of choice: cocaine. It was only a matter of time before I started missing work altogether. To their credit, Pat and Tim Reardon put up with my absences as long as they could, but there was only so much that they could take. Soon, my calling in "sick" taxed even their patience, and they had no choice but to let me go.

I was still on parole and using drugs heavily now, so I knew that it was only a matter of time before my parole officer would find out. When that happened, I would either have my parole revoked or be arrested for a drug-related crime. Either way, I would be on my way back to prison.

Before allowing that to happen, however, I went to my parole officer and came clean about my drug use. I was taking a chance because he could have violated me on the spot, sending me immediately to jail. Instead, he gave me the option of an in-patient drug program, which I immediately accepted.

Binghamton General Hospital has a twenty-eight-day substance abuse program called New Horizons. My parole officer set up an interview for me, and I was accepted into the program immediately. I was grateful for this second chance and planned to do everything that was required of me. I wanted to beat the addiction in the worst way. I certainly didn't want to go back to prison. I knew that with four felony convictions on my record, I couldn't afford another one. I was already over the limit for persistent-felony offender status, and I was very close to a life sentence. Therefore, I knew that I had to get my act together or it would be all over for me. So when I arrived at the New Horizons drug program, I was willing to do whatever was required of me and then some.

I was surprised to see one of my homeboys from Harlem, Ira Mobley, in the program. Ira had moved to Syracuse from New York City some years earlier and had gotten caught up in the drug game as I did. He and I used to sing together on street corners in Harlem, and we would always draw a crowd. Ira is first cousin to Ronnie Spector, ex-wife of the legendary producer Phil Spector and former lead singer of The Ronettes, a popular sixties female group whose big hit was a song called "Be My Baby." So singing was as natural as breathing for Ira, and together we sounded pretty good. We started attracting the attention of the female residents almost immediately, which, in terms of recovery, was a big mistake.

Although frowned upon in most coed drug programs, I had my share of "relationships" during my stay at New Horizons. Now with the benefit of hindsight, I can see why "program romances" are not recommended. They made me lose focus, and I was unable to concentrate on my reason for being there in the first place: recovery. So without fully addressing my addiction, I breezed through the twenty-eight days and was placed in one of New Horizon's outpatient therapy groups.

I attended group therapy Monday through Friday and was beginning to feel good about myself and where I thought I was in my recovery. I felt, for the first time in my life, that I was starting to get a handle on my substance-abuse problem. Then I got kicked out of the group for failing to complete a homework assignment on time.

Being removed from the group was like snatching a lifeline from me, and I was totally unprepared for it. Still, I continued to attend Narcotics Anonymous and Alcoholics Anonymous, but they were not enough to keep me "clean and sober." Since I was able to relate more to the men and women in my New Horizons group, I was more comfortable sharing personal information with them. Now I no longer had them for support.

I was living as an "outpatient" at Fairview, a halfway house that accepted referrals from New Horizons, and first met my best friend, Kent Littlejohn, there. Since we came pretty much from the same background, it was natural for us to become close. Kent was from Brooklyn and had spent some time in prison himself. Having shared that information with me, I told him about my time in prison and how I had used the time to better myself. I told him about the *Good Time* documentary I had written in prison and said it was something the residents at Fairview would probably enjoy seeing.

I went to the director of Fairview and arranged for all of the residents to view the copy of the videotape I had. Kent was impressed with the documentary but was even more impressed with the fact that it was written, produced, and taped behind the walls of a maximum-security prison.

Kent was a member of the outpatient group I got kicked out of and was almost as upset about my being asked to leave as I was.

Like every substance abuser, Kent has his own story to tell, and it is only by the grace of God that he managed to survive his addiction. I remember listening in amazement as he talked about the life-threatening episode that compelled him to seek treatment.

According to Kent, he had just arrived in Binghamton from New York City, seeking a better life for himself. Unfortunately, he brought his alcohol problem with him, and he had been drinking heavily. So much so in fact that he began to hallucinate, seeing "little green men" all around him. At that exact moment, two Binghamton police officers were walking by, and Kent tried to snatch a gun from one of them in order to shoot the imaginary aliens! As Kent and the cop struggled, the officer's partner pulled his own gun. Had he been struggling with a New York City cop, Kent would have almost certainly been killed. Amazingly, though, the cop recognized that Kent was hallucinating and yelled to his partner not to shoot. The cop talked calmly to Kent, finally getting him to release his grip on the firearm. Then, even more amazingly, instead of arresting him, the officers took him to a "sobering-up" station, where he was able to sleep it off, talk with alcohol counselors, and get the help he needed.

For the first time in a long time, Kent's story caused me to think of God and consider just how much of a factor He had been in both of our lives. Too bad it was only a fleeting thought. I'm sure that God, in His infinite love and patience, had to be wondering just what it would take to get my full attention. However, little did I realize that day was not far off.

Learning that I had family in Binghamton, the director of Fairview told me that I could no longer stay there. The halfway house, he explained, was only for residents who had no ties to the Binghamton community. I was given three days to find somewhere else to live and was fortunate enough to find a furnished room almost immediately. I then went to the Department of Social Services and was given a check for one month's security and one month's rent. Exactly three days after being asked to leave Fairview halfway house, I was in my own furnished room. It was the worst thing that could have happened to me.

The day of my relapse began normally enough. I had been working at the Broome County Arena for the past two weeks, and after picking up my first paycheck, I made my monthly report to my parole officer. He asked the usual questions:

"Are you still at the same address?"

"Yes."

"Still drug free?"

"Yes."

"Have you had any police contact?"

"No."

"Anything you want to talk to me about?"

"No."

So with a pocket full of money, I left the parole office feeling pretty good. As I headed home, I found myself in the drug section of town. My thoughts turned to the syringe in the medicine cabinet at home—the one I had stolen from the doctor's office during my pre-employment physical.

At the end of the examination, the doctor had left me alone in the room. As I dressed, I looked around to see if there was anything worth taking. That's when I spotted the brand-new syringe, still in its wrapper. Without giving it another thought, I snatched it and quickly put it in my pocket. I knew it would only be a matter of time before I used it, and sure enough, over the next few days, the syringe was all that I could think about.

Now as I walked through the drug neighborhood, my only thought was to break the syringe in. I knew most of the dealers, so I had no problem locating the one with the best quality cocaine. He had twenty-dollar vials, and I quickly purchased one—as if just one would be enough.

I rushed home, injected the cocaine into my vein, and almost immediately overwhelming ecstasy spread throughout my body. Someone once asked me to describe the feeling I get from shooting cocaine. I told him to think of the best orgasm he ever experienced and then multiply that feeling by a thousand. The rush of the cocaine is uncontrollably sexual—at least it is for me.

So after just one shot, I propositioned a local prostitute and then ran back to the dealer, spending my entire two-week paycheck in a matter of hours. There was no turning back—I was sprung.

It didn't take long after that to get back into my addiction full swing. I began missing work regularly and definitely every payday. Needless to say, it wasn't long before I quit my job altogether to focus on alcohol and cocaine abuse full time. Subsequently, I began to suffer from severe depression, cursing the futility and the worthlessness of my existence. Then one fateful evening in November 1989, while in an alcoholic stupor, it all came to an end.

After a particularly long cocaine binge, I was flat broke and desperate for more. I had just enough money left to buy a pint of wine, which I drank straight down. I then headed down Main Street, in the direction of the twenty-four-hour Price Chopper supermarket. It was just a little before midnight, and I needed to get some money—fast.

I can only imagine how I must have looked to the young white woman approaching her car, struggling with shopping bags, as the alcohol took effect. Appearing in front of her from seemingly out of nowhere, she was clearly startled. With slurred speech, I told her that I was a drug addict and that I needed some money. She immediately handed over her pocketbook, and I ran at top speed from the nearly deserted parking lot.

A few blocks later, I ducked inside of a vacant hallway and looked inside the pocketbook. My jaw dropped as I stared at a lone five-dollar bill. That alone should have been enough to bring me to my senses, but it only made me more determined. I needed much more money than five dollars to feed my addiction, and I was going to get it—simple as that. I headed right back outside, looking for another victim.

I continued up Main Street as if nothing happened, not even considering the fact that the Price Chopper robbery had to have been reported to the police and that they were probably looking for me already. My only thought, however, was to get more cocaine. That was my sole focus. I was on what drug addicts call "a mission."

As my drunkenness reached its peak, I staggered a few more blocks down Main Street and stopped when I saw a woman withdrawing money from an outside ATM machine. As I approached her, I noticed two Binghamton police officers parked about twenty feet away in direct view of the ATM. By this time the wine I consumed had taken full effect. It told me that I had the element of surprise on my side. After all, who in their right mind would commit a robbery in plain view of the police? In my inebriated state, the argument was extremely convincing.

So in plain view of the two Binghamton cops, I approached the woman from behind. I whispered that I was a drug addict and that I wanted her to withdraw one hundred dollars from the machine. She too could see the police car sitting off to the side. For a brief moment, she looked at me as if I had lost my mind— which wasn't very far from the truth. She quickly withdrew the money and handed it to me.

I left the scene running at what I thought was top speed, navigating backyards, fences, and barking dogs. I finally took refuge behind a house some blocks away. Little did I know that someone saw me run behind the house and immediately called the police. In a matter of minutes, the area was crawling with cops and police dogs.

The police quickly located me hiding under a car in the backyard. To their amazement, I had the wallet from the Price Chopper robbery still in my possession. It was in my back pocket, along with my own wallet and personal identification— further proof that I was out of my mind. The drive for more cocaine was so strong that it had taken total control of me. I was like a zombie with tunnel vision moving toward my objective without deviation. Now I was under arrest, charged with two robberies, and starting to return to my senses, but it was much too late for that.

Shortly, another police car pulled up with both robbery victims inside who identified me on the spot. With my record of convictions, I was now facing a life sentence—a hard pill to swallow under any circumstances. On the conscious level, things looked so bleak that I actually contemplated suicide. I felt that I had nowhere to turn and nothing left to live for. Then almost in a whisper, the words "Come to me" echoed in my mind.

For the first time in my life, I felt I had no one else to turn to but God. I closed my eyes and immediately experienced a sense of peace. I would soon come to find that when things are at their worst, God is at His best.

CHAPTER TWENTY-SEVEN

Although I tried not to show it, I was scared to death when I entered the Broome County Jail in downtown Binghamton. Now that I was in my right state of mind, it was hard for me to believe that I had committed two robberies—felonies five and six—just minutes apart from each other. In this equation, however, five + six = life.

So when I was finally alone in my cell, away from prying eyes, it was fear that forced me to my knees. In a halting voice, I began to cry out to a God that I *hoped* was there. I told Him that if He would intervene on my behalf, I would worship and serve Him for the rest of my life. I meant every word of that prayer. I needed a miracle, and I needed it right away. I don't know how long I stayed on my knees, but when I finally stretched out on my bed, I had calmed down to the point that I was able to get some much-needed sleep.

About a month later, a lawyer from the public defender's office came to see me. I was certain he had come to tell me that the district attorney was going to prosecute me as a persistent-felony offender, resulting in an automatic life sentence upon conviction. I took a few deep breaths and slowly exited my cell.

The lawyer was waiting at the end of the gallery to talk with me, and he shook my hand with a smile. *What's he smiling about?* I thought. There was certainly nothing humorous about my situation—at least not as far as I was concerned. I had forgotten all about my prayer and the promise I had made to God. So when I stood before the lawyer, I was prepared for the worst. My only hope was that the district attorney's plea offer—if there was one—would be fifteen years to life rather than twenty-five years to life. The rationale there, of course, was that if I had to plead guilty to a sentence with "life" on the end of it, I would rather have fifteen years as my minimum rather than twenty-five. Those were the thoughts running through my mind as I prepared myself for what the lawyer had to say.

So when he told me that the district attorney was offering me two consecutive four-year sentences in return for a guilty plea, I was stunned. I stood there for a long time, speechless and in absolute awe of God's power. At that moment, I knew that my prayer had been answered. No one could tell me differently; I had asked for a miracle, and God had come through. He stepped in to snatch me from the finality of a life sentence. He upheld His end of the bargain, and I was determined to live up to mine.

Mistaking my silence for displeasure with the district attorney's offer, my lawyer told me that I didn't have to decide right away. He said I could think it over and get back to him. *Think what over?* I thought. I didn't need to think anything over. What I needed to do was accept the DA's offer before he changed his mind. Then I needed to run back to my cell, fall on my knees, and thank God for answering my prayer.

Having already reviewed my criminal history, my lawyer understood my enthusiasm perfectly. He knew I didn't want to take a chance on the district attorney having second thoughts about the plea bargain. I told him to immediately tell the DA that I would accept his offer.

The world had suddenly gotten brighter, as if a veil had been lifted from my eyes. As soon as I entered my cell, I fell on my knees, thanking God repeatedly and vowing to keep my promise to Him.

I still owed six years on parole, so when I received consecutive four-year prison terms, my sentence was automatically revised to include that time. Therefore, I would be serving a term of four to fourteen years. With my record, I knew I would probably not be granted parole after serving my four-year minimum.

However, with good time, the most I would serve would be ten years and eight months. A long time, yes, but still a lot better than fifteen to life.

After spending two months in classification at Wende Reception Center, I was sent to Attica for the third time. I didn't really mind going back to Attica. In fact, since my youngest brother, Marvin, was serving a ten- to twenty-year sentence there, I was hoping I would be sent there. I was looking forward to being with him so that we could keep an eye on each other.

Having been told of my arrival, Marvin arranged for me to be placed on his gallery in D block—the "prison band" gallery. He had taught himself to play the bass guitar, so when I arrived at Attica, he was an active member of the band. My reputation as a vocalist preceded me, so getting assigned to the band was no problem at all. That meant that Marvin and I would be together—not the "reunion" I would have liked; still, it was good for us to be together.

I knew a few of the band members from my previous years at Attica and Auburn prisons. Most of them, however, were new to me, but they still made me feel welcomed. They told me they had heard about me and were anxious to hear me sing. Having already heard some of the vocalists in the band, I was anxious to sing with them as well.

One vocalist who impressed me the most was a guy named Bobby Perkins from Queens, New York. Bobby had a smooth, pure voice with a range that was nothing short of remarkable. He and I hit it off right away, and we became good friends. We were soon performing together on a regular basis for the prison population, and we had quite a following. The only problem Bobby had—which, by the way, wasn't a problem for me—was that he was extremely egotistical. Because of that, he made a lot of enemies, but in all honesty, it was Bobby's talent and friendship that kept me grounded and focused during our brief stay at

Attica. Within months of my arrival, however, Bobby, Marvin, and I would each be transferred to medium-security facilities.

Marvin was the first one to leave, and it depressed me to see him go. I didn't want us to be separated so soon after my arrival—I had only been at Attica three months when his transfer came through. I felt as if a piece of me had been removed when my brother left. I prayed for strength to deal with our separation and asked God to bring us back together soon.

In keeping with my promise to God, I was attending church services on a weekly basis and was also a member of a gospel singing group. Bobby was in the group with me, and we became even closer when Marvin left. Then, just a few months later, he was transferred as well. I didn't know where he had been sent, but I missed him. Now I was completely alone.

Praying that my own transfer would come through, I continued singing at the weekly church services. God knew how badly I wanted to leave Attica, and I trusted Him to answer my prayer. It came sooner than I expected.

A few weeks after Bobby left, I was called to my counselor's office.

"Your classification has been lowered to medium security," he informed me. "Any thought about where you might want to be transferred?"

"Yes, I'd like to go to Groveland, if possible." I knew that my brother Marvin had been transferred there. It would be great if I could get to Groveland with him.

"I'll put the request in," he said, "but I can't guarantee that you'll be sent there."

"I understand," I replied. "I appreciate you putting the request in, though."

I left his office knowing that where I was sent was not under my counselor's control or mine. Therefore, I did the only thing that I could do under the circumstances: I *prayed.*

A few months later, I boarded a bus for my new facility. I prayed it would be Groveland. I was anxious to be with my brother again. The bus made several stops at various correctional facilities along the way, dropping inmates off and picking some up. The trip was long and tiring, and I soon prayed that I would be getting off at the next facility—no matter which one it was. I was tired of riding the bus, shackled and chained, and I just wanted to get settled in.

When the sign that read *Groveland Correctional Facility* came into view, my heart began to beat a little faster. *This is where Marvin is at*, I thought, sitting up a little straighter and peering intently out of the window. My prayers had been answered—this was where I would be getting off.

As the bus pulled on to the grounds of Groveland, I was struck by the size of the facility; it looked like a college campus, with cottages dotting the sprawling grounds. The bus came to a stop in front of the administration building, and I waited anxiously as a correction officer began calling off names from a clipboard that he was holding. I prayed that my name was on the list.

Finally, as he was coming to the end of the list, my name was called. I was so excited that I didn't respond immediately, prompting the officer to call my name a second time. I stood up quickly, shouted out my prison ID number, and exited the bus.

As I stepped down from the bus, I saw a crowd of inmates surrounding the area, anxious to see the new arrivals. I quickly scanned the crowd and saw Marvin among them, smiling at me. He waited as a correction officer removed my shackles, handcuffs, and chains then came over to help me move my property bags to the receiving room where I would be processed into the facility and also assigned to a cottage.

After being processed in, Marvin and a couple of his friends helped me carry my bags to my cottage.

"They got a band here," Marvin said as we walked toward my assigned cottage.

"You playin' with them?"

"You *know* that," he said, smiling. "They needed a bass player—*bad*!"

"What about a singer?"

"They got a dude who *thinks* he can sing," he said. "But when I told the band about you, they're definitely lookin' for you to join."

"Yeah, well, I'm anxious to hear how y'all sound," I said. "But I also want to either join or start a gospel group while I'm here. I made a promise to God that I would serve Him, and I'm determined to keep it."

"No problem, bro," he said. "I'll play for the church. I got you, whatever you want to do."

Arriving at my cottage, I thanked the guys for helping me carry my property bags. It was a long walk, and I sure needed the help. I had the feeling that Groveland was going to work out just fine for my brother and me. Now that we were together again, I felt that the time would pass quickly and worry-free. The fact that we were able to keep an eye on each other meant a lot to me. I turned and thanked Marvin for his help, gave him a quick hug, and then entered my new cottage.

Because of my substance abuse history, I was assigned to the facility's alcohol- and substance-abuse treatment program, better known as ASAT. The program director was a young black woman from Rochester, New York, named JoAnn Marion, or Ms. Marion, as inmate program participants called her.

ASAT had its own cottage, and Ms. Marion was in charge. Each day's activities were highly structured with group therapy in the morning classroom lectures in the afternoon and AA or NA meetings in the evening. It was just what I needed, and I participated wholeheartedly. It was important for me to learn as much as possible about my addiction, because for me it was literally a life or death situation. I didn't know it at the time, but Ms. Marion was observing me closely.

After reviewing my folder and becoming aware of my educational background, as well as my clerical skills, Ms. Marion hired me as the program clerk. She told me that I would be responsible for typing attendance sheets, group meeting schedules, and whatever other paperwork might be required of me. She also said that I would have my own office and typewriter and would be working directly for her. Since I was still working on rewrites of my plays *Transylvania Truckin'* and *Soul Food*, access to an electric typewriter greatly appealed to me. I eagerly accepted the ASAT clerk position, and from that day on, my status in the program was elevated considerably.

In my free time, I sang with the facility band, as well as with a gospel group that I had put together with my former Auburn singing partner, Charlie Hall. Our gospel group was a staple at the weekly church services, and I was extremely pleased with the vocal quality of the group members—especially Charlie Hall. Charlie was from Rochester, New York, and had a pure tenor voice with a range that was unbelievable.

I remember the first time that Charlie and I sang for Ms. Marion in her office. Someone had told her that I could sing, and she asked if she could hear a song. Since I specialized in rewriting secular songs to fit the gospel genre, I asked Charlie Hall to help me with a duet that I had rewritten. The name of the song was "The Closer I Get to You" by Roberta Flack and Donnie Hathaway. My lyrics talked about getting closer to God, as opposed to the original lyrics, which talked about two lovers getting closer to one another.

Ms. Marion was so impressed with our rendition of the song that she asked us to sing at some of the ASAT group sessions as a treat for the men. Since Charlie Hall and I had sung together back in the seventies at Auburn prison, our voices blended extremely well, making singing with him one of the highlights of my two-year stay at Groveland.

Another highlight of my stay was when the deputy superintendent of programs at the facility permitted me to produce a dramatic reading of my play *Soul Food* for the inmate population. In my proposal to the deputy superintendent, I pointed out that for the vast majority of the facility's inmates, it would be their first exposure to theater in *any* form. He was very receptive of the idea and gave me the go-ahead to stage the reading.

I auditioned Groveland inmates for the male roles, and for the play's two female parts, I auditioned two female volunteers from a church in Rochester, New York. After a series of rehearsals, the reading was staged in the gymnasium for both inmates and staff. Since attendance was purely voluntary, I was amazed at the size of the turnout. It looked as if every inmate in the facility was there that evening.

I directed and narrated the reading, singing each of the play's songs as called for by the script. I was also given permission to tape record the production and had a personal copy made for myself. God must have been well pleased, because the reading went off without a hitch.

At play's end, the cast stood to thunderous applause, and I was congratulated on a job well done by inmates, teachers, counselors, and facility administrators. Of course, I appreciated the accolades and praise, but I knew that it had happened only by the grace of God. The same God who had been there for me throughout my life was also present at my reading, and I knew that He had greater things in store—I could *feel* it.

After two years at Groveland, I requested a transfer to Wallkill Correctional Facility. I had heard about the optics program there and was interested in learning how to make prescription eyeglasses. However, because of its status as an "honor" facility at the time, I knew that getting to Wallkill would not be easy.

Through the prison grapevine, I heard that a person could do "sweet" time at Wallkill. The cells were actually rooms with wooden doors that locked with a key, and each inmate had the key in his possession. Wallkill also had a "family reunion program," allowing eligible inmates to spend weekends in a trailer with his family.

I told Marvin that my counselor had put a transfer request in for me to participate in the optics program at Wallkill. I suggested that he ask his counselor to do the same when his transfer review came up, which was months away. If I was fortunate enough to go to Wallkill, I told him I wanted him with me.

As I waited for word on my transfer request, I prayed that God would see fit to keep Marvin and me together. Not only was *that* prayer answered, but God also had an even bigger blessing in store.

CHAPTER TWENTY-EIGHT

I was transferred to Wallkill six months later and was pleased to find that my singing partner from Attica, Bobby Perkins, was there. He was glad to see me and asked about my brother. I told him that Marvin was still at Groveland and would join us soon—God willing.

Bobby told me he was singing with a couple of guys and the only thing missing were decent musicians. He said my voice would round the group out nicely. I joined the group but wasn't really all that impressed with the other members. We sounded okay, but as far as I was concerned, we were nothing to write home about.

Marvin came to Wallkill a few months later, and by then I was pretty much settled in. I was a student in the optics program, and I talked Marvin into taking the entrance exam. I'll never forget how proud I was the day he passed the exam and was accepted into the program.

Since the Optics Shop was considered a part of the prison industry, everyone who worked there received "industry" wages. So not only was the optics training preparation for a good-paying job upon our release, but the prison pay was good as well. By the time Marvin and I went from the classroom to actually making prescription eyeglasses, we were making close to fifty-dollars every two weeks, and that was just to start. Compared to the average prison wages of five to eight cents an hour for a six-hour day, the inmates in the optics program were "corporate" workers. I guess you could say that the Optics Shop was the "IBM" of Wallkill. Many applied for acceptance into the optics program, but few were chosen. I was grateful that Marvin and I were among the chosen few.

Serving time at Wallkill was pretty much low key. The time flew by, and the singing group began to take shape. Bobby and I were able to recruit a couple of better voices, and Marvin concentrated on getting the musicians together.

We were performing at family events on a regular basis, but unlike Marvin and Bobby, I was also attending church services every Sunday. It was at one of these services that I first heard William "Wooga" Pierce sing. I sat in the congregation mesmerized, as his voice blew me away.

Wooga had a life sentence and had served a little over twenty years at the time we met. With a dark complexion, stocky build, and thick glasses, one would never think he was a singer at all, especially a singer of his caliber. He was in charge of the music for the church, and when he heard me sing, he recruited me as a soloist. I had already heard from Bobby that he and Wooga had fallen out with each other shortly before my arrival. However, that had nothing to do with me. Wooga's talent was exceptional, and I felt honored that he asked me to work with him.

I would soon learn, however, that he was extremely opinionated and abrasive in his dealing with others. When it came to music, he had no patience for anything less than the best. That was not a bad thing per se, but when it came to dealing with people one-on-one, he was greatly lacking in the tact department. I have watched him sever more than a few musical associations during my time at Wallkill simply because there was no middle ground with Wooga. It was, as he put it, "My way, or the highway."

To Wooga's credit, however, his intentions were to motivate aspiring singers to strive for perfection, but because he was so abrasive in his approach, he failed to reach most of them. Therefore, it was difficult for him to keep talented singers for any length of time, but God places people as they are needed, and I believe it was meant for Wooga to work with me, my brother Marvin, and a guitar player by the name of Stan Lucas.

BLESSED AND HIGHLY FAVORED

Stan's claim to fame was as former lead guitarist for Gladys Knight & the Pips. He was also a talented vocalist and a God-fearing Christian. His reputation preceded him, and as soon as he arrived at Wallkill, the news spread quickly. Wooga made sure that Stan was placed on the gallery with us.

We took an immediate liking to Stan and were amazed at his guitar skills. He was just what we needed—the missing link, if you will. Now in terms of what we were trying to do musically in the church, we could really stretch out. I felt that God had put us together so that we could give Him, as well as the inmate population, the best we had to offer. And as time passed, that's exactly what we did. We were writing, singing, and praising God to the fullest extent of our musical ability. I knew in my heart that God was pleased, but I was totally unprepared for the blessings soon to come.

One day Wooga and I were sitting in his cell, working on a song that he had written. We were talking about all the years we had in prison and started throwing names out to each other of people we sang with in other prisons. We learned that we were together in Attica in the early seventies just before his transfer to Green Haven prison, where he had served the bulk of his life sentence. It was at Green Haven that he formed the inmate gospel group The Choice Voices, bringing hundreds of inmates to Christ through their music ministry.

Because of its close proximity to the city of Poughkeepsie, Green Haven attracted a number of local churches and community volunteers. Among those coming into the prison in the early seventies were the Rainbow Gospel Singers, an all-female singing group. They were from Holy Light Pentecostal Church in Poughkeepsie, and it was their long association with Wooga that would prove to be a blessing for me.

The successful dramatic reading of my play *Soul Food* at Groveland only served to wet my appetite for a full-blown stage production. I told Wooga about the play and asked about the possibility of performing it at Wallkill. All for the idea, he began making preparations.

Because of my experience with the prison administration at Groveland, I knew we would have to get the green light from the deputy superintendent of programs in order to make a stage production happen, especially since the script called for two female volunteers. That, I thought, would be the biggest hurdle. Wooga, however, assured me that would not be a problem. All he had to do, he said, was tell Reverend Muller that he wanted to put the play on and it would be a done deal.

At the time, Reverend Ed Muller was regional chaplain for the department of correctional services. With offices in Albany, New York, as well as Wallkill Correctional Facility, Reverend Muller was responsible for hiring chaplains and religious leaders for each New York state correctional facility. With a working relationship going back to Green Haven, he and Wooga were extremely close.

The Agape church at Wallkill was hosting an appreciation dinner for volunteers from the local churches, and Wooga told me to bring a copy of the *Soul Food* script to the dinner. He said that two members of the Rainbow Gospel Singers would be there and perhaps they would be helpful in providing the female volunteers the script required. That sounded good to me, so I brought a copy of the script with me that evening and was introduced by Wooga to Pastor Audrey Giles and her sister, Doris Milburn, two of the Rainbow Gospel Singers. They were receptive to the idea but expressed doubts concerning their personal ability to play the female roles.

Pastor Giles, however, went on to say that her sister, Phyllis, would be perfect for the lead female role and asked if she could take the script to her. I, of course, said yes, silently thanking God in the process. I asked Pastor Giles to tell her sister that we would be holding auditions the following Tuesday evening and to call Reverend Muller if she was interested in working with us. I also asked her to see if she could find someone to play the second female role. I felt very confident as I returned to my cell that evening. By the grace of God, it looked as if the play was definitely going to happen.

Stan was as enthusiastic about the play as I was and was happy to serve as musical director. From that point on, he, Marvin, and I worked very closely. During one of our preproduction sessions, Marvin and I happened to be talking about our brother Danny. Stan stopped what he was doing, turned to us, and asked, "Danny Harris?" We nodded our heads, surprised that Stan knew him.

"I was working on Salsoul Orchestra's Christmas album a few years back," Stan explained, "and they needed a strong rhythm guitar player. I recommended your brother Danny Harris."

Marvin and I looked at each other in amazement. We knew that Danny was on *Salsoul Orchestra*'s Christmas album, but we didn't know that it was because of Stan Lucas. The last we heard—after leaving Kurtis Blow—our brother was doing freelance work for various artists.

"How'd you meet Danny?" I asked.

"I was producing a female artist—Jocelyn Brown," Stan said. "Danny played guitar on her album."

I couldn't wait to call Danny and tell him that Marvin and I were working with Stan Lucas. Danny called him "Stan the Man" and told me to put him on the phone. They talked for quite a while, reminiscing about the good old days. Marvin and I drew even closer to Stan after that. I thanked God for bringing us together. I would soon find out, however, that the blessings were only beginning.

The afternoon of our first audition, Wooga came to me and told me that Phyllis, of the Rainbow Gospel Singers, had called

Reverend Muller. She told him that she and her niece would be there that evening to audition for the play. I was excited at that news and waited anxiously for their arrival.

That evening I greeted Phyllis and her niece, Mimi, at the door of the chapel. During the introductions, I locked eyes with Phyllis and felt an immediate connection. I didn't know what it was at the time, but I sensed that there was something very special about her. She gazed into my eyes as I shook her hand, then turned and introduced me to her niece. I nodded hello to Mimi, then turned my attention back to Phyllis. I thanked her for coming on such short notice and then ushered both women into the side room of the chapel, where they read for their parts.

The reading went well enough for me to see that they would be perfect for the roles of Moms and Dee-Dee, a widowed evangelist and her daughter desiring to open a storefront church in their ghetto neighborhood. Also, with Phyllis's own church background and upbringing, the play's storyline was one that she could relate to. In short, she was a natural for the part, and I wasn't about to let her get away. I told her and Mimi that the parts were theirs.

The only concern that Phyllis had was the short amount of time she had to memorize her lines and the songs she would be required to sing. I understood her concern perfectly. The prison administration only allowed rehearsals one night a week with the full cast. *Soul Food* was a three-act musical with a running time of close to two hours, and Phyllis had one of the major roles in the play. It soon became clear to me that if Phyllis and I were to get more rehearsal time, it would have to be done on a one-on-one basis in the visiting room.

I explained to Phyllis that we would have more time to work on our lines if she came to visit me on the weekends. She embraced that suggestion immediately and seemed quite pleased. In all honesty, at the time, my motives were purely professional; my main concern was the play. That, however, would soon change.

Phyllis visited me that coming Saturday along with her sister, Pastor Giles, who came to see Wooga. We greeted each other warmly. I was excited about the fact that we would have the next six hours to work on our lines, or at least that was my intention. After about twenty minutes of play dialogue, we spent the next five and a half hours getting to know one another, prompting Pastor Giles at the next table to jokingly say, "It don't look like there's too much rehearsing going on here."

Phyllis and I both laughed as we continued to talk about ourselves. We were totally honest with one another, and when I talked about my extensive criminal history, it didn't faze her in the least. She said that, in the eyes of God, my past was a clean slate and that I was a new creature in Christ. I sat there staring at her, thinking about how amazing this woman was. I didn't want the visit to end, and I felt like I always wanted to be near her. Phyllis told me she would be back to visit the following Saturday for our next rehearsal. It was almost as if she were reading my thoughts. Our relationship took root after that, with Phyllis visiting me faithfully on a weekly basis.

At the Tuesday evening rehearsals, our chemistry didn't go unnoticed by the rest of the inmates in the cast. One evening in particular, while Phyllis and I were sitting together talking, my friend Howie Harris came over and said that we looked like we were made for each other. Phyllis and I just smiled at each other, not realizing at the time how prophetic that comment would prove to be.

Since I was directing and acting in the play, I was extremely busy. I had to work with the musicians on the songs and the actors on dialogue and delivery. I was proud of Phyllis and Mimi because they were there at every rehearsal, not once letting me down. As opening night approached, I was a bundle of nervous energy, but my saving grace was Phyllis. By now we were undeniably a couple, and I couldn't thank God enough for bringing her into my life.

In the play, Phyllis played my widowed wife, and Mimi the role of my daughter. In an effort to help them realize their dream to have a storefront church next to the *Soul Food* restaurant they owned and operated, I came back into their lives in the form of an angel. Since we had already begun to hint at marriage, we found it ironic that we would be husband and wife in the play.

On opening night, all of the Rainbow Gospel Singers were in the audience, along with other invited community guests. Many were there from the inmate population as well, so the chapel was jam-packed that evening. Everything was in place. The musicians were ready, and I was backstage with the cast. When the lights went down, I went out to welcome the audience and prepared them for what they were about to experience.

The play was well received and ended to thunderous applause. We took a number of curtain calls, and at that moment, I felt good about my future. Standing there on stage, surrounded by the cast members, with Phyllis and Mimi at my side, I said a silent prayer. I thought about the promise I had made to God five years earlier, grateful for how far He had brought me since then. The blessings were so overwhelming; it was difficult for me to take it all in. At that moment, I was happier than I had ever been in my life. *It can't possibly get any better than this*, I thought, but again, the blessings were only beginning.

On September 17, 1994, seven months after the curtain came down on *Soul* Food, Phyllis and I were married. Pastor Audrey Giles, her sister, performed the ceremony. Attending the wedding were my mother, my sister Retie, my brother Marvin, and my friend Kent Littlejohn. Phyllis's sister, Pat, was her bridesmaid, while Kent served as my best man.

After we were married, Phyllis visited Binghamton periodically, making it a point to spend quality time with my mother, along with the rest of my family. My family absolutely loved Phyllis, especially my mother. I "inherited" a family of my own as well.

As a result of our marriage, I inherited four stepdaughters, one stepson, and a bunch of loving grandchildren, all of whom I looked forward to meeting. When I finally got to meet my wife's children and grandchildren, it was love at first sight as far as I was concerned. I bonded quickly with my grandchildren, and nothing would lift my spirits more than having Phyllis bring them to visit me.

Yes, God had blessed me far beyond my wildest dreams. I had a wife, stepchildren, and grandchildren who were all waiting for me to come home. Little did I realize that God was working on that as well.

CHAPTER TWENTY-NINE

I appeared before the parole board for release consideration the year before I met Phyllis, in July 1993. Because of my criminal history, I didn't expect a favorable decision, but I certainly didn't count on the reception I received upon entering the hearing room.

Two parole commissioners were seated at a long table—a black female and a white male—with an empty chair directly in front of them. I approached the chair, nodding politely to each of them, and prepared to take a seat.

"Don't even bother sitting down, Mr. Harris!" the female commissioner barked.

I hovered over the chair, just barely scraping the seat, not sure that I had heard correctly. Once I realized I had, however, I stood up straight, looked directly at the commissioner, and waited.

"Your record is *horrendous*," she hissed. "You are *definitely* not going home!"

I looked toward the male commissioner, who nodded his head in confirmation. Then, after going through some perfunctory motions in the parole hearing, I was summarily dismissed.

"Thank you for your time," I said, anxious to get to the law library.

I appealed the two-year "hit" the parole board had given me on the grounds that the decision was predetermined, and that—for all intents and purposes—I had no hearing at all. I was scheduled to reappear before the parole board in July 1995, so I put the appeal in and waited. Unfortunately, *two years* was precisely how long it took for the appeal to be heard.

In July of 1995, I received notification from the Third Department Appellate Court in Albany, New York, that the

July 1993 decision had been overturned. Considering the fact that I had already completed the two years the parole board had given me, I received the court's decision with mixed emotions. Still, when dealing with the appeal process, a *win* is a win and is extremely hard to come by. So I counted my blessings, simply grateful that the higher court agreed with me that the board's 1993 decision was predetermined. Also, by virtue of receiving the decision the month of my scheduled reappearance, I appeared before the parole commissioners twice in the same day, in effect doubling my chances for a favorable decision.

This time there were two different parole commissioners behind the table, and their demeanor was non-confrontational. As a matter of fact, they were actually polite, taking note of my recent marriage, as well as my extensive involvement in drug-treatment programs. They asked where I would be living if parole were granted, along with a few questions concerning my past drug use. I was totally relaxed and responded well to each question. I was then asked if I had any questions of my own, and I told them no. With that, I was told that the hearings were over and I would receive their decision in a few days.

To this day, I don't know at which hearing parole was granted—the morning or the afternoon session—but near the end of September 1995, Phyllis drove to Wallkill Correctional Facility to bring her husband home. She was so excited that, as I waited for her in the prison lobby, she actually tripped and fell down the stairs. I ran over to help her, and she laughed, assuring me that she was okay. We hugged tightly as I helped her to her feet, both of us overcome with excitement in anticipation of our future together as husband and wife. However, these emotions would soon be overshadowed by a secret I had been harboring from Phyllis from the day we met—a secret I was afraid would threaten our marriage.

Impotency is the one thing that no man wants to admit to and certainly not discuss. I don't know when the condition developed, but I believe that it is a result of many years of incarceration and substance abuse. I didn't tell Phyllis about it because I was afraid she wouldn't marry me if I did. I felt that I would be able to overcome my sexual dysfunction upon my release. I didn't understand that it was a *treatable* medical condition, one that is experienced by millions of men at some point in their lives. Also, I felt that my faith in God would be enough to get back on track in that department. I couldn't have been more wrong.

Knowing my wife as I do now, it is clear that I could have—and *should* have—discussed this problem with her. Phyllis is a kind, thoughtful, caring, and understanding woman, and we would have worked through this together. My male ego, however, would not allow it. Consequently, because of my unwillingness to realistically deal with my problem, our marriage suffered almost as soon as I got home. The fact that we were unable to consummate our marriage was eating me up inside, and I can only imagine what it was doing to my wife. You see, Phyllis, like me, is a "romantic" by nature, which is one of the attributes that attracted us. Every time she would visit me in Wallkill, I would gently caress her, whisper in her ear, and even sing to her from time to time. I even went so far as to make a cassette tape of myself covering Lionel Richie songs, a tape that she played on her job and treasures to this day.

However, because of my sexual dysfunction, my romantic affections diminished not long after my release. At the very least, I know now that I should have made an appointment with a urologist to discuss my problem and see what treatments were available. However, I was hoping that it would somehow correct itself, and therefore, our marriage suffered.

My wife and I were extremely active in the church, so that helped in terms of distraction. I remembered my promise to God and was determined to keep it. Phyllis and I were singing together as The Anointed Two, and it seemed the only time we were truly happy was when we were winning souls for Christ through our music ministry. However, when we were not singing, traveling, or recording, I would simply withdraw, merely going through the motions of being a supportive, loving husband. Little did I realize at the time how much my wife was hurting, but I was too caught up in my own psychological pain to notice hers.

Around Christmas of 1995, The Anointed Two auditioned for a nationally televised Christian talent show called *Gospel Star Seek*, based in Nashville, Tennessee. It was just three months after my release from Wallkill when my wife and I learned that we had been chosen for the competition. Needless to say, we were elated at the news.

At the time, we were working with a fantastic keyboard player named Barry Eggleston. As soon as we learned that we had been accepted by the *Gospel Star Seek* producers, we rented studio time in Poughkeepsie so that we could lay down the soundtracks to the songs we were going to perform. We were told that we would be required to sing a minimum of five songs, so we wanted quality soundtracks.

To our dismay, however, the studio technicians were more concerned with the money we gave them up front rather than in the quality of the finished product. The tracks were so bad that we ultimately had to turn to my brother Danny in Binghamton to bail us out and clean up the tracks as best as possible in his studio on a moment's notice.

Since we were scheduled to appear on the show just two weeks after receiving the inferior tapes, it didn't leave Danny much time to work with, but being the professional that he was,

Phyllis and I worked with him nonstop in his home studio until we had tracks we all were happy with. Danny did such a good job, and Phyllis and I were so grateful to him that, besides paying him for the studio time, we invited him to fly to Nashville with us—our treat. Nothing made me happier than knowing that my brother would be there with me. And just to be fair about it, we invited Phyllis's brother, Freddie, to join us as well. He accepted the invitation, and we all excitedly prepared for our trip to Nashville, Tennessee.

To assist us in financing the trip, our pastor, Debra E. Gause of Holy Light Pentecostal Church, arranged for us to hold a gospel concert at the church the night before our flight. We had lined up quite an array of local gospel groups with The Anointed Two as the featured artists, of course. However, an act of nature caused the concert to be canceled at the last minute.

A heavy and steady downpour of rain had caused the roof of the church to leak extensively, soaking the pews and creating puddles of water throughout the sanctuary. No amount of clean up would have had the church ready in time for that night's concert. So, sadly, the concert was canceled, leaving us with limited funds to cover the cost of the trip.

Knowing that only a miracle would get us to Nashville, I stood outside of the church, thoroughly dejected and depressed. My wife asked me what was wrong, and I told her that our trip to Nashville was not going to happen; there was no way we would be able to raise the necessary funds in a matter of hours. Phyllis simply shook her head. "Oh, ye of little faith," she said, then proceeded to do what she does best: take her troubles to God in prayer. To my amazement, in just a few short hours, my wife had the necessary funds for our trip. To this day, my brother Danny says he has never seen anything like that awesome display of God's power in his life. The next day, he, Freddie, my wife, and I were on our way to Nashville, Tennessee.

The Anointed Two appeared on *Gospel Star Seek*, and when the nationwide tabulations were counted, we were voted among the top twenty amateur gospel singers in the country. As a result, our music ministry was in great demand, and we traveled extensively, praising God in worship and in song. The Holy Spirit was opening doors for us that we could never have accomplished on our own.

We had cassettes for sale, as well as videotapes of our *Gospel Star Seek* performance. We were twice featured on Trinity Broadcasting's *Praise the Lord* television programs—as singers on the first show, then being interviewed between songs on the second. We were also in demand at weddings, funerals, nursing homes, prisons, as well as regulars at the Salvation Army Men's Rehabilitation Center in Poughkeepsie.

All of these things happened for us during my first three years out of prison. It was the longest I had been out of prison in my entire adult life without violating my parole conditions or committing a new crime—a scary thought for me.

CHAPTER THIRTY

I was formally discharged from parole supervision on September 25, 1998. Because that event signaled the first time in my adult life that I was not on probation, parole, or any other kind of court-mandated supervision, my initial reaction was one of complete amazement. Although it felt good not to have to report to someone on a monthly basis, it also felt kind of strange, but because of my continued church involvement, I was living a crime-free life and, as a result, had *earned* my discharge from parole supervision.

I was holding down two jobs—as a ward-aide during the evening at Hudson River Psychiatric Center and as an intake counselor during the day at the Salvation Army's Rehabilitation Center, which kept me extremely busy. Of the two, I enjoyed my position with the Salvation Army the most. Not only was I responsible for bringing new men into the center—mostly referrals by probation or parole officers—I also ran a therapy group twice a week, as well as one-on-one counseling sessions with the men.

As an ex-inmate and former addict, most of the men at the center respected me. If any of them had been drinking or using drugs, they knew they couldn't hide it from me, but they also knew that I was fair and that they could talk to me, unlike my boss and center director, Major Rodriguez. He would kick a man out on the street at the slightest infraction. I can't begin to count the number of times I have butt heads with him in an attempt to prevent a man from having his parole violated and being sent back to prison. Therefore, it was only a matter of time before our confrontations came to a head.

One late afternoon, as I was preparing to leave for the day, Major Rodriguez sent a message by the residential manager that he wanted me to counsel one of the center's residents before going home. I, of course, asked who the man was and what he had done to require counseling. After giving me the man's name, the residential manager told me he had no idea what the man had done. That puzzled me. How could I counsel someone without knowing what he had done?

I picked up the phone and called the major's office, but he had already left for the day. So, because of my lack of information, I decided to go home, talk with the major in the morning, and then counsel the man in question. Reasonable enough, right? Not according to my *good friend* Major Rodriguez.

As soon as I entered my second-floor office the next morning Major Rodriguez came bursting through the door in a rage.

"Did you get my instructions from yesterday?" he yelled.

"Yes," I began in an attempt to explain before being cut off midsentence.

"Did you *counsel* the man, yes or no?" he screamed.

He was raging like a madman, and I knew from experience there would be no reasoning with him. Then, as if someone turned a light bulb on in my head, it dawned on me what he was doing: it was a set-up. For the past couple of weeks, he had been looking for an excuse to fire me, and now this was it. Never mind that his instructions were unreasonable, as well as unclear. The fact was that I didn't obey his orders, and for that I had to go.

"Yes or no?" he hollered once more.

Looking him square in the eyes, I shook my head. My expression clearly indicated that I knew what he was doing, but that didn't stop him. He promptly told me that I was fired and that my check would be in the mail. Without another word, he turned and left the office.

First I was stunned, and then I was angry. I silently collected my belongings from my desk and immediately left the building. The residents, I would later learn, were furious that I had been fired. However, there was nothing that I or, for that matter, anyone else could do. I attempted to appeal my dismissal to the Salvation Army's national office but was informed that since I had not signed a contract clearly outlining my duties and what was expected of me before accepting the job, I didn't have anything to validate my position. What it boiled down to was his word against mine. And since Major Rodriguez was my boss, need I say more? I was, however, fortunate enough to find another job relatively quickly.

My grandson's father, Brian Whitaker, called me at home and asked if I would be interested in working at the Anderson School just outside of Hyde Park, in Staatsburg, New York. Brian had been working there for about a year, and when a vacancy became available, he told his supervisor, Tony Janus, about me. Tony called me in for an interview, and my master's degree, along with my work experience at Hudson River Psychiatric Center, virtually guaranteed me the job.

Because the Anderson School services children with autism, as well as those with behavior disorders, I was apprehensive at first about taking the job, but it turned out to be one of the most rewarding experiences of my life.

Tony and Brian formally introduced me to my coworkers, Rick, Anita, and Karen. Karen's sister, Brenda, was the unit supervisor, and they all made me feel welcome, including Dottie, the unit nurse, and Fred Harris, the school's clinician.

As time went by, I could tell that the staff was impressed with how well the kids related to me and vice versa. I would treat them with respect and always say something to make them laugh. There were the inevitable behavior problems, of course, but I always seemed to be one of the few staff members to have a calming effect on the child in question. However, in those rare moments when I could not get a child to calm down, I would call on the school's clinician, Fred Harris.

Fred is a man with a kind and gentle spirit that really came through in his relations with the kids at Anderson. All of the kids at the school loved Fred, and whenever they were upset, they would always ask to see him.

One day at one of our weekly unit meetings, one of the kids noticed the fact that Fred and I had the same last name. With a straight face, I told him that Fred and I were brothers. Since Fred is white and I am black, he found that statement hilarious, laughing so hard that he literally cried. From that day on, whenever the boy saw Fred and me together, he would point at one of us and say, "He your *brother!*" He would then laugh almost to the point of hyperventilating, whereupon Fred and I would have to calm him down.

After about a year at the Anderson School, Phyllis came to work there as well. We worked in the same building, but I worked upstairs in Upper East, and she worked downstairs in Lower East. We would, however, work together from time to time, taking the kids on off-campus trips. At one point, we even received permission from some of the kids' parents to take them to our church services at Holy Light, as well as to gospel concerts we were singing in.

The kids loved Phyllis from her first day on the job, and they especially enjoyed hearing us sing together. One day we made the mistake of giving a boy a copy of the cassette tapes we had for sale. He would play the tape over and over nonstop, especially enjoying the song "Will You Be Ready When Jesus Comes?" On that particular song, Phyllis and I would end it by singing in unison, "Ready…get ready! Ready…get ready!" fading out as the song came to an end.

Well, of course, he latched on to that cadence, and every time he would see Phyllis or me, he would yell at the top of his lungs, "Ready...get ready! Ready...get ready!" He would then start laughing hysterically, at which point we would have to calm him down before he got completely out of control.

However, times were not always that carefree where interaction with the children was concerned. I remember trying to connect with a particularly hostile boy during my first few weeks of working at Anderson. He would not speak to me, and there was nothing I could do to get him to open up. One day we were sitting together on the housing unit, just he and I, as he waited for a visit from his father. Finally, after an almost unbearable period of silence, the door to the unit opened, and the boy's dad walked in. He immediately jumped up and shouted, "Hi, Dad!"

I made the mistake of asking, "That's your dad?"

As if I was the dumbest person on earth, the boy turned to me and said, "*Duh*...I said...hi, *Dad!*" I stood there with a stupid grin on my face as he ran excitedly over to his father.

Steam was coming out of my ears, but all I could do was swallow it. After all, as much as I hated to admit it, he was right. I took a deep breath, stuck my hand out, and introduced myself to his father—the stupid grin still pasted on my face.

After working three years at the Anderson School, I was given the position of residential manager for two housing units on the campus. I enjoyed my work immensely; still, I could not resist the opportunity to work as a paralegal for Prisoner's Legal Services of New York when an opening became available.

My brother-in-law, Louis Milburn, first told me about the position in April 2000. Louis was married to my wife's sister Doris and was an ex-offender himself, having been in the Attica riot while serving a life sentence and eventually being paroled from Green Haven prison. Elijah Williams, also an ex-offender, was a paralegal at Prisoner's Legal Services and told Louis about the opening.

The job appealed to me for a number of reasons. I would have my own office and would be working just thirty-five hours a week at more than twice my Anderson School salary. Also, with my education and prison background, I was a perfect candidate for the job, returning to the very prisons I had served time in and making my prison experiences count for something by helping other prisoners. So as soon as Louis told me about the position, I decided to interview for it.

I thought I did well at the interview. I was dressed appropriately in a black business suit, complete with briefcase, prepared to answer all questions honestly and intelligently. The panel that interviewed me consisted of Elijah Williams; a Hispanic paralegal, Sylvia Santana, two office secretaries, Mel and Sherry; the lawyers themselves, Joel Landau, Gavin Cook, and Rebecca; and Joan, the office manager.

During the interview, I could sense they were impressed with my educational background, but what really weighed heavily in my favor was the fact that I had spent most of my life incarcerated. I was familiar with the workings of the criminal justice system and would easily be able to build a rapport with the men and women prisoners with whom I would come in contact.

At the end of the interview, I was told that I was one of a number of applicants for the position and that I would be informed shortly of their decision. I thanked them, shook hands all around, and made my exit

Two weeks later I received a phone call at home. It was Joan, the office manager, offering me the paralegal position. Although I wanted to shout for joy, I remained calm enough to accept. Joan wanted to know when I would be able to start. I told her that I was required to give the Anderson School two weeks' notice, and since it was already the middle of April, I would not be able to start until May 1. She said that would be fine, and on that note, we ended the conversation. I immediately called Phyllis to give her the good news, and that evening we went out for a celebration dinner.

On May 1, 2000, I officially started working for Prisoner's Legal Services of Poughkeepsie, New York. I had my pick of three vacant offices and chose the one with a view of the parking lot. I couldn't believe my good fortune. Just five years out of prison, and already God had taken me to another level. I had my own computer, access to an extensive law library, and two secretaries at my disposal.

Sitting in *my* office, behind *my* desk, looking out of *my* window, no one could tell me anything. I was no longer on parole and had been out of prison longer than I had ever been in my entire adult life. I had finally made it! I was in a position to finally make a difference in the prison system, to make all of those years inside count for something, and I was eager to give something back.

But in my excitement, I failed to stop and thank God for blessing me with the job. As a matter of fact, at that time, I had already begun to back away from weekly church services and had completely forgotten the promise I had made to serve Him—a lapse of memory that would come back to haunt me sooner than I expected.

For the moment, though, I was on top of the world about to take it by storm. Little did I realize that the "storm clouds" of sin were looming and that Satan was about to make a grand reappearance in my life. After five years of waiting patiently for me to fall, I had finally given him an opening. The scary part, however, is that I didn't even see it coming.

CHAPTER THIRTY-ONE

S hortly after starting my new job, I started missing church services. At first, it was sporadic, and then it became a more frequent occurrence. Although my wife never really questioned me about it, I knew it was disturbing her. I had been warned about taking my eyes off of God, so I definitely should have known better.

I was at one of our weekly night services at Holy Light when Bishop Gause called me to the altar unexpectedly. I thought that she wanted me to sing, but she said that the Holy Spirit had moved her to pray for me. In front of the entire congregation, she reminded me of her earlier warning that Satan was trying to send me back to prison. I nodded my head obediently, not really taking heed to what she was saying. As she began to pray, I closed my eyes, reflecting on the turn my life had taken up to that point. Although I wasn't drinking or using drugs at the time, I had recently started soliciting prostitutes. Well, to be more exact, my first encounter happened because a prostitute propositioned me.

I happened to be out just driving around when I stopped at the corner for a red light. It was a bright, warm summer day, and all of the windows were down in the car. Then out of nowhere, a woman approached the passenger's side window, stuck her head inside, and asked if I could give her a ride to McDonald's down the street. I knew she was a prostitute, but she was young and attractive, so I went along with the program. Needless to say, we never reached McDonald's. Although I felt guilty about what I was doing, it seemed that once I started I could not stop. Even though I didn't have to go outside the home for sexual fulfillment, I strongly believe that my impotence had a lot to do with the continuation of my clandestine activities—at least on a subconscious level. I was angry and frustrated about my condition and simply withdrew from my marriage until ultimately the romance was gone. That's when I began soliciting prostitutes on a regular basis. Although the sex was always oral—with me as the recipient—I hated myself for what I was doing. Still, I seemed unable to stop.

As I moved further away emotionally from my wife, I also moved further away spiritually from God. I knew that I was loved by both, but at the time I didn't fully realize the extent of that love. Even at that point in my life, where I had given Satan full reign, God still had me in His grace. Sooner than expected, I would come to learn that God had not forsaken me; although, I had turned my back on Him.

It's important to mention that the changes in my lifestyle and behavior were subtle—that's how Satan works. He knew that he could not get me to commit a crime outright, at least not in my normal state of mind. So, what did he do? He drew me into a situation that started me on a journey toward insanity.

Phyllis and I were invited to a lawn party in Binghamton at the new home of our good friends Kent and Doris. Since they also asked us to sing at the party, we decided to bring our kids with us and make it a family thing. Kent and Doris had never met Reginald, Addie, Jeanine, Tamika, and Shashona, so we thought it would be nice to introduce them at the party. Since each of our children, except for Shashona, had kids of their own, it was kind of difficult finding baby sitters for everyone, but Phyllis was determined that we all would be at the party as a family, and that was that. She found babysitters for all of our grandchildren, and we were on our way.

With everyone crowded into my van, we spent most of the trip to Binghamton singing and harmonizing. As a result, the ride was relatively short, and we arrived at Doris and Kent's house early in the evening before the party.

After introducing everyone to our hosts and being settled in, I then took them over to my brother Danny's house so they could see his recording studio. Having already met them months earlier, Danny was glad to see us. We harmonized for Danny, and he told us that he wanted to get us on tape before we left town. He then said that the rest of my family was waiting for us at my brother Marvin's house, so we all went there for a little while. It was getting late, and we were a little tired from the drive, so we only stayed long enough to eat and do a little socializing. After about an hour or so, we excused ourselves and returned to Doris and Kent's, where we retired for the evening.

The following afternoon, Danny assisted me in setting up our microphone stands, speakers, monitors, amplifier, and tape deck. After everything was set up, I put in one of the soundtracks that Phyllis and I sang to and did a sound check. There would be other guests at the party, and I wanted to make sure that nothing went wrong. Satisfied that things were in order with the sound system, I drove Danny home so that he could get ready for the party. He had agreed to DJ for us, and I didn't want him to be late.

When I returned to the house, Phyllis and the kids were helping Doris with the cleaning, cooking, and setting things up for the party. Everyone was laughing, joking, and in the partying mood. Reginald asked me to turn the sound system on so that he and Tamika could do a duet to the soundtrack "Always" by the group Atlantic Starr. I set the tape up for them, and they did a nice rendition of the song. Then to our surprise, some of the guests began to arrive earlier than expected. I immediately shut the system down, and Phyllis and I went upstairs to get dressed.

When we came back down, the party was in full swing. My brother Danny had returned with his wife, Julie, and he had the sound system blaring dance music. There were alcoholic beverages at the party, but since Phyllis and I didn't drink, I didn't think anything of it at the time.

I walked over to where Danny and my daughter Tamika were talking and noticed that she had a drink in her hand. I gave her a kiss on the cheek, and she mentioned how this was the first time that we all were together as a family. I smiled, nodding my head in agreement. Then she said, "This calls for a toast."

"I can't drink, Tamika," I said.

"Why not?"

"Because alcohol is a trigger for me," I replied. "I make bad decisions when I drink, and I can't afford that."

She, however, insisted that just "one drink" wouldn't hurt me—a simple *toast*, nothing more. I kept refusing, and she kept insisting. Finally, just to make her happy, I said, "Okay, just a toast. One drink, and that's it."

"*One* drink," Tamika said, smiling. "What will it be?"

"A glass of Bacardi," I said hesitantly. "And make sure your mother's not around."

I certainly didn't want Phyllis to see me taking a drink of alcohol.

Tamika nodded, slipped unnoticed into the house, and returned with a double shot of Bacardi. I have never been what one would call a "social drinker." Since I don't like the taste of it, I cannot *sip* on a glass of alcohol. So after clinking glasses with Tamika in our toast, I drank the entire contents of my glass straight down. That, of course, was the beginning of the end for me—the monster had been sprung.

Sure, I told Tamika that I was only going to have one drink, but of course that's not how the evening turned out. That single drink was one of many for me that night. When my wife found out that I had been drinking, she was furious with the both of us. Of course I told her that she didn't have anything to worry about, but we both knew that was a lie. We had plenty to worry about—I just couldn't see it at the time.

Although that one episode at the party didn't turn me into a daily drinker, I soon found myself looking for reasons to drink. Since I had cut back on church attendance, it was easy for me to find an outlet for my drinking. Both my nephew Junior and my brother-in-law Randy drank, so it was only natural that I would indulge whenever we "did the town." Although I would never have admitted it at the time, I started looking forward to our times together more for the drinking rather than for the camaraderie the three of us shared.

Not long after his party, Kent invited me to spend a weekend with him and a friend of his named Bob at a time-share property in Virginia. He told me that I could invite two guests of my own, so of course I invited Junior and Randy. I was happy when they accepted the invitation, because I knew we were going to do some serious drinking and have lots of laughs together. Whenever we got together it was usually hilarious, and I knew that we were really going to enjoy ourselves.

Kent drove to my home in Poughkeepsie the evening of the trip, leaving his car in my garage for the weekend. Since there were five of us, including Bob, whom we had to pick up at his home in Maryland, we needed to take my van. So with Randy behind the wheel, we pulled out of my driveway in high spirits. Unbeknownst to the others, I had already purchased a fifth of Bacardi Lemon, and as soon as we hit the open road, I pulled it out. Kent was in the passenger's seat, Junior was alone in the second row, and I was alone in the third row. I started passing the bottle around, so by the time we reached the New Jersey Turnpike, no one was feeling any pain.

At around two in the morning, we approached a self-service tollbooth. There was a sign directly over the change basket that read "Exact Change Only." I asked Randy if he needed some change for the toll, and he told me no. He reached into his pocket and pulled out a handful of change—much more than the toll required. Meanwhile, a line of cars was forming behind us, waiting their turn. I reminded Randy that the toll required exact change only, and he told me not to worry about it. Tossing the handful of change into the basket, Randy waited for the red light to turn green and for the bar blocking our path to rise. The light remained red. Car horns began to honk loudly behind us. Randy reached into his pocket for another handful of change, tossing it into the basket. Still, the light remained red. The impatient drivers in back of us began hollering for us to move it. Kent, Junior, and I were in stitches as Randy shifted into panic mode. He emptied all of his pockets of change and tossed this last batch into the basket. The light was stuck on red. We began to rib Randy unmercifully.

"Write a check!" Junior screamed.

"Throw your credit card in the basket!" I yelled, tears rolling down my face.

Finally, to Randy's relief, a female tollbooth attendant appeared from a side office and manually raised the bar that blocked our passage. She not only motioned us on our way but also the entire line of cars behind us. The cars honked in gratitude as they passed our van because Randy had paid everyone's toll. He waved to them with a sheepish grin as the rest of us howled with laughter.

It was early morning when we pulled into Bob's driveway in Maryland, and we were all tired, but not too tired to recount the tollbooth episode for Bob's benefit. He set out drinks for us, and he laughed hysterically as we told him the story. We then slept for a few hours and were on the road to Virginia before noon.

Our weekend at the time-share resort was one of typical male bonding: eating, drinking, and watching sports on television. Although, during those three days, my drinking was out of control, I was having too much fun to give it any thought. My only regret was that we didn't have more time to spend together.

Needless to say, on the drive back home, when Randy approached the tollbooth that read "Exact Change," he was careful to make sure that his change was just that—exact! To this day, whenever we think about Randy's tollbooth adventure, we all break up laughing.

CHAPTER THIRTY-TWO

Crack cocaine is a new-era drug, belonging to a new generation of addicts. So when I tried it for the first time, I was totally unprepared for its powerful addictive potential. I tried it during a period of alcohol-induced madness, and the "high" completely overwhelmed me. It enhanced my sexual desires greatly, causing me to patronize crack-whores. I was amazed at what that little vial of processed rocks would make a woman do, and I took full advantage of its potential.

I wasn't smoking it every day—at least not in the beginning, so I was able to control my urges for it, but just as any beginning drug use comes in spurts, so did my attempts at leading a normal life. I was still singing, writing, and recording songs. Also, my wife and I were still singing together as The Anointed Two, but it wasn't long before I started feeling like the hypocrite that I was because of the dual life that I was leading. I was no longer singing for the glory of God but for the money the engagements would bring—money that would be used to support my growing alcohol and cocaine problem.

I knew that God was not pleased; I could feel that in my spirit. I could sense that I had hurt Him deeply and, in my mind's eyes, could picture a wise, kind, and loving Creator sadly shaking His head as He watched me throw away the gifts that He had bestowed upon me.

Alcohol was the "gateway" to my crack cocaine use, and I curse the day that I succumbed to temptation and took that first drink after almost ten years of sobriety. The trap was laid, and I went for the bait, so I have no one to blame but myself. Satan had waited almost ten years to snare me, and I walked right in to his clutches.

Shortly after my fifty-second birthday in the spring of 2001, I was arrested for driving while intoxicated. I had just shared a belated birthday celebration with my nephew Junior, my brothers-in-law Randy and Freddie, and my daughter Tamika. Everyone except for Freddie was drinking that evening, and we were using my sound equipment and background tracks to sing karaoke style. The celebration lasted into the wee hours of the morning, with Freddie being the first to leave and the rest following suit shortly after—except for Tamika. Since I knew that her husband, Rod, was home with their three daughters, I thought it would be best if she stayed and got some sleep at my house, and I would drive her home later in the day, but she wanted to go home right then, and she wanted me to drive her. I tried to talk her in to getting some rest first, but she insisted that I take her home—so I did.

It was around 4:00 a.m. when I dropped her off at her apartment, and I was anxious to get home myself. I was tired from all the singing and the alcohol. As I stopped for a red light around the corner from my house, I saw a police car pull up in back of me with two officers inside. They followed me close as I made a left turn on the green light, and I began to get a little nervous. I had one more left turn to make at the corner and then a sharp left into my driveway. I was allowed to do all of that, and then I heard the *whoop-whoop* of the siren.

I just sat there, shaking my head at the approaching police officers. I could only think of what Phyllis was going to say when she learned I had been arrested for DWI. She was working an overnight shift at the Anderson School, and I certainly didn't look forward to calling her from jail.

One of the officers asked me to step out of the car, and I complied immediately. I told him that we were in my driveway. When asked if I had been drinking, I said yes, but it had been a few hours since my last drink. I was then given the sobriety test and was also required to blow into a Breathalyzer. I was placed under arrest for driving while intoxicated; taken to the sheriff's station, where I was fingerprinted; and given an appearance ticket. After spending about half an hour at the sheriff's station, I was then driven back home, where I immediately called Phyllis at her job and told her what had just happened.

Although she was not pleased at the news, I could sense that she wasn't too surprised at it either. Her demeanor and tone of voice gave me the impression that she had been expecting something like that to happen. To her credit, though, she didn't try to make me feel worse than I already did. I was extremely angry with myself and was worried about how news of this would affect my job with Prisoners' Legal Services. After all, I was coming up on my first anniversary as a paralegal with them, and driving to local and even distant correctional facilities to interview inmates was an important part of my job. So knowing that my license was probably going to be suspended, I spent the remainder of the weekend dreading having to break the news to my coworkers on Monday morning.

However, when they found out what had happened to me over the weekend, everyone at the office was supportive. I was totally honest with them, not holding anything back. I went to Gavin Cook first because he was the managing attorney at the time. Gavin told me that the DWI would not affect my job. He said I would more than likely be given a "restricted license," allowing me to continue to drive during work hours. I was relieved to hear that and thanked him for his understanding and support.

Even more supportive of me was Joel Landau, the attorney I was assigned to work with at Prisoners' Legal Services. Joel and I had a close working relationship, and I also viewed him as a good friend. When I told him about my arrest, he immediately offered to loan me the money to retain a lawyer. I told him that I had spoken with Donald Roth, who had recently left our Prisoners' Legal Services office and opened his own practice in Poughkeepsie. Promising that I had nothing to worry about, Donald agreed to represent me for a fee of eight hundred dollars. So, I gratefully accepted Joel's offer, borrowed the eight hundred dollars, and waited for my day in court.

After a negotiated guilty plea by my lawyer, my license was suspended, a four hundred-dollar fine was imposed, and I was required to attend the state's mandated DWI classes. *That's what I paid for?* I thought. None of what Donald said he was going to do for me was actually done. I could have gotten the same, if not better, outcome representing myself! At least the judge allowed me to have a "restricted license," and for that I was grateful. Still, my main objective was to get my license restored as soon as possible, so I was determined to do whatever was required of me, including the DWI classes. I was still upset with Donald for ripping me off, but there was really nothing that I could do about it. After discussing his representation with Joel, I called Donald at his office and asked for my money back. He got very nasty with me and told me that he wasn't giving me anything. I threatened to make a complaint against him and then decided against it. It simply wasn't worth it to me. Besides, I figured, he would get what was coming to him sooner or later—and he did. Just three years later, he would be sentenced to five years in federal prison for witness tampering.

Still, one would think that all of this would have taught me a lesson, right? Wrong! Just weeks after my DWI arrest, my brother-in-law, Randy, and I went up to Binghamton to attend a party at my brother Marvin's house. Because of my "restricted license," Randy was doing all of the driving, so I took it upon myself to do all of the drinking. There was plenty of alcohol at the party, and I wasn't passing up any of it. After all, I reasoned, I wasn't driving, so I might as well enjoy myself. As the party was winding down, someone asked Randy and me if we wanted to go to an after-hours club. We agreed and headed out for more partying.

At the club, while Randy and our host were busy talking, I decided that I needed some fresh air. I asked Randy for the car keys and—not thinking—he handed them to me. As he turned back to our host, I headed out the door straight to my car. By then I was so intoxicated that I couldn't see clearly, let alone drive. Still, I got behind the wheel and roared out of the club's parking lot, heading for downtown Binghamton.

Four blocks from the club, I made an erratic turn in direct view of a police officer that was parked at the curb. He immediately turned on his siren and revolving roof light, and pulled me over about a block away. *Well, this is it,* I thought as I watched the policeman approach the driver's side window. *It's all over for me now…I'm going to jail!* I was sitting there behind the wheel of my van, drunk as a skunk with a *restricted license* in my pocket, clearly marking me as a recent DWI offender. Oh, it was definitely all over for me—of that I had no doubt.

"License and registration," the officer said, peering closely at me through the lowered window.

I tried to appear "normal" as I complied with his demand, handing over the registration and restricted license as if everything were fine.

"Been drinking tonight?" he asked, glancing at the paperwork and then shifting his attention to the restricted license.

"No," I slurred in an attempt to look indignant.

"No?" he shouted, incredulously. "Man, you're *blasted!*"

As he returned to his squad car and got on the radio, I sat there thinking about what I was going to tell my wife and the people at my job—my *second* DWI arrest, and only three weeks apart? I was definitely going to jail—there was no question about that. I thought about my brother-in-law Randy, just blocks away at the after-hours club. There was no way for me to contact him and let him know what had happened to me. As a result, my car would be towed, leaving him stranded in Binghamton. Someone would have to drive up from Poughkeepsie to get him. I just sat there, shaking my head, unable to believe that I had done this to myself again.

Finally, after what seemed like hours, the officer approached the car again, handed the paperwork back, and told me to step out of the car. *Well, this is it,* I thought as I stepped out of the van, waiting to be placed under arrest. To my shock, instead, I was told that I had two choices. I could either be taken to jail and my car towed or I could lock the car and walk. I stood there in a daze, unable to believe what I was hearing. I was asked a second time what I wanted to do, and I looked at him like he was crazy. I wasn't *that* drunk—of course I would walk.

I quickly locked my van and literally ran back to the after-hours club where Randy was waiting. Breathlessly, I told him what had just happened, and he shook his head in disbelief. I couldn't blame him, of course, because I still didn't believe it myself. Again, God stepped in for me, providing the miracle that I so desperately needed. That, alone, should have been enough to convince me that it was time to repent and be thankful for His mercy and grace. For some reason, however, I just could not do it. I didn't realize, at the time, just how strong a hold Satan had on me. Perhaps if I would have been able to recall my sister-in-law's warning to me years earlier—"Satan is trying to send you back to prison"—I would have come to my senses, resumed my Christian walk, and thanked God for His mercy, but unfortunately it was not to be. My sister-in-law's prophecy was about to come true sooner than expected.

CHAPTER THIRTY-THREE

The Poughkeepsie office of Prisoners' Legal Services handled all Department of Correctional Services (DOCS) facilities in New York City, as well as Downstate, Fishkill, Ulster, Eastern, Sullivan, Otisville, Mid-Orange, Woodbourne, Bedford Hills, Taconic, Green Haven, and Sing-Sing Correctional Facility. Because of my long history of incarceration, I felt that I had finally found my niche when I became a paralegal with Prisoners' Legal Services. I say this because my duties required me to go back inside the prisons, interview inmates, and assist them in any way that I could.

I worked closely with attorney Joel Landau, reporting directly to him concerning inmate needs and concerns. Basically, our office dealt with disciplinary and medical issues for New York state prisoners, the majority of which were appealing disciplinary dispositions resulting in six months or more in a special housing unit, or S units, as they are more commonly referred to. We also investigated brutality allegations, with an eye toward litigation for the inmate. For the most part, however, inmates simply requested information relevant to their personal situation at the time: parental/visitation rights, divorces, or how to appeal their conviction. I would mail out hundreds of information packets a month and personalize the response, but the most exciting aspect of my duties at Prisoners' Legal Services was when I was required to visit a client at his or her respective facility.

As a former inmate myself, it was particularly encouraging for the men and women I visited to talk with me. By my example, they were able to see that they too can make it if they apply themselves, and that there is life after prison. However, the absolute best time for me, during my visits to these facilities, was when it was time for me to leave. The guards had to unlock the gates to let me out, and that gave me a "rush" that words cannot convey. When the gates slammed behind me and I headed toward my car, I always felt a sense of relief.

I received mail regularly from prisoners, some of who were simply lonely and wanted someone to write them. However, although I could understand their loneliness, I was not able to have an ongoing correspondence relationship with them. Still, no matter how hard I tried to explain this to those inmates who insisted on writing me each week, none were more persistent than Santé Kimes.

Santé and her son, Kenneth Kimes, were convicted of killing Manhattan socialite Irene Silverman. Santé wrote to me almost daily, asking me to talk with Kenneth, who was being held at Clinton Correctional Facility at the time. She wanted me to make sure that he was okay and was not being mistreated. I tried to explain to her that Clinton was not in our office's region and that I would refer her request to the Prisoners' Legal Services office in the Buffalo, New York area. Santé was at Bedford Hills Correctional Facility at the time, and she begged me to come and visit her as well. I discussed her request with Joel, and he said that it would serve no useful purpose for me to visit her. As a result of their murder conviction, she and her son were both serving life sentences in New York State. They would soon be extradited to California where they faced the death penalty for allegedly killing a California businessman in 1998. I wrote to Santé explaining our decision, but she continued to bombard me with letters. Not long after, her son Kenneth made national news by taking a news reporter hostage in the visiting room of Clinton Correctional Facility. He released her after a couple of hours, but not before proclaiming that he and his mother were being framed. I never went to visit Santé Kimes, and she soon stopped writing all together.

In July 2001, a paralegal position became available in our Ithaca, New York office close to Binghamton, New York. I decided to apply for the job because my mother's health was failing, and I wanted to be closer to her. In addition, I thought a change of environment would allow me to get my life back on track, allowing me to get a handle on my drinking and cocaine use and reconnect with my brothers and sisters in Binghamton.

My wife was eager for the move herself, making relocation even more appealing. So, after expressing my desire for the Ithaca job to Gavin and my supervising attorney, Joel Landau, I went to Ithaca and interviewed for the paralegal position. Because I was already working as a paralegal in the Poughkeepsie office, the job was pretty much in the bag. Two weeks after the interview, it became official—the job was mine.

Since I was scheduled to start on September 1, 2001, my wife and I had less than two months to find housing in the Ithaca/Binghamton area. However, in early August, just one month before I was to begin work, the funding for Prisoners' Legal Services was held up in Albany, and I was laid off as a result. However, believing that the layoff would only be temporary, I was optimistic enough to continue with my move to Binghamton.

Phyllis and I found a lovely, three-bedroom home in the Binghamton suburb of Conklin, New York. So believing that I would only be out of work a month or so at the most, we continued with our moving arrangements. Little did I realize that things were about to go downhill for me from that point on.

Since there were still bills to pay, my wife remained in Poughkeepsie, working at the Anderson School, while I stayed in our new house in Conklin—alone. I searched for jobs in the Binghamton area, but there were none to be found. Months passed without success. Then, in the middle of October, just two weeks after her sixty-ninth birthday, my mother passed away.

My brother Danny called one afternoon to tell me that my mother had been taken to the hospital in the middle of night, unable to breathe on her own. I rushed to the hospital, where Danny, Marvin, Lou Lou, Dee Dee, and Retie met me. We gathered around our mother's bed, maintaining a silent vigil, each of us deep in thought. I don't know what my brothers and sisters were thinking at that moment, but I was thinking how grateful I was that both Marvin and I were not in jail at the time. I thanked God for allowing us to be by her side, rather than hear about her condition from behind prison walls. I don't know how either of us would have handled that, but I was thankful that my mother was able to lay eyes on *all* of her children before taking her last breath. She opened her eyes long enough for each of us to let her know just how much she was loved. Her gaze seemed to linger a little longer when her eyes fell on me, and there was just a hint of a smile as I took her hand in mine.

As her firstborn, my mother and I were extremely close and shared a special bond. I was always able to make her laugh, even when she didn't feel like it. She always looked forward to my visits and was always glad to just have me around. We both shared a healthy sense of humor, and she always got a kick out of my practical jokes—except for one occasion in particular.

My brother-in-law Randy and I had come up from Poughkeepsie early one morning, to surprise her with a visit. My mother had never met Randy, so I was looking forward to introducing them. However, it is important to understand that my mother was a very private person and not very comfortable around strangers. So perhaps that was not the best time to pull one of my practical jokes on her—still, I couldn't resist. I knocked on her door.

"Who is it?"

"Jehovah's witness," I said, disguising my voice.

"I'm on the phone," she said, after a long silence.

I stifled a laugh because not only was she not on the phone, it was also completely out of character for my mother to lie.

"I'll wait," I yelled, still trying not to laugh.

There was an even longer silence this time.

"Long distance," she hollered.

That's when I lost it and started laughing uncontrollably.

Immediately recognizing my voice, she rushed to the door and yanked it open.

"Teddy?" she said, shaking her head in anger.

She spent the next hour or so trying to act like she was really upset with me, but after a while, she had to laugh about it herself. Such was my relationship with my mother, and those are the memories I cherish the most—us joking and laughing together.

I was home alone when my mother passed away, again my brother Danny calling with the news. He was crying hysterically, but I was completely numb. I just didn't know how to process the fact that my mother was no longer alive. I immediately called Phyllis at the Anderson School, and she took the news extremely hard. She and my mother were very close, and my mother loved Phyllis dearly. She was constantly reminding me of the blessing I had in her as a wife, and I knew that they had discussed my growing substance abuse problem. I, of course, tried to act as if everything was fine when I was around her, but mothers know their children, and they cannot be fooled. She implored me not to take Phyllis for granted and to straighten my life out before it was too late. How I wish I had listened to her now—she certainly knew what she was talking about.

My mother enjoyed hearing me sing, and her favorite song was "Alfie." She would always ask me to sing it for her whenever she was feeling down or if she had friends over. So as a tribute to her, I sang "Alfie" at her funeral. As I gazed into the tearful eyes of my brothers and sisters, it was only by the grace of God that I was able to get through it without breaking down. At song's end I felt drained and deeply depressed. However, as the oldest of the family, I was trying to be strong for the others, so I simply stuffed my feelings deep inside. When they finally surfaced, it was overwhelming for me, resulting in actions seemingly beyond my control.

As I waited to be called back to work at Prisoners' Legal Services, I sunk deeper and deeper into depression. I felt that if I could just return to work I would be able to get my life back on track. I was still looking for work in other areas, but my biggest obstacle was my criminal record. Now, as opposed to it being an asset at Prisoners' Legal Services, my past was now coming back to haunt me.

My wife had finally found employment in Binghamton and was now with me in our new home. However, the fact that she was working and I was *not* only served to depress me more. My spirits were somewhat lifted, though, when my daughter Nya flew in from Phoenix, Arizona with my granddaughters, Kira, Jayde, and Onyx. It was the Christmas season, and they stayed with us for a little over a week. When it was time for them to go back to Phoenix, my depression returned even stronger.

The new year 2002 arrived with absolutely no fanfare on my part. As a matter of fact, I slept right through it, not even staying up to watch the Times Square ball drop. By then, I really had no motivation to do much of anything—except drink. My depression had taken root to the point that life for me was just a matter of going through the motions. Phyllis was at work more than she was home, which really didn't make that much of a difference anyway. Even when she was home, I acted as if she wasn't. I was irritable and moody most of the time, so I'm sure that my company left a lot to be desired as far as my wife was concerned. We had stopped doing things together, and I couldn't even remember the last time we had sung together. The

Anointed Two, for all intents and purposes, had simply ceased to exist.

Still, singing is what kept me sane. I had a recording studio in my attic, and I escaped my depression many times by working on my music. I was writing and recording original songs and singing in local clubs and restaurants for extra money. I was also trying to perfect some lyrics for Kurtis Blow and had talked on the phone with him after he had expressed an interest in what I had written. Actually, the idea for the lyrics came from Kurtis himself.

My brothers, Danny and Marvin, and I were visiting with Kurtis at his apartment in the Bronx, which was really a reunion of sorts for us. It had been decades since Danny had played and produced with Kurtis, so he had lost contact with him. Michael "Tony" Jones, a family friend and former head of security for Kurtis, had arranged the meeting. Tony was staying at Marvin's house, and he had come down from Binghamton with us, along with Anthony Foster, another family friend and Kurtis's former road manager.

When we arrived at his apartment, Kurtis told us that he was waiting for Dan-O, our nephew, to arrive. Actually, Dan-O was his stage name, his real name being Daniel England. As a child, the family called him Booby, but he had taken the name Dan-O after breaking into the "rap game." He was now doing studio work with Kurtis, and they had a session to complete that afternoon in Queens.

Meanwhile, as we waited for Dan-O to arrive, Kurtis showed us clips of a hip-hop documentary he was shooting in hopes of getting it produced as a movie. It dealt with the history of rap music and included interviews with such rap legends and pioneers as Grand Master Flash, Run-DMC, and Russell Simmons, just to name a few. It was really impressive work, and I told him so.

My brother Danny had with him a beat that he wrote, and Kurtis asked to hear it. After pumping up the volume, the old Kurtis Blow started to shine, and he began to freestyle to Danny's beat. It was then that I got the idea for the rap lyrics that I wrote for Kurtis later on. For the moment, though, we were all grooving to Kurtis's flow. So much so that by the time my nephew Dan-O arrived, we were all anxious to head out to the Queens studio where Kurtis was recording at the time.

We all piled into my Dodge Caravan with Kurtis taking the seat next me, as I slid behind the wheel. Danny's beat was blasting from the car stereo as Kurtis began to freestyle once more. Before we knew it, we were at the recording studio. I immediately produced my camera, taking exterior and interior shots of all of us. Then Kurtis and Dan-O went to work, doing what they do best. Danny monitored the controls while Marvin and I sat on the couch just outside the recording booth. It was good for us to be together again, and we were enjoying it immensely.

Later that evening, as the session came to an end, my brothers and I prepared for the drive back to Binghamton. We promised Kurtis that we would stay in touch, and he assured us that he would do the same. The ride home was pleasant with all of us laughing, joking, and reminiscing. I was in a good mood the entire ride back to Binghamton, with depression nowhere in sight; little did I realize how quickly all of that would change.

CHAPTER THIRTY-FOUR

Being in the studio with Kurtis Blow stirred something inside of me, and I felt the urge to perform again. I spent the next couple of weeks in my home studio putting together a demo CD and then went around to local clubs and restaurants in an effort to get bookings. The CD, comprised of five love songs, was entitled *For Lovers Only,* and I left it with club or restaurant owners to listen to at their convenience.

The owner of Le Chalet, a French restaurant in the Binghamton suburb of Vestal, New York, loved the CD but was booked up until the summer. He told me to give him a call around late May or early June, and he would have a spot for me. In the meantime, I continued to shop my demo in an effort to get bookings in the area.

Finally, the owner of J-Michaels, an Italian restaurant in downtown Binghamton, contacted me, and I was booked to perform on New Year's Eve 2001. It would not, however, be my first time singing at that particular restaurant. My friend, Dave Robbins, an extremely talented pianist, had asked me to sing on a couple sets with him at J-Michaels a few months earlier, and the patrons loved me. So as a result of that exposure, I opened at the restaurant on New Year's Eve 2001 with my own set entitled: *For Lovers Only—An Evening with Theo Harris.* Because my wife had to work that evening, my daughter Shashona, who was pregnant at the time, came with me for support, and for that I was extremely grateful. Then, just past the halfway point of my performance, Phyllis arrived at the restaurant to catch the end of the show. I was pleased to introduce her to the patrons, and we ended the evening's performance with a number of duets. It felt good to sing with my wife again after such a long layoff, and I was thankful for the opportunity.

A few weeks after my J-Michaels performance, the grandmother of my wife's best friend passed away. Although her friend, Shelly, and I were not on speaking terms at the time, my sympathy went out to her and the family, and I was extremely supportive of my wife singing at the funeral at the family's request. I didn't attend the funeral, but I did accompany my wife to Poughkeepsie, expressing my condolences personally to Shelly later that day at her family's nightclub, Jordan's. Although new to Poughkeepsie, Jordan's was the hottest nightspot going at the time. Not only did Jordan's book name acts, it was also a favorite hangout for ex-heavyweight boxing champion Mike Tyson whenever he was in town.

Shelly introduced me to her cousin, a co-owner of the club, telling him that I was Phyllis's husband and that I was also a singer. He shook my hand warmly and told me how much he enjoyed my wife's song at the funeral. Shelly then told him that my wife and I used to sing together as The Anointed Two and that he should hear me sing. He asked if I had anything that he could listen to, and I told him that I had a demo CD in my van. I hurried back with my *For Lovers Only* CD, and the three of us sat in his office listening to the opening song, "I Believe in You and Me." Watching him, I could sense that he was impressed with my vocals. He nodded his head in appreciation at different intervals, listening to the entire song. He then listened to parts of the remaining songs, showing the same level of interest and appreciation. After turning the CD player off, he sat back in his chair, smiling at me. Breaking the brief silence, he then asked me how I would like to open for the legendary singing group, Blue Magic, at Jordan's upcoming Mother's Day show. I just sat there, too stunned to speak. Finally, regaining my composure, I told him that it would be an honor to open for them, as they were one of my favorite "old school" groups. I was glad that Shelly and I had ironed out our differences, and that we were friends again. I gave her a hug, and her cousin told me that he would have the paperwork ready for me to sign at a later date. In the meantime, we exchanged phone numbers, shook hands, and I exited his office with wings on my feet.

The upcoming gig at Jordan's went far beyond the sheer excitement of opening for Blue Magic; it also meant that I was going to be paid for doing it. That was a good thing because I still had a $400 fine to pay as part of my sentence for my DWI conviction, and the due date for final payment was just weeks away. Because of my unemployed status, I was granted an extension for payment, so if I didn't take care of it on the upcoming date, a warrant would be issued for my arrest.

I drove down to Poughkeepsie City Court on the due date with the $400 in my pocket. When I went to the window to pay, however, the clerk informed me that the computer record showed I had already paid the fine in full! I knew that was wrong, of course, but I certainly wasn't going to inform him of the error. As soon as the clerk uttered those three words, "paid in full," my addiction reared its ugly head. Elated at my good fortune, I almost ran from the clerk's window and to my van.

In all honesty, my original plan was to return immediately to Binghamton, but after purchasing a half-pint of Bacardi Lemon just outside of Newburgh—to celebrate of course—then drinking it straight down from the bottle while driving, that plan had a short shelf life. I drove into the city of Newburgh and bought some crack cocaine, and that was all she wrote. I didn't get home until well after noon the following day—broke, depressed, and disgusted. My wife had been waiting up all night for my return and let me have it as soon as I walked through the door. All I could do was stand there and take it, since there was absolutely nothing for me to say in my defense. I couldn't understand why I was doing what I was doing, and the tears rolled down my face in large, heavy drops. It was as if an unseen force was controlling me, and I was helpless to do anything about it.

Phyllis insisted that I enter a drug treatment program, but I told her that all I needed was for Prisoners' Legal Services to call me back to work. I was certain that all of my problems would simply disappear if that were to happen. My wife was adamant, however, so I finally agreed to look into getting help with my substance abuse problem. Little did I realize at the time that I would soon be employed by one of the best and most respected drug and alcohol programs in the Broome County region: New Horizons—ironically, the very same drug program in which I had been a patient thirteen years earlier!

Still unemployed, I was scanning the help wanted section of the daily newspaper and came across a Program Aid position at Binghamton General Hospital's New Horizon inpatient drug treatment program. Deciding to "kill two birds with one stone," as the adage goes, I applied for the position. I figured that by working around recovering addicts I could address my own problem by osmosis. Of course I didn't tell the interviewer that I had a current substance abuse problem, emphasizing instead the value of hiring an ex-addict. Everything went according to plan—except for the treatment by osmosis part—and I found myself a paid member of the New Horizons staff. I didn't enjoy the job though, because I felt like the hypocrite that I was. There I was counseling others on the dangers of substance abuse and using myself during my off-hours. I was angry with myself for my deception, and I dealt with that anger by drinking even heavier, leading of course to more frequent crack binges on payday. I was completely immersing myself in my addiction, almost as if I was waiting for my demise. And the insane part is that I seemed to be looking forward to it. If returning to prison was my only avenue of relief, well, then so be it! This irrational thought process was not a conscious one of course, but rather the product of a sick and distorted subconscious response. To my bizarre way of thinking, since I couldn't take the necessary steps to get treatment on my own, if I went to prison, I would be forced to get the help I needed. Of course, this makes absolutely no sense, but such is the nature of madness. And just so there is no misunderstanding on the part of the reader, I was, for all intents and purposes, completely out of my mind by that time. The cumulative effects of daily alcohol abuse and random crack binges had turned me into a walking time bomb.

As I sunk deeper and deeper into my alcohol and crack abuse, I went through the motions of leading a normal life. I brought my *For Lovers Only* CD to New Horizons, letting the program clients and my coworkers listen to it. They all liked it and asked if I had any copies for sale. I explained that the CD was just a demo I used to get club bookings, prompting me to tell them about the Jordan's engagement on Mother's Day. When they learned that I would be opening for Blue Magic, a few of my older coworkers said they would be there. I thanked them for their support and told them I looked forward to seeing them there.

In early April of 2002, with the Blue Magic Mother's Day show just one month away, Jordan's booked me for a solo performance. Actually, my wife and I were asked to perform together, but Phyllis had a cold at the time and wasn't up to it. However, she did accompany me to Poughkeepsie, visiting with family as I headed straight to the nightclub. My performance was well received, and I picked up a quick $300 for singing a total of five songs. Phyllis stopped by at the end of the show, and I gave her half of the money. Then after assuring the club owners that I would return to open the Blue Magic show, we drove our son Reginald back to Albany, New York where he was a patient in a drug program there. Having driven down from Binghamton that day, I wasn't really feeling the drive to Albany, but Reginald was out on a weekend pass and had to get back before his curfew was up. Exhausted from the demands of the day, I just wanted to lie down and get some rest.

After dropping Reginald off at the program, I suggested to Phyllis that we stay overnight in a motel. She was tired herself, so she readily agreed to that. We checked into a motel on the outskirts of Albany and headed back to Binghamton the following morning. It was a lovely day; the sun was shining, the birds were singing, and both my wife and I were feeling refreshed. Still, I didn't pay much attention to the scenery because I was lost in thought. My mind was on the money in my pocket and the amount of crack cocaine that it would buy. I didn't realize it at the time, but I only had about a week and a half of freedom left.

CHAPTER THIRTY-FIVE

An addict's sole objective is to try to recapture the rush of his or her very first hit, which of course is an exercise in futility. It's simply not going to happen. Still, an addict never stops trying. Even if there's an abundance of the drug on hand, there comes a point where the addict is simply going through the motions. Crack cocaine is no different. The euphoric rush that comes with crack use is really short lived, with depression following immediately after it is gone.

I once read of a behavioral psychology experiment that involved caged white mice and cocaine. In one cage a mouse was able to dispense food and water as often as he wanted simply by pressing a lever. In a second cage the mouse was provided with two levers. One lever would dispense food and water as desired, and the second would dispense a dose of cocaine directly into his bloodstream. The mouse with the single lever remained healthy and well nourished, while the mouse with two levers literally starved himself to death. He totally ignored the lever for food and water, and pressed the cocaine lever almost nonstop until he died. That is the power of a cocaine rush, and I was just like that experimental mouse. I felt helpless and overwhelmed by my crack addiction, and I knew that if I didn't get help soon, something very bad was going to happen.

Reluctantly, with nowhere else to turn, I phoned my daughter Nya in Arizona. I told her everything, and she said that I needed to get into a drug program right away. She said that she would make some phone calls and try to get me into a program in Phoenix. I told her that I wanted to get away from New York completely, and she agreed that a change of environment was probably best. Phyllis was overjoyed when I told her I had contacted Nya and that she was looking into a drug program in Arizona for me. Well, to be honest, she wasn't all that thrilled about my going all the way to Arizona for treatment, but at that point she would have agreed to a program on the moon if it would get her husband back. I also called my best friend Kent, and he agreed that going to Arizona for treatment would probably be the best thing for me under the circumstances. He offered to help in any way possible, for which I was extremely grateful. At that moment, I could feel a load lifting from my shoulders, and I began to look forward to recovery. I couldn't wait to get to Arizona and begin treatment. Unfortunately, because of insurance problems affecting my ability to pay for treatment, Nya was unable to set anything up for me in Phoenix. Nevertheless, I was so hyped at the prospect of recovery that I didn't let that discourage me. Now that the desire for treatment had taken root, I was determined to get help anywhere I could find it. Anywhere, that is, except New Horizons!

Against my wishes, my wife contacted my supervisor at New Horizons and told her about my substance abuse problem. My supervisor was very understanding and offered to get me into treatment. However, thinking that she was talking about my going into the program where I worked, I firmly rejected that as an option. After working there for the past month or so, there was absolutely no way I would be able to face the same program residents I had been counseling. My supervisor literally begged me to come in and talk with her, but I was too ashamed to do even that. Looking back on it now, I can truly understand the meaning of the term foolish pride. I asked if she could recommend a few treatment centers, assuring her that I would phone them on my own. She agreed to that, and I took her recommendations over the phone. The next few days were spent contacting prospective drug programs, with my wife and I narrowing it down to a treatment center in Beacon, New

York. Again, however, the insurance that my wife carried was not acceptable for inpatient treatment. I knew that I could not trust myself to an outpatient program—I was too far-gone in my addiction for that. So, finding myself back at square one, I of course used that as a reason to get high.

I still had a paycheck coming from New Horizons; so that—combined with my final unemployment check—provided me with the money I needed to go on another crack binge. After a day and night of smoking crack, I called my wife from a gas station in downtown Binghamton, asking her to come and pick me up. My van was parked outside of the crack house where I had spent the night. I had allowed another crack addict to drive it earlier, and he got arrested just before dawn with the van keys in his pocket. So, I needed my wife to bring my extra set of keys from home. I dreaded calling Phyllis, but there was really nowhere else for me to turn.

Needless to say, Phyllis was extremely angry as she pulled into the parking area of the gas station where I was waiting. I climbed into the passenger seat and told her that I didn't want to talk. After giving me an icy stare, she drove straight to the drug neighborhood where I had my van parked. Without a word, I got out of my wife's car and climbed behind the wheel of my van. I immediately checked the overhead visor where I had left my final paycheck from New Horizons, and was relieved to find it still there. Phyllis waited for me to pull away from the curb and then followed close behind me all the way home.

With my wife following me, a wave of depression enveloped me, hitting me like a punch in the face. At that moment, I believe, I stopped caring about anything pertaining to my life. I could feel that something bad was about to happen—a feeling of impending doom that I just could not shake.

My wife pulled into the driveway behind me and went straight from her car into the house. I sat behind the wheel of my van staring at my paycheck. I was literally exhausted from a night without sleep, but sleep was the last thing on my mind. I could sense Phyllis watching me from our bedroom window, so I exited my van and went into the house.

Our daughter Shashona was up and about but stayed silent for the most part. The tension in the house was palpable, and I knew that she and my wife were waiting to see what I was going to do next. I went to the bathroom, washed up, and changed clothes. Then, making sure that Phyllis was still in our upstairs bedroom, I headed back out to my van. Of course she heard me start the car and came running out of the house as I sped off.

I headed straight for the ATM at my credit union where I cashed my paycheck then drove straight to the crack house where I had spent the previous night. To my shock, Phyllis pulled up just as I was about to enter, yelling my name from inside the car. I glanced at her briefly, pausing for just a moment, but by that time, I was too far-gone.

With my wife still shouting my name, I walked inside the crack house and closed the door behind me. Still, my wife didn't give up on me—I could hear her repeatedly blowing the horn, shouting my name over and over. By now, the drug dealers and addicts inside the house were beginning to get upset, threatening to make me leave if I couldn't get her to stop drawing attention to them. I knew that the only way to make her stop was to go out to her, but there was no way I was going to do that—I simply could not face her.

Finally, after about another five minutes or so of shouting my name, Phyllis gave up and drove off. I found out later that she went in search of my brothers, Danny and Marvin, in the hope that they would be able to talk some sense into me. However, when they came looking for me at the crack house I was gone. Knowing that my wife would not let the matter drop, I only stayed there long enough to buy enough crack to hold me for another night then checked into a motel.

I was so exhausted from the previous night's drug binge that I fell asleep the moment my head hit the pillow. When I awoke late the following day, I turned on the television news to see the date—Friday, April 13, 2002 scrolled across the bottom of the screen. *Friday the thirteenth,* I thought, wondering if turning on the news at that moment was an omen. Not being superstitious, I quickly dismissed that from my mind, going instead to my stash of crack cocaine. It was the day before my fifty-third birthday, and I was going to celebrate, but celebrate *what?* I was a middle-aged, ex-convict, crack cocaine addict about to throw the rest of his life away, hiding from my wife and family in a motel room! Oh, yeah, I had a lot to celebrate! How sick was I?

It was close to checkout time, so I showered and dressed then returned the room key to the office. I still had quite bit of crack left, but I wasn't about to spend another $50 for one more night at the motel. Instead, I drove to my friend Anthony's house, where I stayed until well after midnight smoking crack with him. At one point, my brother Marvin showed up looking for me, but I hid in the back room while Anthony answered the door.

To be honest, I was secretly hoping that Marvin would check all of the rooms in the apartment in his search for me. My van was parked across from the house, so I'm sure he knew I was in the apartment, but he simply told Anthony to tell me that I wouldn't be able to drive my van, and then he left.

I watched from the window as Marvin got into his Jeep and drove off. Concerned that he had done something to my van, I ran outside and tried to start it—nothing happened. He had obviously done something to the van, but I didn't know what. However, at that point, I didn't really care. I still had some crack left, so I simply returned to the Anthony's apartment and continued to smoke with him.

On April 14, 2002, just after midnight, the crack ran out; it was my fifty-third birthday. It felt as if I was functioning in the *Twilight Zone*—I was down to my last twenty dollars, exhausted, deeply depressed, and suicidal. I ran out of the apartment, yelling over my shoulder to Anthony that I would be right back. I had no real plan in terms of getting more money, but in my state of mind, there was no way I could stay inside that apartment.

As I headed toward the downtown area trying to get my thoughts together, it never really occurred to me that it was my birthday. My head was throbbing, and my heart was still racing from the crack binge. I didn't know where I was going; all I knew was that I had to keep moving. I also needed a drink to calm me down so that I could think more clearly.

After crossing the pedestrian bridge separating Court and Main Street, I stopped at a bar on the corner of Main and Front Street. I ordered a Bacardi double—straight, no chaser—and drank it down in one gulp. I then stepped back out into the cool night air, turned left on Front Street, and headed straight for the Ramada Inn.

The hotel had a nightclub, and I saw a crowd of people in the parking lot. I was starting to feel the effects of the alcohol I had just consumed, so I took a seat on the steps of a clothing store across from the Ramada Inn. The registration desk of the hotel was in clear view. Through the large plate-glass window, I could see the lone desk clerk behind the counter. I don't know when the decision to rob the hotel was made, but as I watched the nightclub patrons spilling out into the parking lot, I figured the element of surprise would tip the scales in my favor. After all, I reasoned, no one would expect a person to be so brazen as to rob a hotel clerk in front of dozens of witnesses! Although I liked the idea of hiding in plain view, my nerves would need an extra boost to pull this one off, but another double shot of Bacardi would take care of that.

I sprinted back to the corner bar, ordered a second drink, and pitched the burning rum straight down my throat. I then slammed the glass down on the counter and headed directly back to the Ramada Inn. With people still milling around in the parking lot just outside the registration area, I walked straight through the crowd into the hotel.

Once inside, I confronted the clerk as he was returning to his station behind the registration desk. I waited for him to unlock the door leading to that area and then quickly rushed to his side.

"This is a robbery," I said, startling him. "I'm a drug addict—I need some money."

He had no way of knowing that it was just my bare hand beneath my shirt, so as far as he was concerned I had a gun. I led him over to the cash register, telling him to open it and to give me all of the money. As he complied with my instructions, I was shocked to see a middle-aged, white man staring at me from the other side of the counter. I didn't know it at the time, but he was one of the hotel's security guards. He didn't say a word or move to intervene; he just stood there, staring at me. He thought I had a gun as well and didn't want to take a chance on someone getting hurt or possibly killed. Still, his presence was quite unnerving for me, but by that time I was deeply committed to the robbery, so I went ahead with it.

I snatched a wad of money from the clerk's hand and ran outside into the parking lot. The guard followed close behind me and was immediately joined by another security guard. He was talking on a cell phone, and it didn't take an Einstein to figure out who was on the other end. At that point, my fate was sealed.

I could already hear the sound of police sirens in the distance, and I knew it would only be a matter of minutes before the parking lot was swarming with cops. The guards would not let me out of their sight, and there was nowhere for me to run—I was trapped.

The sight of Binghamton police cars roaring into the parking lot from all sides was something straight out of a Hollywood movie. I stood there, as if a mere spectator, frozen for a moment, then made a futile attempt to run for it. However, my heart was no longer in it. At that point, I was functioning on pure adrenaline.

All I remember thinking as the police dog appeared out of the darkness, tearing the flesh from my upper left arm, was that I was going to spend the rest of my life in prison. It was then that the prophetic words of my sister-in-law, Pastor Debra Gause, came to mind: *Satan is trying to send you back to prison!* Tears rolled down my face as the combined force of the snarling dog and arresting officers brought me to the ground. *Happy birthday to me,* I thought bitterly. *You just threw your life away.* Satan had won.

EPILOGUE

Broome County Courthouse
Binghamton, New York
February 6, 2003

I have just been sentenced, and am being transported back to the Broome County Jail. I am feeling a little melancholy and somewhat pensive. The past ten months have been an emotional roller-coaster ride for me. I know just how blessed I am to have received a ten-year-flat sentence. With time off for good behavior, I will be home in approximately eight and a half years. Not too bad—considering that I was originally facing a life sentence.

Still, I didn't lose focus on the judge's words, and I know that this will absolutely, positively be my last chance to get it right. There is no room for games or fantasy. If I don't fully address my addiction this time around, I will either die in the streets or in prison—one or the other.

Judge Smith said that I had a lot to offer, and I believe that. He also said that the word *horrible* doesn't begin to do justice to my criminal record, and I know that. So my job, as I see it, is to synthesize the two so that I can use my past to guide someone else's future.

Perhaps that was God's plan for me all along. I would like to think that there is a reason for all that has happened to me throughout my life. It is certainly evident that God is not through with me and that there are greater things in store, but I must do my part so that God can use me at my full potential. I'm just disappointed that it has taken over four decades of incarceration for me to see that.

Many years before meeting and marrying Phyllis, a girl I was involved with asked me, "How come every time you go to prison, you find God?" Being young—and dumb—at the time, I didn't really know how to respond. And even though the answer remained a puzzle, the question stayed in the back of my mind, but now that I am old—and dumb—I believe that I have found the answer. The only place that God could get my attention was in prison, and I am so very grateful for His patience.

With the ridiculous amount of prison time that I have served over the course of my life, God had every right to give up on me, but He didn't. I know in my heart and in my spirit that God has a purpose for me, and that is why I am still alive—even after having been pronounced dead! God's purpose must be fulfilled, and His Word will not return to Him void—there is work for me to do.

Such were my thoughts as the jail van turned onto the long driveway leading to the Broome County jail reception building. Even after just being sentenced to ten years in prison, I was at peace. I marveled at the thought of such a loving God, who continued to bless me even in my sin.

As the van pulled to a stop outside of the jail's prisoner reception area, a smile appeared on my face, and I began to softly sing:

Amazing Grace, how sweet the sound
That saved a wretch like me
I once was lost but now am found
Was blind but now I see

I continued to sing softly as the heavy, steel doors of the Broom County jail clanged shut behind me. I was grateful that—as far as God was concerned—I was still a work in progress.

CONCLUSION

I served eight years of the ten-year sentence I received in February 2003. As usual, I let the time serve me rather than the other way around. In June 2008, I earned a second master's degree at Sing Sing prison. The school was New York Theological Seminary, and the degree was master of professional studies. As the elected class speaker, I was honored to share the podium with *Sojourners* president Jim Wallis, the keynote speaker for the graduation ceremony. Before leaving the prison, Mr. Wallis asked me for a copy of my valedictorian speech, excerpts of which were published later that year in *Sojourners* magazine.

Since my release from Fishkill Correctional Facility on April 30, 2010, life has not been the proverbial bowl of cherries. Still, my frame of reference, in terms of my most recent incarceration, has given me a unique perspective. No matter what difficulties life throws at me, I can honestly say that my worst day out here in the free world is better than my best day behind prison walls.

In June 2011, I was blessed with a part-time job at the Hudson River Presbytery, working as their prison partnership associate. My job is to speak, teach, and preach at the Presbytery's eighty-eight churches in our district in an effort to get them involved in prison ministry. This gives me the unique opportunity to use my past experiences as a testimony to God's forgiveness and saving grace, as well as to the very real possibility of redemption.

My wife and I continue to sing from time to time as the Anointed Two, and it is always a blessing whenever that happens. Our music ministry is the foundation of our spiritual life. It is one of the things that keep us grounded, allowing us to testify to God's goodness in song. We have been on a number of gospel programs since my release, and I am always grateful for the opportunity to sing with my wife. Besides my relationship with God, she is truly the best thing that has ever happened to me.

I am also grateful to be surrounded by family and friends who continue to love and believe in me in spite of my past. Although I would certainly change a number of things if I had a chance to do them over, I do not regret where I have been or what I have been through. My story is just that—*mine!* No one can tell it like me; no one can tell it but me. And if that story keeps others from making the same mistakes, from choosing the same path of destruction as me, then my life will have counted for something.

My experiences have molded and shaped me into the person that I am today, and I really do like the person that I have become. Having spent almost forty years in and out of prison, I am certain that many people do not understand how I can make a statement like that. I look at those years in prison as my wilderness experience—where God was preparing me for such a time as this. In other words, in terms of where I am today as opposed to where I have been, I know that I am exactly where I am supposed to be.

A WORD FROM THE AUTHOR

Although writing this memoir had a truly cathartic effect on me, that was not my primary intention. I wrote about my struggles with substance abuse, and subsequently my life of crime, in order to reach out to those who are struggling with their own demons. My target audience is, of course, our youth because they are the most misunderstood, and the most difficult to reach. However, if this book has connected with you on an emotional, psychological, or spiritual level I would like to hear from you regardless of your age. I am available as a criminal justice consultant, and for speaking engagements. To contact me, please write to:

Theo Harris
P.O. Box 2963
Poughkeepsie, NY 12603
Internet Address: www.singertharris@verizon.net